D1242435

Wills and Administrations

of

Elizabeth City County, Virginia

1688-1800

Wills and Administrations of ELIZABETH CITY COUNTY, VIRGINIA 1688-1800

With Other Genealogical and Historical Items

By Blanche Adams Chapman

Reprinted in an Improved Format

**With a New Index by
Gary Parks**

Baltimore
GENEALOGICAL PUBLISHING CO., INC.
1980

Originally published: 1941
Reprinted in an improved format and with a new index by
Genealogical Publishing Co., Inc.
Baltimore, 1980

Library of Congress Catalogue Card Number 80-68127
International Standard Book Number 0-8063-0909-1
Made in the United States of America

To

Catherine Lindsay Smith (Greer)

(Mrs. Hermann August Knorr)

of

Virginia Ancestry

in whom

the State may take pride.

CONTENTS

PREFACE

VER SINCE THE PUBLICATION of *Virginia Wills and Administrations, 1632-1800*—the Virginia genealogists' Bible—in which the compiler, Dr. Clayton Torrence, inadvertently omitted the material still extant in Elizabeth City County, I have been abstracting and compiling the original wills and administrations. In spite of the county being placed in the column marked "records destroyed," there is a record of some kind in the Clerk's Office for every year from 1688 to 1800. For this present compilation the Deed and Order Books were also examined, but only if a will or administration was proven.

Owing to a personal interest in the county I have collected much additional material from printed sources and have included it here, hoping it will be of service to genealogists and researchers in other parts of the United States who do not have access to printed source material. Unless otherwise stated, printed information has been gleaned from the following sources: *The Virginia Magazine of History and Biography*, the *William and Mary College Quarterly Historical Magazine*, *Tyler's Quarterly*, the *Calendar of Virginia State Papers*, *Journal of the House of Burgesses*, and the *Council Journals*.

BLANCHE ADAMS CHAPMAN
Smithfield, Virginia

N.B. *The attention of the researcher is called to the fact that Elizabeth City County was created in 1634 and comprised territory that was ultimately laid off for the counties of Nansemond, Norfolk, and Princess Anne. Since 1952 it has been incorporated as the Independent City of Hampton.*

WILLS AND ADMINISTRATIONS

ADAMS, John Nelson. Leg.- sister Rosea Field, with a reversion of the bequest to her sons, Robert Field and John Field. Ex. sister Rosea Field. D. March 2, 1789. R. April 22, 1790. Wit. Gerrard Seymour, Bartlit Field, Mary Field. Original Will.

ADDOMS (Adams), Mary. Leg.- daughter Hannah Adams; son John; daughter Rosea Fields; grandson Robert Fields. D. 1779. Wit. Ann Latimer, Moseley Armistead, James Bray Armistead. Original Will.

ALFORD, William. Indexed in Book 1689-1699, but recorded on a lost page.

ALKIN, Emanuel. Leg.- wife Susanna whole estate and a plantation adjoining Mr. Anthony Armistead. D. September 27, 1722. R. June 21, 1727. Wit. John Roe, Ellen Roe. Book 1704-30, p. 74.

ALKINGS (Alkin), Susanna. Leg.- friend Roscow Sweny, son of Captain Merrit Sweney; friend Jane Curle; friend Mrs. Jane Sweny all my personal estate. Ex. friend Captain Merritt Sweny. D. February 5, 1733. R. December 19, 1744. Wit. Jane Curle, Mary Hamilton, John Kerby. Book 1737-49, p. 194. Original Will.

ALKIN, Susanna. Appraisal by William Tucker, John Nelson and John Dunn. R. January 16, 1744. Book 1737-49, p. 195.

ALLAINBY, Captain Thomas. Administration requested by Elizabeth Allainby his wife. D. January 27, 1692/93. R. April 29, 1693. Book 1688-1699, p. 117.

ALLAINBY, Captain Thomas. Walter Innis gave bond as marrying Elizabeth Allainby, the Administratrix of Thomas Allainby. Book 1688-1699, p. 117. Appraisers of his estate were, Edmund Sweny, George Waffe, Petter Hopson, Robert Tucker. R. February 10, 1692/93. Book 1688-1699, p. 144. Appraisers appointed for the widow, Edmund Sweny, George Wauffe; those appointed for the orphan, Robert Tucker and Peter Hobson. Mr. Pascho Curle and Mr. William Clerke are desired to be present. Jan. 27, 1692/93. Signed, Walter Innis and wife Elizabeth Innis. Order Bk., p. 11 & 13.

ALLEN, Ealenor. Leg.- daughter-in-law Elizabeth Allen, the widow of my son Thomas Allen. Extx. Daughter-in-law Elizabeth Allen. D. November 21, 1754. Wit. Robert Brough, Jean Sqaring (?), Sarah Patton. Original Will.

ALLEN, Henry. Leg.- Elizabeth Moss, John Moss and Margaret Tabb Moss, the children of Sheldon and Mary Moss. Ex. friend, Captain Miles King. D. November 8, 1784. March 24, 1785. Wit. Dianah Allen, Lucy Holloway; Sheldon Moss qualified as Ex., his security, William Moore. Original Will.

ALLEN, James. Administration of his estate granted Hannah Allen. Her securities, Curle Tucker and William Wager. Appraisers appointed, John Casey, Anthony Hawkins, King Humphlet, Nicholas Bayley. June 5, 1759. Order Book 1755-60, p. 230. Estate appraised by John Casey, Anthony Hawkins, Nicholas Bayley. R. August 7, 1759. Book 1758-64, p. 76. Account estate examined by Thomas Dixon, Curle Tucker, Joseph Jeggitts,

Anthony Hawkins. Book 1758-90, p. 439.

ALLEN, John. Ordered that his widow, Ann Allen return an account of his estate. December 18, 1695. Order Book 1688-1699, p. 80.

ALLEN, John. Leg.- John Bayley and James Bayley, sons of James Wallace Bayley. I gave their mother in her lifetime by deed of gift, all that I ever intended she should have of my estate; nephew John Allen, son of my brother Henry Allen, decd, the plantation given me by my father William Allen, decd, also a plantation bought of Dunn Armistead; reversion of the bequest to nephew John Allen's brother Henry Allen, reversion to Henry Allen's next eldest brother; to William Smith, son of Elizabeth Smith; brother Abraham Allen a plantation bought of Martha Gamblin (?), adjoining Edward Yergin's land; to Elizabeth Smith as long as she remains a single woman; to William Smith and his guardians are to be Captain John Tabb and Captain Henry King. Exs. nephew John Allen, son of my brother Henry Allen and William Mallory. D. December 4, 1771. R. January 28, 1773. Wit. Starky Armistead, Samuel Sandefur, Sarah Sandefur. John Allen qualified as Ex., security, Moseley Armistead, William Moore. Original Will.

ALLEN, John. Leg- brother Henry, a tract of land adjoining the land which was given me by my uncle John Allen decd., being the land which was bought by my father of Francis Mallory; reversion of this bequest to my brother Edward; to William Smith, son of Elizabeth Smith, when he becomes of age; brother Thomas; brother William; my two youngest sisters, Ann and Dianah Allen. Exs. brothers Henry and Edward Allen. D. July 8, 1776. R. February 27, 1777. Wit. Proved by Thomas Allen. Original Will.

ALLEN, Phillip. Leg.- son William; wife Elesha my estate of 11 years and at the end of that time to be divided among my six youngest children, viz.-Philip, Savage Prieston, Mary, Elesha, Elizabeth and Henry. If my wife should die my estate is to be turned over to my brothers, John and Henry Allen for the 11 years. Extx. wife Elesha Allen. D. October 22, 1753. R. December 4, 1753. Wit. Thomas Roberts, Mary Roberts, Henry Allen. Codicil, witnessed by Thomas Roberts, Mary Roberts, John Allen. Original Will.

ALLEN, William. Appraisal of his estate ordered recorded. September 15, 1731. Order Book 1731-47, p. 10. Eleanor Allen, Extx. of William Allen summoned to appear in Court to answer a petition. Ibid, p. 63. William Allen an Ex. of the estate, renounced his executorship and John Allen qualified. September 17, 1735. Appraisers appointed, John Tabb, William Parsons, Mr. Lowry, Thomas Smith. Order Book 1731-47, p. 97. Settlement of the estate of William Allen, Pilot. Each of following were paid legacies, John Allen, William Henry Allen, Jane Allen, now Cavinis, the widow and Ann Allen. Signed by Eleanor Allen the Admtx. R. August 15, 1744. Audited by R. Brough, Robert Armistead, Will Tucker. Book 1737-49, p. 188.

ALLEN, William. Pilot. Leg.- son Edward; wife Bethair; daughter Judith; daughter Mary; daughter Margaret; daughter Frances Allen. Wife Extx. D. June 21, 1749. R. August 1, 1749. Wit. Robert Brough, George Watkins, William Naylor. Security for Extx. Mark Parish and Pennuel Penny. Book 1737-49, p. 345.

ALLEN, William. Leg.- son John; wife Jane; son William; daughter Mary; son Henrey; son Johnson. (Children not of age) Wife,

Extx. D. June 11, 1752. Wit. Anthony Armistead, Thomas Palmer, John Allen. Original Will. Settlement of the estate, September 7, 1763. Equal parts alloted to the following heirs, William Allen, Henry Allen, Johnson Allen, Mary Allen and Jane Allen. Audited by John Tabb, John Parsons and John Armistead. Book 1758-64, p. 505.

ALLMON, John. Of the Town of Hampton. Leg.- to son Edmund and "Little Billey"; son Solomon; daughter Mildred; wife Mary, at her death to be divided between Mary Allmon, Ann Allmon, Sarah Allmon, Edmond Allmon and Billy my grandson. Wife, Extx. D. July 14, 1759. R. January 1, 1760. Wit. Benjamin Ham, John Sheppard, Jr., James Manson. Security for Extx. Thomas Wootten. Book 1758-64, p. 109. Original Will.

ALMAND, (also written Allmon), John. Appraisers appointed, Francis Parker, James Wallace Bayley, James Nobbs, William Simmonds. January 1, 1760. Order Book 1755-60, p. 268.

ANDREWS, Elizabeth. Inventory returned by Richard Nusum. Sale of estate, returned by Simon Hollier, Sheriff. January 3, 1716. Book 1715-21, p. 55.

ARCHER, John. Probation granted Charles Courts and wife Elizabeth, relict of ye said decd. March 18, 1696/97. Book 1689-1699, p. 112. (See will after Armistead, inadvertantly omitted.)

ARMISTEAD, Anthony, Sr. Leg.- son Westwood (not of age) land given me by my father, Anthony Armistead's will, also land I bought of Edward Myhill; wife Elizabeth; son Anthony land which I purchased of Dunn Armistead, being the tract given him by the will of Pasco Dunn; daughter Hannah. Exs. brother Robert Armistead, brother-in-law William Westwood, friend, Charles Jenings, Jr. and cousin Robert Armistead. D. February 22, 1727/28. R. December 18, 1728. Wit. Moss Armistead, C. Jenings, Charles Avery, John Lowry. Elizabeth Armistead qualified as Extx. Book 1704-30, p. 150. Appraisal estate of Colonel Anthony Armistead, by Simon Hollier, John King, John Lowry, John Tabb. R. March 19, 1728. Book 1704-30, p. 174.

ARMISTEAD, Anthony. Leg.- wife Margaret, with reversion of the bequest to son Anthony; son William (not 21) born before wedlock with my now wife; son John; son Benit; son Anthony my plantation in Warwick called "Renolds". Exs. wife Margaret and son John Armistead. December 29, 1737. R. February 15, 1737. Wit. Robert Brown, Argil Blaxton, Edward Parish, Andrew Giles. Book 1737-49, p. 32. Original Will. Appraisal of estate. March 15, 1737. Book 1737-49, p. 42. Settlement of estate. Signed Margaret Armistead. Paid - John Armistead, Benit Armistead and the widow. Audited by John Brodie, William Smelt and William Allen. February 18, 1740. Book 1737-49, p. 99.

ARMISTEAD, Colonel Anthony. Estate account. Signed by Mrs. Elizabeth Armistead. Cash paid Mr. NIcholas King his wife's estate, cash paid Mr. William Smelt his wife's estate. Audited by Joseph Banister, Thomas Mingham, John Selden. March 18, 1740. Book 1737-49, p. 102.

ARMISTEAD, Booth. Leg.- land in York county, which I bought is to be sold for the benefit of my son Robert (not of age) with reversion to my son John; all of my negroes to be equally divided among my heirs, with the exception of those which were vested in me by my intermarriage, which are to be vested in my wife and daughter Betsey, with reversion to her brothers and sisters, with Booth excepted; daughter Betsey is to be under the sole management of my wife; provision for an unborn child. Exs. brother Robert Armistead, William Mallory, William Armistead and wife Frances Armistead. D. April 13, 1770. R. June 28, 1770. Wit. Robert Armistead, Francis Jones, William Selden. William Mallory qualified, security-Thomas Kirby and John Brodie. Robert Armistead, Jr. qualified, security-James Wallace. Frances Armistead qualified, security-John Allen and James Bray Armistead. Book 1763-71, p. 353. Original Will.

ARMISTEAD, Booth. Administration of estate, granted to Robert Armistead, security-John King. June 21, 1727. Order Book 1723-29, p. 12.

ARMISTEAD, Edward. Leg- wife Martha, negroes reversion at her death to my son Samuel, daughter Rebecca and the children of Mrs. Frances Allen; to all my children, viz.-William, John, Moss, Ann, Edward, Samuel and Rebecca. My wife to forfeit negroes, if she allows John Allen, Jr. or his wife Frances to live upon her plantation. Exs. wife, son William Armistead and William Armistead, Sr. D. February 19, 1771. R. March 1, 1771. Wit. Clausel Clausel, William Read, Clayton Rogers, Callohill Mennis. Martha Armistead qualified, security-Simon Hollier and Alexander Graham. Book 1763-71, p. 414. Original Will. A suit is recorded, original papers, which is brought against the estate of Edward Armistead, by Robert Armistead, William Armistead, James Armistead by Robert Armistead his next friend, Samuel Armistead, an infant, by his guardian William Garrow, William Smith and wife Elizabeth, late Elizabeth Reade, daughter of William Reade and Patrick Walker. Appraisal of estate by Robert Sandefur, Clausel Clausel, Will Mallory. May 23, 1771. Book 1763-71, p. 431.

ARMISTEAD, Elizabeth. Appraisal ordered July 22, 1942 by Charles Jenings and James Manson. R. September 15, 1742. Book 1737-49, p. 144.

ARMISTEAD, Elizabeth. Leg.- son Westwood; son Anthony; daughter Mary Wills; granddaughter Mary Allen, daughter of William Allen; granddaughters Elizabeth and Mary Allen the daughters of John Allen; granddaughter Sarah Smelt; daughter Hannah Allen. Exs. son Anthony Armistead and Mr. John Allen. D. September 28, 1750. Wit. Judith Robinson, Robert Armistead, Margeat Thuntear (?). Original Will. Settlement of estate, June 3, 1760 by Robert Armistead, Booth Armistead and Thomas Smith. R. July 1, 1760. Book 1758-63, p. 159. Account current. Refers to former settlement. John Allen Executor. By Westwood Armistead decd., account for necessaries while under age and living with his mother, to be paid Mr. William Westwood. Audited by George Wray, James Wallace and John Riddlehurst. Also a private account listed between John Allen and Anthony Armistead. December 7, 1762. Book 1758-64, p. 372.

ARMISTEAD, Dunn. Appraisal, dated August 15, 1715. Appraisers, Ban. Smith, Francis Rodgers, Thomas Read. September 10, 1716. Book 1715-21, p. 48.

ARMISTEAD, Hannah. Leg.- grandchild Judith Armistead; son Robert; grandchild Hannah Armistead; son Anthony. Ex. son Anthony Armistead. October 26, 1726. R. 19 of Xber 1728. Wit. Wil. Westwood, Robert Armistead, Jr. Will presented by Elizabeth Armistead, who qualified. Book 1704-30, p. 160.

ARMISTEAD, Hind. Hannah Armistead appointed Admtx. Security, Brien Penne and Thomas Watts. August 15, 1722. Book 1721-23,

p. 65. Estate appraised by William Spicer, John Moore and Thomas Hawkins. September -- 1722. Book 1721-23, p. 74. ccount current estate of Hind Chandler Armistead. Charles Jenings, Ad. Bill for schooling and bringing up Hind Armistead. The profits of Hannah Armistead's estate. Charles Jenings to retain one-third of estate as his wife's dower. June 22, 1738. Audited by Alexander McKenzie, David O'Sheal and John Selden. Book 1737-49, p. 131.

ARMISTEAD, James Bray. Leg.- to Diana Wallace Bayley during her widowhood, if she should marry the negroes to be free upon paying Wilson Wallace Bayley 3£ annually; to Gill Armistead the son of Captain William Armistead. Extx. Diana Wallace Bayley. D. August 31, 1790. R. April 28, 1791. Wit. James Goodwin, Samuel Cunningham, Samuel Burket. Book 1787-1800, p. 19. Original Will. Estate appraised by Thomas B. Armistead, Bartlett Fields and John Skinner. June 23, 1791. Book 1787-1800 p. 30. Account estate. Signed, Diana W. Bayley. Audited by Thomas B. Armistead, John Skinner, William Sandy. June 28, 1792. Book 1787-1800. p. 78.

ARMISTEAD, John. Leg.- wife Elizabeth; son John land in Northhampton County, N.C.; son Robert land in Elizabeth City and York, to his male heir, with reversion to eldest male heir of son John. Exs. wife Elizabeth, Robert Armistead and my son-in-law Thomas Smith. D. March 26, 1787. R. January 27, 1791. Wit. Michael King, George Booker, R. Armistead, John Cary Robert Armistead qualified, security-George Booker. Book 1787-1800, p. 1. Original Will. Estate appraised by Thomas Allen, James Dixon, Johnson Tabb. July 28, 1791. Book 1787-1800, p. 36.

ARMISTEAD, Katherine. Leg.- I desire that Woodhouse Wood be maintained out of my estate as long as he lives, also Susannah Powers until she be fit to be bound out; to Sarah Broadnax; daughter Angelica; son Booth; son Robert. Exs. friends, John Lowary and Ellyson Armistead. D. November 6, 1745. R. May 3, 1748. Wit. Woodhouse Wood, Tarlton Allmand. 1737-49. p. 286.

ARMISTEAD, Martha. Leg.- my grandchildren, Mary Bell, Martha Tompkins Armistead, William Allen, Patrick Walker, Frances Mennis Armistead and Samuel Armistead. Exs. Miles King and grandson William Allen. D. November 15, 1788. R. February 28, 1799. Wit. M.M. Robinson, Everard Robinson. Book 1787-1800, p. 449. Original Will. Estate appraised by Thomas Robinson, Charles Collier, Samuel Thomas. June 27, 1799. Book 1787-1800, p. 472. Account estate. Signed William Allen, Ex. Audited by Robert Armistead, William Armistead and William Allen. February 27, 1800. Book 1787-1800, p. 527.

ARMISTEAD, Mary. Widow. Leg.- daughter Elizabeth; daughter Mary to live with my sister Elizabeth Tabb; son Westwood; to God daughter Elizabeth Smelt for her education, which is to be under the direction of Mrs. Jane Allen. Exs. brother William Tabb and cousin Captain John Tabb. D. March 22, 1760. R. May 6, 1760. Wit. John Brodie, William Smelt, Sr. Codicil-Wit. William Smelt, Sr., Samuel Jones. John Tabb qualified, security, John Tabb, Sr., James Wallace. Book 1758-64, p. 153. Appraiser appointed, John Allen, John Armistead, Henry Allen, William Smelt, Jr. Order Book 1755-60, p. 286. Appraisal recorded, August 5, 1760. Book 1758-60, p. 163.

ARMISTEAD, Moseley. Leg.- wife Whiten; son William; son Moseley; son Anthony; daughter Judith Curle Armistead; daughter Elizabeth

Moseley Armistead; to my three God children; to John King Bayley; to Robert Armistead, the son of Westwood Armistead. Ex. friend William A. Bayley. February 4, 1781. R. November 22, 1781. Wit. Westwood Armistead, Thomas Crandol, James Dixon. Original Will.

ARMISTEAD, Moss. Leg.- brother Robert; Mr. Samuel Sweny is to have the privilege of getting his firewood from my land during his lifetime; nephew William, son of Robert Armistead; niece Mary, daughter of Robert Armistead; nep- James Armistead; to Ann Sweny, daughter of Mr. Samuel Sweny; to Martha Sweny. Ex. brother Robert Armistead. August 9, 1736. R. November 1736. Original Will.

ARMISTEAD, Moss Wallace. Of the Town of Hampton. Leg.- wife Catherine; all the goods I have in the hands of Samuel Beal, Esq. to be returned; at death of wife, estate to my children, viz.- Mary, Ann, Moss and Priscilla; my military and provision certificates to be divided among my children, also the money due me from Col. Richard Randolph, Executor of the late Col. David Meade; I desire that my negroes be continued on Mr. Curle's estate to make a crop. Ex. wife and friends William Armistead and Miles King. D. February 25, 1786. R. June 22, 1786. Wit. John Ashton Wray, Francis Riddlehurst, Mary Tarrant. Catherine Armistead and William Armistead qualified, security-John Cary. Original Will.

ARMISTEAD, Moss. Estate appraised by George Wray, Jr., Joseph Needham and Charles Jennings. R. June 28, 1792. Book 1787-1800, p. 79. Account of estate. Moss Armistead account as Executor of the estate of Joseph Selden audited. Examined by Miles King, Charles Jennings, William Brough. July 26, 1792. Book 1787-1800, p. 86. Account estate, William Armistead, Executor. Paid Wilson Curle the balance of his legacy; paid Mrs. Mary Curle; paid Elizabeth Kello Curle, per proportion of her father's estate; paid board for Nancy and Priscilla Armistead. Audited by Miles King, George Booker, Charles Jennings. October 25, 1797. Book 1787-1800, p. 380.

ARMISTEAD, Robert. Of York County. Leg.- son Booth my land in Elizabeth City County, with reversion to son Robert, with reversion to son Ellyson and reversion to daughter Angelica; wife Katherine; provision for unborn child. February -- 1737. Wit. Miles Cary, John Brodie, John Lowry. Codicil: Son Booth all the negroes I was in possession of before my last marriage and an equal share of my personal estate with all my children by my present wife; son Robert land in Hanover County, which I bought of Col. Thomas Jones. March 19, 1741/42. R. May 19, 1742. Wit. John Brodie, John Dewbre, Sarah Brodnax. Book 1737-49, p. 127. Inventory of Captain Robert Armistead, Sr., presented by Katherine Armistead. March 16, 1742. Book 1737-49, p. 157. Additional inventory of money in England. March 25, 1744. Book 1737-49, p. 197.

ARMISTEAD, Robert, the Elder. Leg.- son William; son James; son-in-law Joseph Selden (? torn); son Thomas; son Moss Wallace Armistead; son Robert; granddaughter Euphan, daughter of my son William Armistead. Exs. son William Armistead and friend Richard Cary. D. July 28, 1771. R. November 24, 1774. Wit. Richard Cary. Original Will. (In very bad condition).

ARMISTEAD, Robert. Division of slave between Robert Armistead and Westwood Armistead by William Brough, Joseph Needham and William Smith. May 26, 1791. Book 1787-1800, p. 24.

ARMISTEAD, Robert, Sr. Leg.- daughter Elizabeth; mother Elizabeth Armistead; wife Ann; son William (not of age) land in York County. Exs. Col. John Cary, Robert Armistead, son of William Armistead, Sheldon Moss, Johnson Tabb. D. November 12, 1792. R. January 24, 1793. Wit. Johnson Tabb, Thomas B. Armistead, William Armistead, John Nettles. Robert Armistead qualified, security-Miles King. Book 1787-1800, p. 111. Appraisal taken after the death of the old lady, Mrs. Armistead, April 28, 1794, by W. Armistead, Jr., Thomas Allen and Thomas B. Armistead. Book 1787-1800, p. 253.

ARMISTEAD, Samuel. Leg.- wife Franky, who is to keep my estate in her hands until one of my children becomes 21, when provision is to be made for my six children. D. August 17, 1784. R. March 24, 1785. Wit. Hinde Russell, William Smith, Eli Smith. Original Will.

ARMISTEAD, Starkey. Leg.- brother Robert Armistead a tract of land given me by my father John Armistead by deed of gift, August 26, 1770, which adjoins the land of Edward Lockey Collier and John Read, decd.; wife Mary, reversion at her death to my niece Mary Smith; my mother Elizabeth Armistead. Exs. friends Thomas Smith of York County and Robert Armistead of this county. D. January 16, 1775. R. Wit. John Armistead, Andrew Ma-- (?), John Armistead, Jr. Original Will.

ARMISTEAD, Westwood. Leg.- wife Mary the land I purchased of my brother Anthony Armistead; daughter Elizabeth; daughter Mary; son Westwood. Exs. wife, Col. John Tabb and Anthony Armistead. D. February 9, 1756. R. January 1, 1760. Wit. John Tabb, Hannah Tabb, John Frazier. Book 1758-64, p. 95. Original Will. Will proven by John Tabb and John Frazier. Mary Armistead qualified, security-John Tabb and John Tabb, Jr. Appraisers appointed, John Allen, John Armistead, Henry Allen, William Smelt, Sr. Order Book 1755-60, p. 267. Appraisal of the estate of Captain Westwood Armistead by John Allen, Henry Allen and John Armistead. April 1, 1760. Book 1758-60. p. 145. Estate account, administered by Mary Armistead and since her death by John Tabb, Gent. Audited by Augustine Moore, John Lowry, Will Mallory. R. July 2, 1765. Book 1763-71, p. 51.

ARMISTEAD, Westwood. Leg.- son Robert my plantation on Back River, adjoining the land of Thomas Kerby and Charles Miles Collier, orphan; son Westwood. (Neither son of age) Exs. wife Mary and son Robert Armistead. D. January 18, 1782. R. June 22, 1786. Wit. Edward Allen, Robert Kerby, James Dixon. Robert Armistead the surviving Ex. named, qualified. Original Will. Appraisal of estate by W. A. T. Parsons, Thomas Allen and William Moore. April 28, 1791. Division of estate between Robert and Westwood Armistead was made by William Brough, Joseph Needham and William Smith. May 26, 1791. Book 1787-1800, p. 21 & 24.

ARMISTEAD, William, Sr. Leg.- wife Rebecca at the decease of my mother Hannah Armistead; son Anthony; son William; son John; son Hind a tract of land bought of Thomas Cary and his wife; son Robert; son Moss, a tract formerly granted John Ingram; son Edward land leased to Benjamin Clifton, Sr.; provision for unborn child; mother Hannah Armistead. Exs. wife Rebecca and sons Anthony, William and John. D. January 5, 1714. R. January 18, 1715. Wit. Anthony Armistead, Robert Armistead, Thomas Charles, George Cooper. Book 1715-21, p. 19. Appraisal of the estate of Major William Armistead by John King, Francis Ballard and Joseph Banister. May 17, 1718.

Book 1715-21, p. 113.

ARMISTEAD, William. Leg.- son Dunn, wife Judith son William; daughter Ann; daughter Francis; son Simon; son Henry. Exs. uncles, Anthony Armistead and Robert Armistead and son William Armistead. D. February 15, 1724. R. June 21, 1727. Wit. Anthony Armistead, Jr., John King, Dunn Armistead. Book 1704-30, p. 66. Administration granted Judity Armistead, security-John King, Charles -----. Order Book 1723-29, p. 12.

ARMISTEAD, William. Leg.- wife and four children; daughter Hannah; wife Elizabeth with the reversion of the bequest to my two youngest sons, Anthony and the child yet upbaptised; son William Armistead. Exs. wife and brother Dunn Armistead. D. July 7, 1741. R. May 19, 1742. Wit. Mary Sloughtenburg, Judith Hatton, Miles Cary, Charles King. Book 1737-49, p. 119. Original Will. Appraisal by William Smelt, William Allen, John Allen. Signed, Elizabeth Armistead. July 21, 1742. Ibid, p. 138. Account of estate. Examined by John Brodie and Robert Armistead. November 18, 1742. Book 1737-49, p. 148. Account of estate, signed George and Elizabeth Barbee, Extx. of William Armistead. Examined by John Lowry and John Allen. June 19, 1745. Book 1737-49, p. 197. The subscribers have examined the accounts of Elizabeth the wife of George Barbe and Extx. of William Armistead. Signed, John Lowry and John Allen. May 2, 1749. Book 1737-49, p. 333.

ARMISTEAD, William, Jr. Leg.- wife Constance; son Robert; daughter Mary; son William. Extx. wife Constance Armistead. D. February 24, 1772. R. Wit. John Tabb, John Parsons, John Cary. Original Will.

ARMISTEAD, William, the Elder. Leg.- son Robert; son William the plantation called "Baker", purchased of Miles King; son Moss; daughter Euphan Graves; my three youngest children, William, Moss and Rebecca; daughters Sarah and Mary; my daughter Robinson has had all of my estate I intend to give her; my wife's dower to be divided among my three youngest children; rest of my estate after my debts are paid to my children, Robert, Sarah, Euphan and Mary. Exs. son Robert Armistead and friend Richard Cary. D. August 23, 1799. R. September 26, 1799. Wit. Worlich Westwood, Samuel Selden, James Davis, Samuel Cook. Book 1787-1800, p. 486.

ARCHER, John. Leg.- son Thomas; daughter Hannah; daughter Elizabeth; daughter Sarah; wife Elizabeth. Extx. wife Elizabeth Archer. February 17, 1695/96. R. March 18, 1696/97. Wit. Thomas Allen, William Williams, Thomas Williams. Book 1689-99, p. 231.

ASSON, John. Leg.- to Mary Thurmore; to James Cotsell, the son of Elizabeth Cotsell; to John Barnes the plantation bought of Gain Fraeman; to Thomas Casey, the son of William Casey, with reversion of the bequest to James Cotsell's two children. Ex. John Barnes, who is to keep Thomas Casey until he is sixteen. D. December 11, 1688. R. February 18, 1688/89. Wit. Edward Loftis, Richard Joanes. Book 1689-1699, p. 112.

ATKINS, Andrew. Nuncupative Will. Leg.- daughter Sarah; daughter Ann; daughter Elizabeth; wife Lucy. D. 13 of Xber 1690. R. January 19, 1690. Proved by depositions of Richard Hursley, aged 54 and Ann Hursley aged 56. Book 1689-1699, p. 113. Probation granted Joseph Parish, who married the relict of Andrew Atkins. April 28, 1691 Book 1689-99, p. 81. Account of the estate of Sarah, Ann and Elizabeth, orphans of Andrew Atkins, returned by Joseph Parrish, who married the relict of Andrew Atkins. September 11, 1693. Order Book 1689-99, p. 23 & 49.

AVERA, Charles. Leg.- son Charles the plantation I purchased of Christopher Copeland, reversion of bequest to son William; reversion to grandson Thomas Avera; wife Ursula; rest of estate to my three sons and four daughters. Extx. wife Ursula Avera. D. February 12, 1745/46. R. June 18, 1746. Wit. Thomas Mingham, Falvey Copeland, James Latimer. Ordered that Henry Avera, heir-at-law be summoned to contest the validity of this will. Henry Avera appeared in Court and said he had no objection to the probation of his father's will. Book 1737-49, p. 219.

AVERA, Hannah. Leg.- nephew Thomas Avera; sister Hurstly Brittain; to Robert Rebling Brown, who now lives in my house, a home until my son Thomas Avera comes down; to Elizabeth Brown, the wife of Robert Brown; I acknowledge I have no claim or title to a negro the property of Mr. James Ball of Lancaster County. Ex. Captain Miles Cary. D. September 15, 1784. R. September 23, 1784. Wit. John Tabb, John Randle. Original Will.

AVERY, Henry. Receipt of Henry Avery to his mother Jane Avery for the estate left him by his father, Henry Avery November 11, 1695. Book 1689-1699, p.

AVERRA, Henry. Appraisal of the estate in the hands of his brother, Charles Averra, John Stores, William Frazey and John Whitfield by John Dunn, Thomas Needham and Moses Davis. Estate paid John Stores his account for buying Jane Averra. The estate to be divided into four equal parts. February 22, 1721. Book 1721-23, p. 44.

BABB, John. Inventory signed by John Moussit. July 2, 1719. Book 1715-21, p. 197.

BADGETT, William. Leg.- wife my plantation in Warwick County adjoining the land of John Lewelling, with reversion to son Thomas; daughter Ann; provision for any future children. Exs. Mr. Thomas West and Josiah Massenburg, Jr. D. September 21, 1786. R. December 28, 1786. Wit. Miles King, John Field. Original Will. Appraisal of the estate by Miles King, Thomas Jones and John Perry. Signed, Thomas West and Josiah Massenburg. October 27, 1796. Book 1787-1800, p. 324.

BAINES, BAINS AND BANES

BAINS, Eleanor. Widow. Leg.- son George; son Henry; grandson Thomas Bains; son John, who is to live with his brother George until he is 21. Ex. son George Bains. D. April 2, 1727. R. July 19, 1727. Wit. Richard Nusum, Thomas Skinner, Judith Humphlett. Book 1704-30, p. 79. Inventory. September 21, 1727. Book 1704-30, p. 102.

BANES, Henry. Leg.- son Thomas; son Henry; to Samuel Banes (the same legacy as the previous two he called sons) daughter Mary; wife Sarah and at her death to my children by my present wife. Exs. wife and Joseph Jegitts. D. February 19, 1758. R. Wit. Ezekiah Smith, Thomas Skinner, Mark Parrish. Original Will. Appraisal of estate by Mark Parrish, Thomas Hatton and Nicholas Bayley. September 5, 1758. Book 1758-64, p. 6.

BAINES, Henry. Leg.- brother Sammuel. Ex. brother Sammuel

Baines. February 19, 1766. R. August 5, 1766. Wit. Thomas Dixon, Richard Burt, J. Casey. Samuel Baines qualified, security, Thomas Dixon. Original Will. Book 1763-71, p. 84. Appraisal of estate by Thomas Skinner, Richard Burt and William Loyall. Book 1763-71, p. 99.

BAINES, John. Estate appraised by John Massenburg, Alexander Carver and William Tucker. Ordered, May 16, 1742. R. April 20, 1743. Book 1737-49, p. 160. Estate account, signed by John Jones, Administrator. Examined by Thomas Everard and Robert Armistead. R. September 19, 1744. Book 1737-49, p. 190.

BANES, John. Leg. - son Mathew; son John; son William; son Henry; son Richard Banes. Ex. Robert Armistead of Sawyer's Swamp. D. February 15, 1798. R. February 22, 1798. Wit. James Davis, John Allen, Fanny Baines. Book 1787-1800, p. 410. Original Will.

BAINS, Thomas. Leg.- wife and children. Wife, Extx. D. July -- 1726. R. June 21, 1727. Wit. John Faulkner, Allen Shaw, William Morehead, John Skinner. The Extx. died before probation of will, Henry Bains qualified. Book 1704-30, p. 68. Administration granted Henry Bains, security-Samuel Cade. Order Book 1723-29, p. 12. Appraisers of the estate, Richard Hawkins, William Morehead and Richard Nusum. July 19, 1727. Book 1704-30, p. 83.

BAKER, James, Sr. Leg.- son James; son John; son-in-law Thomas Lattimer in full of my daughter Rebecca's estate. Ex. son James Baker. D. April 8, 1735. R. June 1736. Wit. Thomas Tucker, Mary Jenings, Mary Tucker. Original Will.

BAKER, James. Leg.- eldest son William, with reversion to the first son he should have, for want of such heir to his daughters, Elizabeth and Susanna; daughter Elizabeth Jenings; daughter Jane Purrier; son James; son Timothy Blodworth Baker; two youngest sons, John and Thomas. Exs. son-in-law Peter Purrier and friends Hursley Carter and Cary Selden. D. January 25, 1758. Wit. Cary Selden, Thomas Palmer, William Randulph, Hursley Carter, William Carter. Original Will. Will proved by William Randolph, Hursley Carter. Ordered William Baker his heir-at-law to be summoned. Appraisers, James Naylor, Banister Minson, John Minson and James Wallace. Peter Puryear qualified, security- Cary Selden and Ursley Carter. February 7, 1758. Order Book 1755-63, p. 163. Appraisal by Banister Minson, John Minson and James Wallace recorded January 2, 1759. Book 1758-64, p. 27. Account estate, examined by John Riddlehurst, H. King and W. Wager. August 5, 1766. Book 1763-71, p. 80.

BAKER, James. Leg.- wife Elizabeth; daughter Susanna; son James the plantation on which I live given to my wife by her brother, Robert Carter, decd. and a lot in Hampton which I bought of Thomas Butts, decd. adjoining William Skinner and James Wallace; son Timothy Bloodworth Baker, a lot in the Borough of Norfolk, that I bought of Richard Knight, which he had of John Smith; provision for an unborn child. Exs. wife Elizabeth and Mr. Robert Bright. D. January 19, 1781. R. April 25, 1782. Wit. William Carter, William Jenings, Robert Bright, John Carter. Original Will. Robert Bright qualified, security, Joseph Needham.

BAKER, John. Leg.- after a division between my estate and brother Thomas, my estate to be equally divided between James Baker, Timothy Bloodworth Baker, Thomas Baker, and Thomas Jenings and their heirs; to Elizabeth Baker; to Sarah Baker. Exs. brother James Baker and Thomas Jenings. D. September 14, 1766. R. October 7, 1766. Wit. Edward Parish, William Bennet. Security for Exs. Peter Puryear. Book 1763-71, p. 100.

BAKER, Joshua. Appraisal of estate by John Henry Rombough, John Nelson and John White. Ordered, April 16, 1746. R. May 21, 1746. Book 1737-49, p. 217.

BAKER, Moses. Suit brought by Moses Baker against Edward Ruddle, his father-in-law of the estate left him by the last will and testament of his father, Moses Baker. September 29, 1693. Order Book, 1688-99, p. 18.

BAKER, Peter. Joiner. Leg.- wife Jane Baker and her heirs. Extx. wife Jane Baker. D. February 24, 1717/18. R. January 21, 1718. Wit. John Bayley, Joseph Banister, Susanna Banister. Book 1715-21, p. 157.

BAKER, Sarah. Widow. Leg.- mother Elizabeth Pool to have the care of my children, Elizabeth and Susanna Baker, at the death of my mother, brother Robert Pool and sister Elizabeth Pool are to have my children. Ex. mother Elizabeth Pool. D. January 20, 1764. R. February 7, 1764. Wit. James Bullock Sarah Parish. Elizabeth Pool qualified, security, Robert Pool. Book 1758-64, p. 536. Estate appraised by Samuel Watts, Thomas Latimer and James Naylor. April 3, 1764. Book 1763-71, p. 8. Account of Estate, signed Elizabeth Poole. June 4, 1765. Book 1763-71, p. 46.

BAKER, William. Estate appraised by Cary Selden, John Sheppard, Jr. and R. Brough. Ordered August 7, 1759. R. July 1, 1760. Book 1758-64, p. 157. Estate account, returned by Charles Jenings, Administrator. Audited by George Wray and H. King. R. July 7, 1761. Book 1758-64, p. 263.

BALFOUR, Mary Jemima. Widow of Hampton. Leg.- daughter Charlotte;son George; to friend Mrs. Sarah Cary. Ex. Mr. Wilson Miles Cary. D. July 24, 1781. R. January 27, 1785. Wit. Eleanor Bowser (?), William Brough. Original Will.

BALLARD, Edward. Estate appraised by John Massenburg and William Tucker. Ordered, June 7, 1728. R. June 19, 1728. Book 1704-30, p. 126.

BALLARD, Francis. Leg.- son Servant; daughter Frances; daughter Mary; daughter Lucey; daughter Ann; son Francis; to Mr. Perry. Exs. Joshua Curle, Sr., Alexander McKenzie and son Servant Ballard. D. March 10, 1719. R. March 16, 1719. Wit. Robert Armistead, Mary Jenkins, Jo. Wragg. Book 1715-21, p. 244. Appraisal of the estate of Captain Francis Ballard by James Ricketts, Joseph Banister, John Bordland and Joseph Wragg. April 30, 1720. Book 1715-21, p. 261.

BALLARD, James, Sr. Of Hampton and belonging at present to the schooner Dove. Leg.- brother Edward; eldest brother Francis; to my cousin or niece Sarah, daughter of Edward Ballard. Ex. brother Edward Ballard. February 21, 1782. R. April 25, 1799. Wit. John Seymour, William Dunn. Book 1787-1800, p. 463. Original Will.

BALLARD, William. Of the Town of Hampton. Pilot. Leg.- son Francis; son Edward; son James Servant Ballard; son Edward; the house adjoining Mr. William Armistead to my son Francis, reversion of the bequest to my two grandchildren, William Servant and Ann Ballard; to Mary the daughter of John Ballard. Exs. son Francis and friend Henry King. D. April 22, 1775. R. Wit. Edward Hurst, Banister Minson, Moseley Armistead. Codicil: revocation of negro given to granddaughter Ann Ballard, which I desire to go now to son James Servant. D. September 21, 1781. R. February 28, 1782. Wit. Francis Riddlehurst, John Hunter, Miles King, Edward Ballard qualified, security, John Robinson. Original Will.

BANISTER, Joseph Jr. Appraisal of his estate by John Webb, Charles Jenings and John Dunn. R. May 21, 1740. Book 1737-49, p. 90.

BANISTER, Joseph. (badly torn) Leg.- daughter Affiah Shepard; grandson Banister Minson; daughter Sarah Needham; granddaughter Mary Cooper, with reversion of the bequest to Anne, daughter of William Carter; to Whiting Minson the daughter of Banister Minson; to Mary the daughter of William Carter; to Joseph Needham; to Joseph and John Cooper; mourning rings to Francis Parker, Joannah Carter, Mary Parker and Susanna Skinner; my clothes to Banister Minson, William Carter and Samuel Watts. Refers to lawsuit with the Adms. of Blomfield's estate and specifies that certain negroes are not to be delivered to Col. Selden until he paid for them. Exs. my two daughters, following the advice of Mr. George Wythe. D. October 29, 1760. R. February 3, 1761. Wit. Thomas Latimer, William Bean. Affiah Shepherd qualified, security-Samuel Watts and Banister Minson. Book 1758-64, p. 191. Original Will. Account of the estate of Joseph Banister presented by Apphis Tompkins. Mrs. Tompkins is to furnish rings to Francis Parker, Joannah Carter, Mary Parker and Susanna Skinner persuant to the will of Mr. Banister. Mrs. Needham agrees to pay one-half the charges. Examined by George Walker, Jr., James Wallace, Joseph Selden and Thomas Latimer. R. August 7, 1764. Book 1763-71, p. 12. Estate appraised by Joseph Selden, James Naylor and Hursley Carter. April 7, 1761. Book 1758-64, p. 200.

BANKS, James. Appraisal of his estate by Thomas C. Amory, John Skinner and John Minson. Ordered October 8, 1795. R. October 24, 1799. Mary Banks, signed the return of the sale of the estate. Book 1787-1800, p. 499.

BARBEE, Gray. Mariner. Leg.- brother George Barbee. Ex. brother George Barbee. D. September 29, 1735. R. July 1736. Wit. Isaac Rambow, Samuel Markom, William Dudley. Original Will.

BARNES, John. Leg.- brother Henry Barnes, to John Barnes ye son of Henry Barnes. Ex. brother Henry Barnes. D. December 8, 1689. R. February 18, 1689. Wit. Richard Jones, Thomas Wethersby. Book 1689-1699, p. 109.

BARRADALE, Mathew. Margaret Riddick, Extx. Received of Mills Riddick and wife Margaret, the estate given my wife by her father Martin Goodwin. Signed Jesse Barrett. R. July 9, 1764. Book 1763-71, p. 22.

BARRON, Richard. Of the Town of Hampton. Leg.- wife, reversion at her death to sons, Thomas Cary Barron, Miles Selden Barron and Richard Barron; plantation bought of William Jennings on on the James River to be sold for debts; daughter Elizabeth Jones; my military certificates to my wife; daughter Mary Graves. Exs., wife and Mr. Miles King. D. June 26, 1787. R. January 24, 1788. Wit. William Johnston, Ann Harper, Henry Dunn. Security for Exs., William Armistead and Wilson C. Selden. Original Will.

BARRON, Samuel. Leg.- son Robert Barron. Exs., son-in-law Bartian Servant and friend Robert Brough. Wit. Elennor Roe, Nathaniel Allen, Robert Brough. D. August 15, 1757. Original Will. Security for Exs., Bertrand Servant and Robert Brough, John Minson and William Wager. Appraisers appointed were Cary Selden, John Minson, John Bennet and Willis Scott. April 5, 1758. Order Book 1755-60, p. 106.

BATTS, Henry. Leg.- brothers John and Thomas; Godson Wm. Wood; sister Elizabeth Wade; each of my sisters. Exs., brothers John and Thomas Batts. D. December 30, 1717. R. May 21, 1718. Wit. Charles Jenings, William Westwood, Bridget Chaven. Book 1715-21, p. 121.

BATTS, Thomas, Sr. Leg.- son Henry; daughter Elizabeth Wade; son John; daughter Martha Wood. Ex., son Thomas Batts. D. October 2, 1717. R. January 22, 1718. Wit. Charles Jenings, Elizabeth Cole. Book 1715-21, p. 158.

BATTS, Thomas. Leg.- son John; son Thomas; daughter Lydia Batts. Exs., friends William Westwood and Thomas Tabb. D. March 21, 1737/38. R. May 18, 1738. Wit. John Webb, Susannah Webb, John Cook. Book 1737-49, p. 50. Original Will. Appraisal of estate by Thomas Baker, Thomas Smith and Ed. Parish. February 21, 1738. Book 1737-49, p. 60.

Bayley and Bailey

BAILEY, Charles. Leg.- wife Frances; son William; son Charles; son Thomas Bailey. Exs., wife, son William Bailey and friend George Wray. D. March 8, 1794. R. September 25, 1794. Wit. Pascow Herbert, Samuel Healy, James Cunningham, Seawel (?) Armistead. Book 1787-1800, p. 177. Original Will.

BAYLEY, Diana Wallace. Leg.- son Wilson Wallace debt from Mr. Francis Riddlehurst of Hampton, with reversion of bequests to daughter Elizabeth Wallace Bayley and my sister Rachel Mallory. Ex., Mr. Johnson Mallory. D. January 27, 1792. R. February 23, 1792. Wit. Robert Armistead, David Lively, Rebecca Russell. Johnson Mallory qualified, security-George Booker. Book 1787-1800, p. 64. Original Will. Appraisal of estate by Thomas B. Armistead, John Skinner, William Sandy. R. July 24, 1794. Book 1787-1800, p. 167.

BAYLEY, James. Nuncupative Will. Leg.- mother Judith Bayley to take his estate into her possession toward the maintenance of the child Anne Cordert now goes with, in case the said child dies reversion to his brother Pasco Bayley. D. March 11, 1741/42. R. December 15, 1742. Proved by Judith Bayley, Pasco Bayley and Sarah Bayley. Book 1737-49, p. 155.

BAYLEY, James. Division of estate; to John Stith Westwood and wife Judith 1/5; to William King and wife Mary 1/5; to James Bayley 1/5; to Walter Bayley 1/5; to orphans of William A. Bayley, decd. Division by Thomas B. Armistead, Bartlet Fields and Joseph Needham. March 27, 1793. Book 1787-1800, p. 142. Appraisal of the estate by Thomas B. Armistead, Sheldon Moss and John Skinner. Book 1787-1800, p. 373. Another division of estate to Mary King, John S. Westwood in right of his wife Judith and the orphans of William A. Bayley, decd., by Charles Jenings, Edward Face and John Banks. R. July 27, 1798. Book 1787-1800, p. 411.

BAYLEY, John. Leg.- eldest son Walter; wife Judith to all my children. Wife Extx. March 25, 1720. R. May 18, 1720. Wit. Joseph Wragg, Joshua Curle, Margaret Needham. Book 1715-21, p. 248. Appraisal of the estate by Samuel Sweeny, Joseph Banister and John Moore. June 9, 1720. Book 1715-21, p. 265.

BAYLEY, John Wallace. Leg.- to my half brother, Walter Wallace Bayley, with reversion to my half brother Charles Lee Wallace Bayley, who is also to have a negro sold by Henry Allen, Sr. to Mrs. Mary Pride, for Mr. John More Bayley's lifetime, John More Bayley has since died and the said negro descended to James Wallace Bayley, Jr., and after his death fell to me as heir at law; to my half brothers and sisters, Robert, Wilson, Charles Lee and Elizabeth Wallace Bayley; to Edward Mallory, Sr.; I desire that a house be built on the plantation on Back River on which my father dwelt for my step mother Dianah Wallace Bayley. Exs., friends Thomas Baker Armistead, Capt. Miles King. D. December 9, 1784. R. January 27, 1785. Wit. John Seymour, James Bray Armistead, Thomas B. Armistead. Original Will.

BAYLEY, John. Division of estate among legatees; to William King, William Redwood, Walter Bayley, James Bayley and John Stith Westwood. Divided by Miles King, Joseph Needham and George Booker. February 4, 1796. Book 1787-1800, p. 286. Appraisal by Thomas B. Armistead, Bartlett Field and Sheldon Moss. Book 1787-1800, p. 374.

BAYLEY, Judith. Leg.- daughter Sarah; son Pascow; son Nicholas Bayley. Exs., my children, Sarah, Nicholas and Pascow Bayley. D. January 2, 1752. Wit. J. Wallace, Priscilla Michell, Mary Mall (ory ?). Original Will.

BAYLEY, Margaret. Widow. Leg.- granddaughter Margaret daughter of my son Walter; granddaughters Mary and Betty, daughters of my son Walter; to Sarah the daughter of Walter Bayley; grandson Christopher Needham, the son of Thomas Needham; daughter Margaret Needham; son John Bayley. Exs., son Walter Bayley and daughter Margaret Needham. D. December 8, 1719. R. July 20, 1720. Wit. Samuel Selden, John Selden, Thomas Jones. Book 1715-21, p. 267.

BAYLEY, Nicholas. Leg.- son John Moore Bayley; with reversion to daughter Fanny; the reversion of my land to the second son of my cousin John Bayley called John; to my cousin James Wallace Bayley's son James Bayley, Exs., cousins John Bayley and James Wallace Bayley. D. July 29, 1765. R. September 3, 1765. Wit. William Minson, Mark Parrish, Willis Skinner. Security for Exs., Moseley Armistead, Samuel Thomas, Thomas Wootten. Book 1763-71, p. 62. Appraisal of the estate of Nicholas Bayley by Thomas Dixon, William Minson, Anthony Hawkins. October 1, 1765. Book 1763-71, p. 71.

BAYLEY, Sarah. Leg.- son James Wallace Bayley all of my part of the estate of my mother and father. Ex., son James Wallace Bayley. March --, 1754. Wit. Pascow Bayley, Hen. King, Francis Parker. Original Will. Security for Ex., Henry King and Pascow Bailey. Appraisers appointed, Cary Selden, Thomas Dixon, George Wray, Jr., and William Wager. April 5, 1757. Order Book 1755-60, p. 85 & 108.

BAYLEY, Sidwell. Administration granted James Nobbs, security, Wilson Roscow Bayley and Francis Parker. Appraisers appointed were William Armistead, John Moore, John Herbert and Thomas Dixon. November 4, 1760. Order Book 1755-60, p. 11 & 12.

BAYLEY, Walter. Estate appraised by Richard H. Hurst and John Banks. October Ct. 1797. Book 1787-1800, p. 373.

BAYLEY, William. Leg.- son Wilson Pasco Bayley (not 21); wife Sidwell; if my wife should remarry my estate to be equally divided between my children by friends Charles Jenings, John Jenkins and William King. D. April 10, 1746. R. August 20, 1746. Sidwell Bayley qualified, security, Samuel Galt and Angus McCoy. Book 1737-49, p. 220. Appraisers of the estate were William King, John Jenkins and Anthony Tucker. September 17, 1746. Book 1737-49, p. 226.

Balis and Baylis

BAYLIS, Humphrey. Leg.- son John land adjoining William Baylis; son Thomas Baylis. Exs., wife and sons John and Thomas Baylis. D. September 8, 1716. R. July 17, 1717. Wit. Thomas Baylis, John Whitfield, Thomas Poole. Book 1715-21, p. 84. Inventory returned by Jane Baylis. July 2, 1719. Book 1715-21, p. 196. Estate appraised by Edward Lattimore, James Naylor and William Coopland. R. August 25, 1719. Book 1715-21, p. 211.

BAYLIS, Thomas. Gent. Planter. Leg.- eldest son Thomas, second son Humphrey; third son John; fourth son William. Refers to plantation on which my son-in-law Thomas House is going to situate; wife. D. R. 18 of Xber 1696. Wit. Thomas Carter, Samuel Tompkins. Book 1689-1699, p. 223.

BAYLIS, Thomas. Leg.- son Thomas; son William; daughter Mary Abrahams; daughter Eadith; son John Baylis. Exs., sons Thomas and William Baylis and wife Mary Baylis. D. September 14, 1741. R. June 18, 1746. Wit. Humphrey Baylis, Thomas Baylis, Thomas Latimer. Book 1737-49, p. 276. Appraisal of estate by Thomas Latimer, Baldwin Sheppard, James Latimer and Thomas Minson. July 16, 1746. Signed, Thomas and William Baylis Exs. Book 1737-49, p. 221.

BAYLIS, William. Of the Town of Hampton. Mariner. Leg.- son William lot bought of William Wager; son George; wife Ann; daughter Susanna Baylis. D. January 2, 1760. R. January 1760. Wit. John Brodie, Pascow Curle. Ann Baylis qualified, security, David Curle and Robert Hundley. Book 1758-64, p. 107. Original Will. Appraised by Charles Pasteur, Francis Ballard, Francis Parker and Francis Riddlehurst. Order Book 1755-60, p. 270.

BEAN, John. Estate appraised by John Jenkins, John Moore and Anthony Tucker. Ordered September 4, 1746. R. September 17, 1746. Book 1737-49, p. 225. Elizabeth Bean was appointed Admtx. Her security, William Parsons and Samuel Galt. August 20, 1746. Order Book 1731-47, p. 505.

BEDINGFIELD, Nathaniel. Of Hampton. Leg.- wife Mary; Captain Samuel Ellis is to be given a good right to my tract of land in Surry County. Exs., William Bennett of the County of Surry and John Hardyman of Elizabeth City County. D. March 9, 1798. R. June 28, 1798. Wit. John Britain, James Banks, Timothy Baker. Book 1787-1800, p. 406. Original Will.

BELL, Mrs. Margaret. Estate appraised by Charles Collier, Samuel Thomas and Thomas Robinson. R. December 27, 1798. Account of estate, examined by Michael King, Thomas Robinson and Charles M. Collier. William Allen, Jr., Administrator. August 24, 1799. Book 1787-1800, p. 509.

BELL, Nathaniel. Leg.- daughter Mary; daughter Jane; daughter Sophia Maney; daughter Diana Holloway; at the death of my wife my plantation to be sold and the money divided between my children, John, James, Mary, Jane and Nathaniel Cay Bell; wife Margaret Bell. Exs., wife Margaret and Mr. Miles King. D. July 18, 1787. R. June 25, 1789. Wit. William Hicks, William Kirby, Miles King. Original Will. Account of estate. Paid Mary and Jane Bell; paid Robert Maney's wife; paid Robert Holloway's wife; paid the widow Bell. Account given of the estate of William Sandifur of which Nathaniel Bell was Ex., Paid Mrs. Elizabeth Sandifur her proportional part of her husband's estate, paid Robert Sandifur, paid William Sandifur. R. September 27, 1792. Signed, Miles King, Shf. Book 1787-1800, p. 100.

BENNETT, John. Leg.- son William, land bought of Bartrand Servant; daughter Mary Bennett. Ex., son William Bennett. D. December 24, 1769. R. January 26, 1770. Wit. Cary Selden, James Wood, William Harper. Book 1763-71, p. 321. Original Will.

BERRY, Eleanor. John Tucker brings suit for her maintenance during her lifetime. March 18, 1723. Order Book 1723-29, p. 9.

BERRY, James. Leg.- wife Ann Berry. Exs., son James Berry and Elizabeth Davis. D. February 7, 1800. R. February 27, 1800. Wit. R. Armistead, John Wilson. Book 1787-1800, p. 522.

BLACK, John. Wills dated March 27, 1669. This fact found in a deed when John Colwell sold land left him in his last will and testament. June 18, 1691. Book 1689-1699, p. 111.

BLAND, Samuel. Estate appraised by John Cooper, Thomas Fenn and Thomas Latimer. Ordered January 26, 1798. R. February Court 1798. Book 1787-1800, p. 390.

BLAND, Rev. William. Estate in account with Robert Pool. Audited by Joseph Cooper, Thomas Fenn, John Lewis. May 24, 1792. Book 1787-1800, p. 87.

BLUMFIELD, Francis. Administration granted Cary Selden, security, William Wager and William Young. Appraisers appointed Thomas Lattimer, Samuel Watts, John Minson, James Manson. R. July 1, 1760. Order Book 1755-60, p. 297.

BLUMFIELD, Joseph. Estate appraised by James Wallace, John Selden, Baldwin Shepard, Robert Brough. February 17, 1741. Book 1637-49, p. 117. Account of estate. Mrs. Frances Blumfield Admtx. and assigned her dower; to maintenance of Joseph Blumfield an infant. Audited by T. Michell, John Brodie, Wilson Curle, George Wray and Robert Armistead. Among items, paid passage for nine persons and three negroes from the West Indies. August 15, 1744. Book 1737-49, p. 189.

BOID, John. To estate of John Creek decd. money for coffins for Boid and wife. Paid board for children. Audited by Robert Armistead and Thomas Dixon. September 3, 1765. Book 1763-71, p. 64.

BORDLAND, John. Appraisal ordered recorded. June 16, 1736. Book 1737-49, p.

BORDLAND, Mrs. Mary. Estate appraised by William Tucker, George Wray, Servant John Proby. January 21, 1746. Book 1737-49, p. 234. Estate settled by W. Wager, William Tucker, George Wray. December 6, 1748. Book 1737-49, p. 306.

BOSSELL (Boswell), William. Leg.- son William (not 16). daughter Agnes land in Nansemond County; daughter Grace; wife Eleanor Bossell. Exs., wife, George Walker and son William Bossell. D. June 28, 1718. R. September 17, 1718. Wit. William Brough, Elizabeth Howard, Joseph Wragg. Book 1715-21, p. 146. Appraisal of the estate of Captain William Boswell by Thomas Wythe, Joshua Curle, J. Ricketts, taken at the house of Mrs. Boswell. November 24, 1719. Book 1715-21, p. 221. Inventory of certain things for the use of the family, taken at the house of Mr. Yeo, by Thomas Wythe, Joshua Curle and James Ricketts. June 22, 1721. Book 1716-21, p. 306.

BOULT, Charles. Appraisal by Sir George Eland and Robert Holmes. November 22, 1689. Book 1688-1699, p. 80.

BOUTWELL, Adam. Leg.- son John; son Samuel; son Edward; son Roe; daughter Ann; wife Katherine; daughter Elizabeth; provision for an unborn child. Exs., wife Katherine and friend James Cuningham. D. November 14, 1754. R. July 2, 1755. Wit. Nathaniel Cuningham, William Avera, Ann Cuningham. Original Will. Ordered that James Cunningham be summoned to take upon himself the executorship of the will of Adam Boutwell. October 7, 1755. Order Book 1755-60, p. 26.

BOWTELL (Boutwell), William. Leg.- son William; son Adam; daughter Sarah; wife. D. May 11, 1714. R. May 16, 1717. Wit. Thomas Naylor, Ann Roe, John Skinner. Probation granted Elizabeth Bowtell, widow. Book 1715-21, p. 72. Appraisal of the estate by Thomas Tucker, Robert Bright, and Charles Cooper. August 30, 1717. Book 1715-21, p. 86.

BOYS, Michael. Administration granted Barbara Boys, security, John Loyall and Josiah Massenburg. Appraisers appointed, Carter Tarrant, James Westwood, Thomas Dixon, Charles Pasteur. July 6, 1756. Order Book 1755-60, p. 58.

BRADFIELD, William, Sr. Will dated September 26, 1664. Land Book 7, p. 712.

BROWNE, William. Administration granted Thomas House. February 18, 1694/95. Book 1689-1699, p. 155.

BRIGHT, ------- Estate, ----- Tucker Adm. Indexed but account destroyed. Book 1689-99.

BRIGHT, John. Estate appraised by Thomas Jenings, William Carter and Thomas Wootten. July 6, 1762. Book 1758-64, p. 345.

BRIGHT, John. Nuncupative Will. Leg.- to brother Samuel Bright and my mother. September --, 1797. Book 1787-1800, p. 365.

BRIGHT, Robert. Leg.- son Robert Bright. Ex., son Robert Bright. D. 21 of 8ber 1715. R. October 16, 1717. Wit. Thomas Naylor, Charles Cooper, Stephen Lillis. Book 1715-21, p. 89.

BRIGHT, Robert. Leg- son John; wife Hanah; daughter Elizabeth; daughter Anne. Exs., wife, my brother Charles Tucker and my cousin Anthony Tucker. January 19, 1722/23. R. May 19, 1723. Wit. William Lowry, Fleet Cooper, Wil Westwood. Book 1721-23, p. 169. Appraisal of the estate by Charles Jenings, John Robinson, Joseph Harris. February 5, 1725/26. 1704-30, p. 48. Hannah Skinner qualified on the will of her late husband, Robert Bright. Order Book 1723-29, p. 92.

BRIGHT, Robert. Leg.- Land bought of Littleton Watts to be sold; son Robert the plantation I was to have in right of Littleton Watts, after the death of Samuel Watts, Sr., who now holds it; son Samuel; son John; son Francis; wife Mary. Extx., wife Mary Bright. D. April 22, 1784. R. January 23, 1785. Wit. Samuel Watts, Worlich Westwood. Mary Bright qualified, security-Samuel Watts, Sr., Charles Jenings, John Cowpier. Original Will.

BRIGHT, Robert. Leg.- brother John (not of age); reversion of bequest to brother Francis Bright. Ex., mother Mary Bright. D. September 12, 1788. R. October 28, 1790. Wit. Charles Jennings, Thomas Latimer, Samuel Watts. Original Will. Account of estate examined by Joseph Needham, Thomas Watts and Samuel Selden. September 26, 1799. Book 1787-1800, p. 489.

BRITTAIN, John. Estate appraised by Thomas Sorrell, Christopher Needham and Christopher Peirce. William Brittain, administrator. December 15, 1742. 1737-49, p. 149.

BRODIE, Elizabeth. Of the Town of Hampton. Leg.- son John; son Lodowick; son David lot in the town of Warwick; daughter Elizabeth S. Brodie. Exs., son David and daughter Elizabeth S. Brodie. D. July 30, 1784. R. September 25, 1788. Wit. Benjamin Bryan, George Wray, Charles Jennings. Original Will.

BRODIE, James. Appraisal of the estate by Max[l]. Calvert, Richard Scott and William Orange. November 2, 1762. Signed by Florence McNamara. Book 1758-64, p. 368.

BRODIE, John. Leg.- wife Elizabeth if she will give ten pounds each to John Brodie, Lodowick Brodie and Elizabeth Brodie; son David Brodie. Extx., wife Elizabeth Brodie. D. R. July 22, 1784. Wit. Westwood Armistead, Charles Jenings, John Banks. Original Will.

BROUGH, Mary. Leg.- daughter Sarah McCo ------ (torn) Ex., daughter Sarah McCo----. E. March 21, 1778. Wit. John Cowling, Elizabeth Cowling. Original Will.

BROUGH, Robert. Leg.- son William, the plantation purchased of Bartrand Servant; son Robert a plantation in Princess Ann County; daughter Bowrey has received her part of my estate; provision for settlement of a mill owned with Cary Selden. D. March 1, 1770. R. June 28, 1770. Exs., wife and son William Brough. Wit. Wa. McClurg, Joseph Selden, Cary Selden. Grace Brough and William Brough qualified. Book 1763-71, p. 355. Original Will.

BROUGH, William. Will proved by William Smelt and Robert Brough. Mary Brough qualified. Appraisers appointed George Waff, John Henry Rombo, William Tucker and John Nelson. December 17, 1735. Order Book 1731-47, p. 102.

BROWN, James. Leg.- wife Margarett, land bought of William Bayley; son James; son William; daughter Sophia; daughter Euphan; reversion if my children should die to my brother William Brown, reversion to James Wallace. D. March 15, 1718. R. January 21, 1718. Wit. William Baylis, Hanah Whitfield, James Wallace. Probation granted to Margarett Brown. Book 1715-21, p. 156.

BROWN, James. Leg.- daughter Martha (not 18); daughter Mary (not 18); wife Elizabeth Brown. D. October 11, 1739. R. February 21, 1739. Wit. Robert Tucker, Hugh Ross. Book 1737-49, p. 77. Original Will. Appraisal of the estate by John Howard, Rt. Cross, William Morehead. R. August 20, 1740. Book 1737-49, p. 94. Estate of James Brown. Paid Elizabeth Davis one-third of the estate as the late widow of the said Brown. Examined by Merritt Sweny, Miles Cary, Rt. Armistead. R. September 15, 1749. Book 1737-49, p. 348.

BROWN, Mary. Nuncupative Will. Leg.- sister Betty; sister Patty Ross; sister-in-law Margaret Ross; brother-in-law John Ross. D. October 15, 1753. R. February 6, 1754. Proved by Ann Ross. Original Will.

BROWN, Philip, Jr. Leg.- wife Elizabeth; daughter Mary Wilson Brown; daughter Elizabeth, if my daughters should die without heirs my estate to be divided between Robert Pressey, son of my sister Ann, James Saunders, Jr., Judith Wood Saunders and Martha Allen. My daughters to be bound out until 18 or married, if the profits of my estate does not take care of them. Exs., friends Westwood Armistead, John Allen and wife. D. January 24, 1778. R. November 26, 1778. Wit. John Armistead, William Smelt, Elizabeth Smith. Mary Brown qualified, security-Mary Wood and William Brown. Original Will. Account of estate, returned by Mary Brown. Examined by Will Mallory, C. Clausel, Robert Sandifur. July 23, 1767. Book 1763-71, p. 169.

BROWN, Sophia. Leg.- mother Margaret Phillips money which Phillip Cowper has on interest; daughter Margaret Dean; son James Brown. Ex., Nathaniel Bell. D. December 2, 1755. R. April 8, 1761. Wit. J. Westwood, Daniel Routon, Robert Brown. James Brown entered a caveat against probation, saying she had a husband then living. Book 1763-71, p. 169. Original Will.

BROWNE, William. Leg.- to Edward Jegetes; son William; wife Susan; daughter Sarah, reversion of bequests to my children to Edward Jegetes and Elizabeth Tully. Exs., wife and son William Browne, overseer- Thomas House. D. November 4, 1694. R. February 18, 1694/95. Wit. Thomas Francis, Thomas Pool. Book 1689-1699, p. 181. Administration granted Thomas House. February 18, 1694/95. Book 1689-99, p. 155. Administration granted Thomas House in behalf of William Browne. Appraisers for the widow, Worleich Westwood and Gabriel Dunn; for the orphan, Christopher Copeland and Thomas Bayley. R. February 18, 1694/95. Order Book 1689-1699, p. 54.

BROWNE, William. Rebecca Browne qualified as Admtx., security, John Jones, Thomas Jones, Leonard Whiting, Thomas Baylis. May 16, 1722. Book 1721-28, p. 49. Appraisal of the estate of William Browne by John Bushell, James Naylor and John Poole. June 20, 1722. Book 1721-28, p. 54.

BROWN, William. Leg.- wife Diana, all the estate I received by my marriage with her; granddaughter Mary Landrum; daughter Mary Landrum; daughter Nancy Brown. Exs., wife, friends George Booker and George Wray. D. December 9, 1797. R. June 26, Wit. George Bates, Mallory Ross, George Wray, Ginthea Smelt. Original Will.

BRYAN, Benjamin. Leg.- son William; daughter Sarah Marchant; daughter Mary; daughter Patsey; my house to be rented out by Mr. Thomas Jones. D. May 28, 1797. R. June 22, 1797. Wit. John Applewhite, Minson T. Proby. Book 1787-1800, p. 353. Original Will.

BRYAN, Richard. Leg.- son John; wife Mary to bring up my younger children. Ex., Mr. Bartlett Field. D. January 23, 1784. R. February 26, 1784. Wit. Gerrard Seymour, Ann Seymour. Bartlett Field qualified, security-Thomas Humphlett. Original Will. Account estate, paid for the lodging Richard Bryan, orphan; cash paid William Langley for boarding the orphans. Examined by Gerrard Seymour, Thomas Allen, William Lively. January 25, 1787. Original papers.

BURT, Richard. Leg.- wife Sarah; daughter Elizabeth; daughter Rebecca; daughter Sarah. Extx., wife Sarah Burt. D. August 31, 1784. R. March 24, 1785. Wit. James Bullock, Ellyson Skinner, John Skinner. Original Will.

BURTELL, James. Leg.- to Childermus, third son of Madam Katherine Croft, my lot adjoining Robert Taylor; to brother Edward Burtell; to brother John Burtell; to Abraham, the youngest son of Madam Croft; to Mrs. Marthay Taylor. Ex., friend Mr. Cole Digges. D. September 10, 1716. R. September 19, 1716. Wit. George Waffe, Joseph Banister, John Smith. Book 1715-21, p. 49. Administration granted John Burtell. 19 of Xber 1716. Book 1715-21, p. 9. Appraisal of the estate, produced by Simon Hollier, Sheriff and Joseph Banister by F. Ballard, Thomas Howard and William Bossell. December 24, 1716. Book 1715-21, p. 86.

BURTON, Peter. Administration granted John Weymouth. Security, Henry Rombough and John Middleton. Wit. Robert Irwin and Isaac Rambow. July 18, 1721. Appraisal estate by Joseph Banister, William Loyall, Jo. Wragg. July 24, 1721. Book 1721-28, p. 1.

BUSHELL, John. Leg.- son William; son John; son Andrew; to son Joseph a bed, which he carried to William Randolph's when he left me; daughter Ann Randolph; daughter Frances Farefield. Ex., son Andrew Bushell. D. November 5, 1747. R. February 2, 1747. Wit. James Brown, Ann Brown. Book 1737-49, p. 270. Appraisal of the estate by Thomas Latimer, Baldwin Sheppard, Thomas Bayley. Signed, Andrew Bushell. June 7, 1748. Book 1737-49, p. 288.

BUSHELL, John. Leg.- wife Ann; daughter Frances Butt; son William; son John (aforesaid sons not of age); son Thomas; son James, land bought of my brother William Bushell; to son James ye younger. Exs., wife and son Thomas Bushell. D. February 21, 1754. R. Wit. Andrew Bushell, Thomas Fenn, William Dunn. Original Will.

BYLLINGS, William. Administration of the estate granted Thomas Allen. November 20, 1699. Order Book 1689-1699, p. 160.

CAMPBELL, Priscilla. Leg.- daughter Mary, the wife of William Armistead. Ex. son-in-law William Armistead. D. October 6, 1784. R. December 22, 1785. Wit. Hannah Armistead, Wilson Curle, Darby Tuel. Original Will.

CARNIBEE, Daniel. Probation was granted Philipa Carnibee on his will. Appraisers appointed were John Roe, Robert Brough, Bertrand Proby and James Servant. April 16, 1735. Order Book 1731-47, p. 92.

CARTER, ------. Probation indexed, page destroyed on which recorded. Book 1689-1699.

CARTER, Hursley. Leg.- wife Ann; son Robert; son William (not 14); daughter Elizabeth; son John; son Lemuel; son Hursley; provision for unborn child. My will is that the lottery for land drawn or about to be drawn in Petersburg and entered by Chapman Manson shall be sold. Extx. wife Ann Carter. D. February 4, 1763. R. April 5, 1763. Wit. Francis Riddlehurst, William Carter, James Baker, James Bullock, Joanna Carter. Ann Carter qualified, security-William Carter and Francis Riddlehurst. Book 1758-64, p. 432. Original Will. Estate appraised by James Naylor, Banister Minson and Thomas Jenings. July 5, 1763. Book 1758-64, p. 416.

CARTER, William. Leg.- daughter Anne; son John; daughter Mary; son William Carter (not 15). Ex. Captain Joseph Selden. D. December 26, 1768. R. January 27, 1769. Wit. James Baker, William Face, Elizabeth Baker, Robert Carter. Joseph Selden qualified, security-William Armistead. Book 1763-71, p. 275. Estate appraised by Robert Bright, George Latimer, James Baker. December 27, 1770. Book 1763-71, p. 400.

CARTER, William. Leg.- brother Lameuell Carter. Ex. brother Lameuell Carter. D. November 12, 1781. Wit. Thomas Fenn, Joseph Cooper, Hursley Carter, William Carter, Jr. Original Will.

CARVER, Alexander. Ann Carver his wife qualified on estate, security-William Spicer and Brian Penny. Appraisers of the estate were Francis Rogers, Thomas Allen and Charles Tucker. Ordered May 21, 1718. R. July 18, 1718. Book 1715-21, p. 131.

CARY, John. Leg.- wife Susannah the land bought of Capt. John Parsons decd., in Charles Parish, York County; to my children; Miles, Hannah Armistead, Betsey Allen, Gill Armistead, John, Judith Robinson, Susannah and Nathaniel Robert Cary; sale of property in York County to be divided among my children as I ow have or hereafter may have by my wife Susannah; the claim I have in the right of my wife against the estate of Mr. Gill Armistead to be used for certain debts; negroes which came by her to be divided among her children only. Exs. wife, brother Robert Cary, friend William Armistead of the mill, Richard Cary and Miles Cary of Warwick County. D. October 28, 1794. R. July 23, 1795. Wit. J.M. Galt, John Kirby, William Brown. Book 1787-1800, p. 247. Original Will.

CARY, Miles. Of Ceeley. Leg.- sister Mary Selden; nephew Cary Selden; brother Wilson Cary; nephew Miles Selden; niece Sarah Fairfax; niece Mary Cary, niece Ann Nicholas; niece Elizabeth Cary; nephew Wilson Miles Cary, with reversion of bequest to his father Wilson Cary; land in King and Queen County to brother Wilson Cary; refers to his brother William

Roscow Cary decd., leaving a bequest to his son James Roscow Cary, with a reversion to his brother Wilson Roscow Cary; to Mrs. Catherine Burkelow with reversion of bequest to nephews Cary, Samuel and Miles Selden. Ex. brother Wilson Cary, in case of the death of my brother my Exs. Mr. Robert Carter Nicholas and nephew Wilson Miles Cary when he is 21. D. October 11, 1752. Wit. George Wray, Jr., Charles Pasteur, James Wallace, William Diston. Original Will. Wilson Cary, Gent. qualified, security-Cary Selden, Gent. Appraisers appointed in Elizabeth City County, Robert Armistead, Charles Jenings, Anthony Tucker and Francis Jones. Appraisers appointed in King and Queen County, George Pigg, John Forster, Richard Crittenden, William Collier and Alexander Wederburn. Appraisers appointed in Albemarle County, John Cobb, Joseph Thompson, Guy Smith, Samuel Hopkins, Jacob Moon, Samuel Jordan, John Cannon, John Firn, Henry Martin, John Bryan. November 2, 1756. Order Book 1755-60, p. 77 & 82.

CARY, Wilson. Of Ceeleys. Leg.- wife Sarah; son Wilson Miles Cary to pay his mother in lieu of dower 100 pounds from income from lands in Albemarle, Henrico, Warwick, Gloucester and King and Queen Counties; a legacy has been left me by the widow of George Dudley, formerly my overseer, which I leave to her son living in King and Queen near Poropotank; granddaughter Sarah Cary; granddaughter Mary Munro Cary; at request of my son I am omitting a provision formerly made for my daughter Mrs. Sarah Cary in case I outlived my son Wilson Miles Cary; to my four daughters, Sarah, Mary, Anne and Elizabeth-refers to their husbands; daughter Elizabeth Fairfax's part of estate in trust, without intervention by her husband Bryan Fairfax, with reversion to her daughters and son William Fairfax; nephew Colonel Cary Selden; reference to money for which Colonel Lem. Riddick is liable; to Mrs. Elizabeth Eyre a suit of mourning out of Col. Prentis Staro; ring to sister Selden; Robert Carter Nicholas to be paid for his advice; grandson Miles Cary. I was appointed Ex. with Hon. John Blair and Col. John Bolling to will of my sister Anne Whiting, a bond being paid her by Col. Henry Whiting before I qualified and John Blair loaned it to James Shields, my Exs., to secure full discharges etc. Exs. son Wilson Miles Cary, son-in-law Robert Carter Nicholas and kinsman Richard Cary of Warwick County. D. October 10, 1772. R. February 25, 1778. Wit. Samuel Rowland, James Gill, William Roade, Thomas Wooten, Jr., Abraham Parish, Keziah Wood. Original Will.

CASEY, John. Appraisal ordered July 10, 1746 by John Jenkins, Anthony Tucker and John Moore. November 20, 1746. Book 1737-49, p. 232. Account of estate audited by Charles Jenings, Robert Armistead, John Moore, Francis Jones and Anthony Tucker. August 3, 1756. Order Book 1755-60, p. 68.

CASEY, John. Account of estate presented by Robert Tucker and wife Ann, who was Admtx. Examined by George Wray, W. Wager, Francis Riddlehurst. May 1, 1759. Book 1758-64, p. 48. Ordered that Cary Selden, George Wray, William Wager and Francis Riddlehurst settle estate. February 7, 1759. Order Book 1755-60, p. 216.

CASEY, Thomas. Leg.- son John (not 21); son Thomas, with reversion of bequest to his two sisters; rest of estate between my three youngest children. D. February 2, 1718. R. May 21, 1718. Wit. Richard Hawkins, Thomas Powell, John Howard. Appraisal of the estate by Hind Armistead, John Skinner, John Howard. May 30, 1718. Book 1715-21, p. 122 & 123.

CATSELL, James. Ordered that Ruthe Street return an inventory of his estate. December 18, 1695. Order Book 1689-99, p. 79.

CAY, Gabriel. Comptroller of his Majesty's Customs in the Lower District of the James River. Leg.- to friend Miles Cary, Esq., Naval Officer of the said district all my effects which are to be sold to defray expense of my burial. December 15, 1769. R. January 24, 1771. Proved by Cary Selden. Original Will.

CEELEY, Thomas. Administration of estate granted his son Charles Ceeley. September 20, 1697. Cassandra Ceely aged 10, orphan of Thomas Ceely bound to John Fiquett and wife Judith. 1698. Rebecca Ceely aged 9, bound to George Gigly and now wife, until she is 18. 1697. Order Book 1689-1699, p. 119, 130 and 217.

CELE, Charles. Leg.- son Daniel Cely; daughter Mary Cely. Ex. son Daniel Cely. D. August 9, 1738. R. March 21, 1738. Wit. John Moore, William Creek. Book 1737-49, p. 63. Original Will.

CHAMP---, John. Indexed, page on which recorded has been destroyed. Book 1689-1699.

CHANDLER, Danll. Ordered Thomas Waterson who married Susanna the relict of the said Chandler give security for the estate of the orphans. May 18, 1694. Order Book 1689-1699, p. 35.

CHANDLER, Hannah. Account of estate returned. Sarah Williams made oath to the truth of the account. July 18, 1739. Book 1737-49, p. 70.

CHANDLER, John. Appraisal of his estate by John Collwell, Henry Barnes. February 18, 1698/99. Signed by Phebe Chandler. Goods given to my son Alexander Strange by my husband John Chandler. February 22, 1698/99. Signed Phebe Chandler. Book 1689-1699, p. 271.

CHANDLER, John. Leg.- wife Hannah; daughter Sarah. Extx. wife Hannah Chandler. D. July 1, 1727. R. June 19, 1728. Wit. Richard Hawkins, Thomas Jones, William Creek. Hannah Cole, Extx. qualified. Book 1704-30, p. 127. Inventory of the estate of John Chandler returned by Hannah Chandler. 18 of Xber 1728. Book 1704-30, p. 162.

CHAPPELL, James. In perfect health, but traveling to North Carolina. Leg.- to John Cross; to Ann Cross; to Elizabeth Cross; to William Cross; to Robert Cross. D. February 2, 1739/40. R. November 19, 1740. Wit. Robert Tucker, Vialeto Keble. Book 1737-49, p. 94. Original Will.

CHAPPEL, Zachariah. Leg.- cousin William Allen land in Warwick County. Ex. cousin William Allen. D. January 13, 1726. R. June 21, 1727. Wit. John Jones, Thomas Allen, Thomas Dewberry. Book 1704-30, p. 75.

CHEELEY, Joseph. Administration granted Mary his relict now wife of John Nelson. Appraisers for the widow Edmond Swany and Augustine Moore and those for orphans Robert Crook and Hugh Ross. September 18, 1696. September 18, 1696 Rebecca Ceely bound to George Gigly. Book 1689-1699, p. 156. Order Book p. 104 & 119. Appraisal by Augustine Moore, William Malory, Robert Crooke and Hugh Ross. October 5, 1696. Book 1689-99, p. 222. Administration granted to son Charles Ceely.

Order Book 1689-1699, p. 119.

CLEILAND, James. Estate settled by George Wray, Wil. Westwood and Alexander Hamilton. December 19, 1739. Book 1737-49, p. 75.

CLEILAND, William. Lucy Cleiland the widow refused to qualify. Administration granted James Turner, who was also made the administrator of the estate of James Servant. Appraisers for the two estates appointed were Samuel White, Henry Robinson, Robert Brough and John Roe. December 17, 1735. Order Book 1731-47, p. 102 & 103.

COLE, William. Leg.- cousin Henry Robinson all of my land. Ex. cousin Henry Robinson. D. September 22, 1720. R. June 21, 1721. Wit. C. Jenings, Benjamin Rolph, Joseph Milby. Book 1715-21, p. 305.

COLTON, Job. Of the County of Gloucester. Leg.- wife Ann one-half of my estate; son Samuel Colton; provision for unborn child, reversion to friend Robert Brough and his sister Amelia Brough. Exs. wife and friend Robert Brough. D. August 28, 1787. R. February 24, 1796. Wit. Miles King, Charles Jenings, W. Kirby, John Ashton Wray. Book 1787-1800, p. 288. Original Will.

COLWELL, John. Administration of his estate granted Elizabeth his relict. November 18, 1700. Book 1689-99, p. 217.

COMBS, Elizabeth. Administration of her estate granted to William Williams. January 20, 1700. Book 1689-99, p. 217.

COOKE, Elizabeth. Appraisal of her estate at the homes of Evan Randall and James Baker ordered. December 18, 1695. Order Book 1689-1699, p. 79.

COOK, John. Indexed but page on which recorded has been destroyed. Book 1689-1699.

COOPER, ------. Indexed, but recording destroyed. 1689-1688.

COOPER, Abraham. Estate appraised by Baldwin Sheppard, Thomas Latimer, John Bushell. July 29, 1749. Signed by Sarah Cooper, Admtx. Book 1737-49, p. 344.

COOPER, Charles. Will proved by William King and Joseph Skinner. Extx. Barbara Cooper. Appraisers appointed William King, John Cooper, Charles Jenings and William Copeland. June 18, 1735. Order Book 1731-47, p. 95.

COOPER, John. Leg.- son Joseph my plantation adjoining Mr. John Selden; son John my land adjoining my cousin John Cooper; wife Susanna Cooper. D. December 3, 1748. R. June 6, 1749. Wit. John Selden, John Cooper, Charles Cooper. Codicil appointing John Cooper the guardian of my children in case of the death of my wife. December 20, 1748. Wit. Joseph Banister, Apphia Minson, John Selden. Susanna Cooper qualified, security-Joseph Banister and John Selden. Book 1737-49, p. 335.

COOPER, John. Dr. the orphans of John Cooper the elder to Joseph Banister. To cash paid John Shepherd in right of his wife, balance due the orphans. June 3, 1761. Book 1758-64, p. 256.

COPELAND, Christopher. Leg.- eldest daughter Ann Poole; son Falvi; son Elyas land adjoining William Phrasis and Charles Averit; son William a tract which Phrasy is going to seat after the death of the said William Phrasy and Mary his wife, my daughter; daughter Hannah; daughter Mary Phraser; daughter Hursley Averett; daughter Elizabeth Firmer; daughter Jane Peirce. Wife Extx. D. January 12, 1710/11. R. March 21, 1715. Wit. Thomas Baylis, Moses Davis, William Dunn, Mycall Peirce. Book 1715-21, p. 39.

COPELAND, Henry. Leg.- to William Copeland the son of Christopher 120 acres; to Martha Daniel 120 acres; to my brother Samuel Daniel; to mother Ann Daniel my seal rings; uncle Christopher Copeland; friend Henry Royall to see me decently buried in ye Church yard. Ex. uncle Christopher Copeland. D. June 11, 1693. R. 18 of Xber 1693. Wit. Joseph Farneworth, Darby Daniel, Henry Royall. Book 1689-1699, p. 138. Probation requested by Christopher Coapland on the estate of Henry Coapland. December 18, 1693. Book 1689-99, p. 153.

COPELAND, Mary. Leg.- cousin William Allen son of Philip Allen; cousins Mary and Eleshe Allen; cousin Littleton Wats; son of Samuel Wats; cousin Mary Savage Wats, daughter of Samuel Wats; to daughter Eleshe Allen. February 4, 1753. Wit. Thomas Latimer, James Naylor, William Latimer. Original Will.

COPELAND, William. Leg.- daughter Mary Latimer; daughter Elizabeth White, her husband Charles White; daughter Elsha (not 18); daughter Copeland Copeland (not 18); brother Falvy Copeland; wife Mary Copeland. Wife, Extx. D. March 29, 1738. R. November 21, 1739. Wit. John Selden, Falvy Copeland, John Gorder (?). 1737-49, p. 74. Original Will. Inventory presented by Mary Copeland. August 20, 1740. 1737-49, p. 93.

CORBIER, Paul. Estate appraised by William Latimer, Joseph Cooper, William Latimer, Jr., William King, Jr. Ordered, March 27, 1794. R. July 24, 1794. Book 1787-1800, p. 168.

CORNELIUS, Jane. Leg.- son Spicer; son Jacob; two sons to be left with George Ware; rest of estate to friend George Ware. Ex. George Ware. D. August 24, 1736. R. February 16, 1736. Wit. Tucker Smith, Thomas Kyble, Isaac Rambow. Original Will. Account settled by Thomas Mingham and John Moore. September 15, 1742. Book 1737-49, p. 14[illegible].

CORNELIUS, Thomas. Leg.- son Jacob; son Spicer; daughter Mary; daughter Elizabeth; daughter Hannah; wife Jane. Wife Extx. D. November 7, 1728. R. February 19, 1728. Wit. Richard Hawkins, Sarah Williams, Isaac Rambow. Book 1704-30, p. 163. Appraisal of estate, not signed. March 19, 1728. Book 1704-30, p. 173.

COTSELL (Catsell), James. Appraisers appointed were Walter Bayley and William Hudson. May 18, 1696. Order Book 1689-99, p. 86.

COTTEN, John. Leg.- John Powers; James Fosen (?), Jr. Godson John Fleu; cousin Thomas Freeman; Godson James Wilson. Extx. wife Bridget Cotten. D. February 17, 1726. R. June 21, 1727. Wit. Anthony Armistead, Darby Muline, Charles Avera. Book 1704-30, p. 76. Inventory returned. July 19, 1727. Book 1704-30, p. 88.

COUPLAND, Henry. (See Copeland). Probation granted Christopher

Coupland, security-Anthony Armistead and George Burtenhead. December 18, 1693. Order Book 1689-1699, p. 24.

COWPER, Phillip. Leg.- land adjoining James Stores to be sold for my debts; daughter Elizabeth; to my children: Mary, Jane, Charlotte and Courtney Cowper; other bequests to my wife Elizabeth and children: Chittey, Abraham, Mary, Jane, Charlotte, Courtney and Robert Cowper as they come to age or married. Exs. Edward Cowper and Roe Cowper. D. December 16, 1773. Wit. George Watkins, Margaret Latimore, Jane Barron. Original Will.

COX, Henry. Ordered Michael King, Moss Armistead and Thomas Mingham to settle estate. February 16, 1731. Order Book 1731-47, p. 17.

CREEK, John. Administration of estate granted Sarah Creek, security-John Brodie, Banister Minson and John Casy. Appraisers appointed John Moore, Samuel Roland, King Humphlet, John Casey. January 2, 1760. Order Book 1755-60, p. 271. Appraisal by John Moore, John Casey, King Humphlet. August 5, 1760. Book 1758-64, p. 168. Account of estate settled by Robert Armistead, William Armistead and James Westwood. September 3, 1765. Book 1763-71, p. 61.

CREEKE, William. Leg.- wife Hannah; son William; son George; daughter Elizabeth; daughter Hannah; son Samuel; son-in-law Thomas Powell; son-in-law Marke Powell; son-in-law Mathew Powell. Wife Extx. D. September 22, 1697. R. July 18, 1698. Wit. Thomas Powell, Mathew Powell, Charles Jennings. Book 1689-1699, p. 243. Probation granted Hannah the relict of William Creeke. July 18, 1698. Estate appraised by Charles Jennings and Richard Streete. Signed Hannah Creeke. September 14, 1698. Book 1689-1699, p. 260.

CREEKE, William. Leg.- daughter Hannah Henderson; daughter Elizabeth; son William; son John; son Samuel. Extx. wife Philis Creeke. D. April 9, 1737. R. May 20, 1738. Wit. Thomas Jones, John Jones. Book 1737-49, p. 63. Original Will.

CREEKITS, Reynolds. Appraisal of estate by George Eland and Mark Parrish. Signed Anne Milby. January 26, 1690/91. Division of estate:-the widow's share; Lucy Creekits share; John Creekits share Susannah Creekits. Signed Joseph Milby. 18 of Xber 1693. Book 1689-1699, p. 140.

CROOK, Penuell. Leg.- brother Thomas Crook; sister Deborah Parrish; to Jane Roe, two gold rings at Mr. Galt's; to Abraham Parrish. Ex. brother Thomas Crook. D. June 4, 1741. R. March 17, 1741. Wit. R. Armistead, Ed. Parrish, Agness Cook. Abraham Parrish qualified as Ex. Book 1737-49, p. 119. Original Will. Appraisal of the estate by Thomas Reado, Rt. Armistead and Thomas Williams. May 19, 1742. Book 1737-49, p. 123.

CROOKE, Robert. Administration granted to his son Penuell Crooke. July 18, 1701. Book 1689-99, p. 217.

CROOK, Thomas. Account of the estate examined by Rt. Armistead, George Wray and W. Wager. Paid Roscow Sweny for boarding the orphans. Signed Roscow Sweny. August 7, 1759. Book 1758-64, p. 78.

CROSS, John. Leg.- to my Mother; to brother Edward Cross. D.

February 16, 1742/43. R. May 18, 1743. Wit. Robert Tucker, Mary Tuell. Probation granted Rebecca Cross, security-Thomas Wilson and John Casey. Book 1737-49, p. 166.

CROSS, Rebecca. Estate appraised by Anthony Tucker, John Jenkins and Joseph Jeggitts. Ordered May 15, 1745. R. June 19, 1745. Signed Thomas Wilson, Adm. Book 1737-49, p. 196.

CROSS, Robert. Leg.- son Edward at 21; wife Rebecca; son John; daughter Anne; son William; daughter Elizabeth. Exs wife Rebecca and son John Cross. D. October 19, 1742. R. May 18, 1743. Wit. Charles Tucker, Thomas Wilson. Rebecca Cross qualified, security-Thomas Wilson and John Casey. Book 1737-49, p. 166. Estate appraised by John Moore, Charles Jenings, Jr. and Anthony Tucker. September 21, 1743. Book 1737-49, p. 175. Account estate, examined by Miles Cary, Anthony Tucker, Thomas Everard. June 19, 1745. Book 1737-49, p. 197.

CRUSSELL, Richard. Leg.- wife Mary; son Richard; daughter Elizabeth; provision for unborn child. Extx., wife Mary Crussell. D. April 8, 1718. R. July 16, 1718. Wit. Charles Powers, William Wood, Thomas Delaweny (?). Mary Crussell qualified, security-Charles Powers and Edward Myhill. Book 1715-21, p. 134.

CUNNINGHAM, Nathaniel. Leg.- wife Ann; reversion to my surviving children. D. April 27, 1762. R. July 6, 1762. Wit. James Bullock, John Sheppard, Francis Ballard. Ann Cunningham qualified, security-Henry Sinclair and William Cunningham. Book 1758-64, p. 342. Original Will. Appraisal by George Johnson, Edward Ward, Peter Puryear July 3, 1764. Book 1758-64, p. 532.

CUNNINGHAM, William. Inventory ordered recorded. June 16, 1731. Order Book 1731-47, p. 2.

CUNNINGHAM, William. Leg.- wife Mary; son William, at the death of my wife my estate to be divided among my children. Extx. wife. D. April 7, 1787. R. April 27, 1787. Wit. Thomas Humphlett, Benjamin Cark (Clark), William Cunningham, Jr. Original Will.

CURLE, Andrew. Of Liverpoole in the County of Lancaster. Mariner. Leg.- wife Ann Curle. Extx. wife Ann Curle. D. March 27, 1762. Wit. John Wilson, Michael Robinson, Samuel Selden. Original Will.

CURLE, David Wilson. Appraisal of estate by Rt. Brough, John Riddlehurst, Benjamin Crooker. Ordered June 1767. Signed W.R.W. Curle. Account of sales, signed William Roscow Wilson Curle. February 22, 1770. Book 1763-71, p. 324. Since the within Inventory two negroes have come to my hands, being the dower negroes, which David W. Curle bought of Mrs. Stretch and sold at public auction to William Selden. The negroes were sold during the life of Mrs. Stretch, an explanation is given why they brought such a low price.

CURLE, Hamilton. Priscilla Curle the mother of Hamilton Curle relinquished administration and William Roscow Curle qualified. Security, David Wilson Curle. May 6, 1760. Order Book 1755-60, p. 283. Inventory returned by William Roscow Curle. Book 1763-71, p. 61.

CURLE, John. Bond for Mary Jenkins as Admtx., signed by Thomas Wythe and Joshua Curle. Wit. Charles Jenings. Book 1715-21, p. 170. Henry Jenkins also qualified later. Bond dated February 19, 1718. Appraisal of estate taken at the house of Mrs. Mary Jenkins by Hind Armistead, John Moore, Henry Irwin. November 17, 1719. Ibid, p. 233.

CURLE, John. Administration granted John King on the part of the estate yet unadministered. February 21, 1732. Order Book 1731-47, p. 47.

CURLE, Joshua, Jr. Administration of estate granted Rosea Curle. Appraisers appointed Anthony Tucker, Servant Ballard, John Moore and Richard Hawkins. February 21, 1732. Order Book 1731-47, p. 46.

CURLE, Joshua. Appraisal of estate by William Tucker, Samuel Hawkins and George Wray. May 18, 1737. Book 1737-49, p. 9.

CURLE, Mary. Appraisal estate by William Latimer, John Nicholson, William King. Ordered August 15, 1798. R. September 27, 1798. Book 1787-1800, p. 431.

CURLE, Nicholas. (Original will found among the papers of Northampton County.) The will names wife Jane Extx. Exs. George Walker, John Curle and Henry Jenkins. Leg.- son Pasco; son Wilson, provision for unborn child; brother John Curle; to Nicholas Curle son of Joshua Curle; to Nicholas Bailey, son of John Bailey; kinswoman Lydia Curle, to each of his natural brothers and sisters. Dated August 12, 1714. William & Mary College Quarterly, vol. 26, p. 9-15. Nicholas Curle died August 15, 1714 leaving issue Wilson Curle his eldest son born December 18, 1709. Order Book 1704-30, p. 45. Appraisal of the estate by William Bossell, Edmund Kearny, Thomas Tucker. ------15, 1715. Book 1715-21, p. 35. Henry Jenkins and John Curle, Jane and James Ricketts qualified as Exs. of the will of Nicholas Curle. Security, Anthony Armistead, John King, Thomas Wythe and John Bayley. Book 1715-21, p. 9 & 21. Book 1736-70, p. 54. Estate account, to estate of James Ricketts, decd. due to Mr. Curle's children, to Mrs. Ricketts. Estate of James Ricketts in account with Major Merrit Sweny, examined by Joseph Banister, Jacob Walker and Will Westwood. July 17, 1745. Book 1737-49, p. 207.

CURLE, Nicholas Wilson. About to leave the country; to brother Will Roscow Wilson Curle to hold my estate during the life of my mother, reversion at her death to my said brother. Ex. brother Will Roscow Wilson Curle. D. May 31, 1768. R. June 27, 1771. Wit. James Armistead, Francis Mallory, William Face. Security for Ex. Richard Cary. Book 1763-71, p. 435. Original Will.

CURLE, Pasco. To sundry debts paid for his estate and his schooling in England; received of Mr. Dandridge for a legacy left him and his part of his father's estate. August 21, 1745. Signed by Merrett Sweny. 1737-49, p. 208.

CURLE, Joshua. Division of slaves according to suit. Mr. David Wison Curle came into court and made choice of lot #2 for his brother Nicholas Curle, he to pay Mr. George Walker, Sr., as guardian to Mary and Jane Curle, orphans, he also made choice of lot #5 for his brother Andrew Curle and William Roscow Curle made choice of lot #3 and is to pay the difference to Andrew Curle and George Walker, Sr., guardian to Mary and Jane Curle, orphans. Division made by Rt. Brough, John Jones and W. Wager. February 6, 1760. Book 1758-64, p. 143.

CURLE, Samuel. Leg.- son Samuel after bequests to bring up three youngest children, Sarah, John and Mary Baker Curle; son Darby Tools Curle; son John land on Harris' Creek, adjoining John Shepherd, William Lattimore and Hannah Avent; daughter Mary Baker Curle a negro bought of my brother Joshua Curle; wife Mary Curle. Exs. wife Mary Curle, friends Daniel Barraud and Colonel Cary Selden. D. October 25, 1766. R. June 26, 1767. Wit. Charles King, Robert Kipplin Brown, Robert Bowrey. Mary Curle qualified, security-Thomas Dixon, Curle Tucker and William Wager. Book 1763-71, p. 160. Original Will. Appraisal of the estate by Samuel Watts, James Naylor, William Lattimer. November 26, 1767. Book 1763-71, p. 176.

CURLE, Sarah. Leg.- daughter Mary Jenkins; son-in-law Captain Henry Jenkins; daughter Sarah, wife of Joshua Curle; daughter Judith Bayley; son Joshua; son John; son Nicholas. D. March 19, 1713. (Recorded before September 15, 1715.) Wit. Elizabeth Jenings, Mary Ballard, Euphan Roscow. Book 1715-21, p. 13. Ex. son Nicholas Curle.

CURLE, Sarah. Leg.- niece Sarah Curle Barraud; nephew Thomas Pierce; niece Frances Prevost Barraud, provided brother-in-law Daniel Barraud will pay Mary Herbert, the daughter of beloved niece Sarah Herbert money; sister Catherine Barraud; niece Martha Pierce; niece Sarah daughter of Samuel Curle; nephew Darby Curle; niece Jane Summerell; sister Judith Pierce; niece Mary Bridger. Exs. brother-in-law Daniel Barraud, Mr. James Westwood and Colonel Joseph Bridger. D. February 25, 1764. R. August 5, 1766. Wit. Augustine Moore, Ann Moore, James Westwood. Security for Ex.-James Balfour. Book 1763-71, p. 81. Original Will. Appraisers of the negroes,-sworn by John Hutchings, Justice of Norfolk County, who were John Sprowl, Robert Crooks and John Schaw. August 3, 1767. Book 1763-71, p. 118.

CURLE, Thomas. Cordwainer. Probation granted Ann Curle his relict as Extx. August 20, 1699. Order Book 1689-1699, p. 153. Will recorded May 31, 1700 leaving a bequest to Pasco and Joshua Curle, sons of Pasco Curle. Pasco Curle died intestate leaving his brother Nicholas Curle, who died August 15, 1714 leaving issue Wilson Curle, born December 18, 1709. Order Book 1731-47, p. 292. Thomas Curle's probation granted Nicholas Curle. September 18, 1700. Thomas Curle, Cordwainer. Administration granted John Dixson. June --, 1701. Book 1689-99, p. 217.

CURLE, Wilson. Leg.- wife Priscilla; son Wilson (not of age); son David lots contiguous to George Waffe, reversion to son Hamilton; son Nicholas a tract called Scones Dam plantation; son Andrew land at Foxhill and Harris' Creek; son William Roscow land called Ridgeland; son Hamilton a lot adjoining Henry Irwin and George Waffe; son Wilson the land on Back River bought of Merrett Sweny, he paying to his sister Jane money when she is 18; daughter Mary Curle. Son David is to be left to the management of David Meade until he is of age. Exs. Miles Cary, Cary Selden and David Meade. D. December 15, 1746. R. June 7, 1748. Wit. Alexander Rhonnald, Wilson Curle, Catherine Batts, Mary Hamilton. Priscilla Curle renounced the will. David Meade qualified as Ex. Book 1737-49, p. 289. Inventory returned to David Meade. June 2, 1749. Book 1737-49, p. 329. Wilson Curle, grandson and devisee of Colonel

William Wilson, born December 18, 1709. Order Book in 1704-30, p. 19.

CURLE, Wilson. Leg.- lands in North Carolina to be sold for my debts; beloved wife all the slaves I acquired by her; daughter Elizabeth, reversion to the children of Moss Armistead; to William and Moss Armistead, sons of William Armistead; sister Elizabeth Curle; to relation Wilson Wallace; wife lots in Norfolk and Hampton. Exs. William Langhorne the Elder, Richard Cary and Maurice Langhorne. D. May 25, 1792. R. July 26, 1792. Wit. George Booker, William Diggers, Augustine Moore. William Langhorne qualified, security-Richard and Miles Cary. Book 1787-1800, p. 84. Original Will.

DAILEY, Owen. Leg.- wife; daughter Hannah; daughter Frances Dailey. Wife Extx. D. 1762. R. July 5, 1763. Wit. Thomas Dixon, John Hay. Ann Dailey qualified, security-Signe Parish and Thomas Webster. Book 1758-64, p. 418.

DAMES, John. Leg.- son George; grandson John Dames Ralls; daughter Jane Ralls; to William Dunn; daughter Mary Dunn; granddaughter Rebecca Mowbarry; daughter Ann Boutwell; granddaughter Elizabeth Boutwell; son-in-law William Dunn. Exs. son-in-law William Dunn and daughter Ann Boutwell. D. August 25, 1784. R. October 28, 1784. Wit. Joseph Cooper, Robert Bright. Original Will.

Daniell and Daniel

DANIELL, Ann. Leg.- son Samuel, cattle at Thomas Skinner's plantation; to Ann, Jonathan, Martha, Mary and Darby Skinner; to Samuel Skinner and his mother Elizabeth Skinner; to Martha Pitt (or Pett); to Sarah Pitt; to Ann Mitchel; to my daughter Catherine Pitt; to Elizabeth Riddlehurst. Ex. son Samuel Daniel. D. October 3, 1715. R. August 15, 1716. Wit. John King, Edward Richards, Joseph Skinner. Book 1715-21, -. 41.

DANIELL, Darby. Probation granted Ann Daniell, Extx. Appraisers for the orphans, Henry Robinson and John Cooper. Appraisers for the widow, Henry Royall and George Cooper. March 18, 1697/98. Order Book 1689-1699, p. 130.

DANIEL, John. Appraisal of estate by William Tucker, John Nelson and George Waff. December 15, 1742. Book 1737-49, p. 149.

DANIEL, Samuel. Leg.- nephew Samuel Skinner; wife Jude all the tobacco left to her before marriage; sister Hannah Mitchell and her husband; to the child unborn of Hannah Mitchel; sister Elizabeth Skinner; nephews Robert and Martha Taylor. Ex. brother-in-law John Mitchel. D. March 25, 1718. R. February 19, 1718. Wit. Abraham Mitchel, Nicholas Parker, Jo. Wragg. Book 1715-21, p. 165. John Mitchel qualified, security-William Coopland, James Naylor and Thomas Jones. Wit. Charles Jenings. February 19, 1718. Book 1715-21, p. 196. Appraisal of the estate by Samuel Sweny, Joseph Banister and Jo. Wragg. July 2, 1719. Book 1715-21, p. 171 and 197.

DAVIDSON, David. Leg.- daughter Martha with reversion of bequest to friend John Allen. Ex. John Allen who is also to be guardian to my daughter. D. May 27, 1745. R. July 17, 1745. Wit. William Tuell, Thomas Skinner, Daniel Ceely. John Allen qualified, security-William Allen. Book 1737-49, p. 206.

DAVIS, Charles. Jacob Davis qualified on will, which was proven by Richard Harman and William Davis. Appraised by John Howard, Richard Hawkins, Hugh Ross and William Morehead. Order Book 1731-47, p. 97.

DAVIS, Mary. Joseph Henderson appointed administrator, security- John Casey, William Loyall and William Baker. Appraisers appointed by John Smith, Samuel Roland, John Creek and William Roland. March 7, 1758. Order Book 1755-60, p. 170.

DAVIS, Thomas. Leg.- wife and my dear children. Wife Jane and Edward Davis to see my will performed. D. July 26, 1694. R. March 18, 1694/95. Wit. Augustine Moore, William Mallory. Book 1689-1699, p. 175. Probation granted Edmd. (?) Davis his son March 18, 1694/95. Book 1689-99, p. 155.

DAVIS, Thomas. Account estate, paid widow's part, to the four children's part. Examined by Anthony Hawkins, James Bullock and Samuel Rowland. June 26, 1771. Book 1763-71, p. 440.

DAWS, John. Leg.- son Gilbert; son Ezekial; son John; son Bartholomew; son William; daughter Rachell; daughter Sarah. Ex. Gilbert Daws. D. January 3, 1797. R. January 26, 1796 (?). Wit. John Skinner, Thomas Webster Bullock. Book 1787-1800, p. 338. Original Will.

DAWSEY, Christopher. Ex. Benjamin Ridge. May 18, 1698. Appraiser appointed, John Harron, Charles Combs and William Williams. Order Book 1689-1699, p. 130 & 132.

DEFOY, Jeremiah. Ann Defoy was granted administration. Appraisers appointed Thomas Craghead, James Wallace, Francis Parker and Charles Pasteur. August 7, 1758. Order Book 1755-60, p. 194. Appraised by Charles Pasteur, James Wallace and Francis Parker. January 2, 1759. Estate settled by H. King, W. Wager and James Wallace. June 5, 1759. Book 1758-64, p. 25 & 67.

DELANEY, Edward. Leg.- wife Elizabeth; son Edward; daughter Pamelia; son John. Extx. wife Elizabeth Delaney. D. April 21, 1796. R. July 28, 1796. Wit. John Perry, John Parish, Richard Gilliam. Book 1787-1800, p. 309. Original Will.

DENT, Lawrence. Merchant. Leg.- son Robert; wife Dorothea. Extx. wife Dorothea, who is to be guardian to my son until 21. D. August 6, 1755. R. Wit. Rt. Brough, Henry King, Keatinge Fleetwood. Original Will. Extx. qualified October 7, 1755. Estate ordered to be settled by George Wray, Robert Brough, George Wray, Jr. and James Westwood. September 8, 1756. Order Book 1755-60, p. 24.

DERAY, Francis. Estate appraised by James Nobbs, John Riddlehurst and Francis Riddlehurst. July 8, 1761. Book 1758-64, p. 264.

Duberry, Dewbre and Dewbry

DUBERRY, Giles. Hugh Ross qualified as executor, security-Francis Mallory. Wit. on bond, John Thomas, John Fitzgerald and John Hares. May 18, 1721. Thomas Duberry, the orphan of Giles Duberry. Book 1704-30, p. 319 & 321. Estate appraised by William Armistead, Thomas Road and John Cook. June 22, 1721.

DEWBRE, John. Leg.- wife Rebecca land in Warwick; son Thomas W. Dewbre at 21; daughter Elizabeth; son John. Extx. wife

Rebecca Dewbre. D. April 3, 1777. August 26, 1779. Wit. William Selay, John Banes. Original Will.

DEWBREY, (DEWBRE), Rebecca. Leg.- son John, money in hands of Miles King with reversion to my children, Elizabeth Davis; Thomas W. Dewbre and James H. Dewbre; granddaughter Elizabeth Davis. Ex. James Davis. D. October 23, 1792. R. February 26, 1795. Wit. John Baines, Mathew Baines, Mary Wilson. Book 1787-1800, p. 223. Original Will. Estate appraised by William Allen, John Allen, Jr., John Allen, Sr. and John Baines. June 26, 1795. Book 1787-1800, p. 240. Account of estate audited by George Wray, John Bright and William Kerby. February 23, 1797. Book 1787-1800, p. 342 & 345.

DIXON, James. Mariner, on his Majesty's ship the Pearl, now engaged in battle. Nuncupative Will. We George Guy and James Cousins did hear the said Dixon say to Mr. Evander Meckover, that the longest liver should take all, meaning their estates to which Mr. Meckover readily agreed and both desired the said Guy and Cousins to bear witness. D. November 22, 1718. R. February 19, 1718. Book 1715-21, p. 168.

DIXON, Richard. Account of the sale of his estate. September 28, 1797. Book 1787-1800, p. 359.

DIXON, Thomas. Leg.- wife Sarah with reversion of bequest to son Anthony Tucker Dixon; plantation bought of Thomas Hawkins to be sold; my slaves at the death of my wife are to be divided among all my children except Rosea Bryan. Exs. wife, Col. Cary Selden and Mr. Wm. Roscow Curle. D. June 11, 1773. R. January 27, 1774. Wit. Edward Hurst, Samuel Rowland. Original Will.

DOLBY, Rebecca. Single woman. Leg.- George Eland, to whom she leaves whole estate. Ex. George Eland. April 22, 1693. R. February 19, 1693/94. John Dawson, Mary Dawson, John Heyward. Book 1689-1699, p. 151.

DOLBY, Thomas. The Admtx. of his will was Mary, who married Thomas Morgan. December 18, 1690. Mary and Rebecca Morgan, the daughters of Elizabeth Morgan decd. one of the daughters of Thomas Dolby, decd. sued for their part of their grandfather's estate. William Browne, decd. married Susannah another daughter of Dolby and Peter Pierce married Sarah another daughter. Book 1689-99, p. 114. Order Book, p. 81. Sarah Dolby an orphan petitioned for her part of the estate of Thomas Dolby. Ordered James Baker and Evan Randle deliver to her the estate which Mrs. Elizabeth Cooke died possessed of in their custody. November 18, 1695. Book 1689-1699, p. 77. Order Book. Account of estate. 1690. Book 1689-99, p. 119.

DORAN, David. Of the Island of St. Cruix. Leg.- son Gabriel Doran. Exs. friends David Wilson Curle of Elizabeth City and Benjamin Crooker of the town of Halifax in the Province of North Carolina. The said friends guardians of son. D. November 30, 1759. R. December 4, 1759. Wit. John Jones, Francis Riddlehurst, James Westwood. Book 1758-64, p. 93. Sale of estate. Book 1758-64, p. 215.

DRAPER, Archer. Administration granted Edward Yergin, security-Thomas Tabb and William Evans. Estate appraised by Josiah Massenburg, Curle Tucker, Robert Massenburg and Thomas Webster. April 4, 1758. Order Book 1755-60, p. 173.

DREBLE, Walter. Indexed, page on which it was recorded has been destroyed. Book 1689-1699.

DRISKELL, Florence. Inventory. November 1727. Book 1704-30, p. 116 (b).

DUDLEY, William. Estate appraised by Thomas Smith, Thomas Baker and William Predy. February 15, 1737. Book 1737-49, p. 34.

DUNLOP, John. Estate appraised by William Hunter and John Brodie. (Many Books). July 17, 1728. Book 1704-30, p. 145.

DUNN, John. Appraisal of his estate taken at the house of John Bayley, Gent., by Thomas Batts, Bryan Penny and John Chandler. November 9, 1719. Book 1715-21, p. 287.

DUNN, William. Leg.- son William; daughter Elizabeth; daughter Ann; daughter Catron; daughter Mary; to my wife. Ex. daughter Elizabeth Dunn. Overseers, Henry Dunn and Thomas Wilson. D. March 9, 1724/25. R. January 18, 1726. Wit. Coules Avera, Edward Williams. Book 1704-30, p. 58. Estate appraised by Edward Lattimer, James Naylor and Charles Jenings. January 28, 1726. Book 1704-30, p. 91.

EATON, Thomas. Of Back River. Leg.- for the love I bear to the inhabitants of the County of Elizabeth City, 500 acres of land for a free school, being part of a patent granted me June 5, 1638; rest of estate to the maintenance of a school master to educate and teach the children born within the County of Elizabeth City. Trustees to be the Commissioners, Minister and Church wardens. The overplus of funds to be used for poor, impotent persons, widows and orphans of this county. D. September 19, 1659. Wit. Leonard Yeo, William Hill, Henry Poole.

ELAND, Anne. Estate appraised by Thomas Smith, Thomas Baker and John Powers. May 19, 1742. Book 1737-49, p. 130. Estate settled by Miles Cary, Anthony Tucker and John Moore. Signed Joseph Jegetts, Adm. Book 1737-49, p. 209.

ELLIOTT, Chevers. Estate appraised by John Cooper, James N. Cooper and Thomas Latimer. Reference to Mrs. Elliott's estate. February 24, 1796. Book 1787-1800, p. 289.

ELLIOTT, Robert. Leg.- sister Martha Elliott, sister Ann Buxton; brother William; brother Harry; brother Thomas at 21. D. December 5, 1793. R. July 28, 1796. Wit. Joseph Cooper, Thomas Latimer, John Latimer. Ex. Mr. George Booker. Book 1787-1800, p. 309. Original Will.

ELLIOT, William. Will proved October 15, 1700. William Elliot the heir apparent. Book 1734-70, Ejectments, p. 65.

ELLIS, Dr. William. Administration given Ann his wife who has since married Thomas Midleton. May 18, 1698. Order Book 1689-1699, p. 131.

ELLYSON, Anne. Leg.- son John property in Nansemond County; son Gerrard; son Thomas; to my sister Myhill; brother Lockey Myhill. Ex. Locky Myhill. D. June 1, 1727. R. July 19, 1727. Wit. John Young, Samuel Young, Anne Paris, Nehemiah Nichols. Book 1704-30, p. 78.

EVANS, William. Administration granted William Westwood,

security-Charles Jenings. Appraisers appointed, Curle Tucker, Thomas Webster, Josiah Massenburg and Edward Yergin. May 2, 1759. Order Book 1755-60, p. 221. Appraisal recorded by Thomas Webster and Edward Yergain. April 5, 1763. Book 1758-64, p. 429.

FACE, William. Of Town of Hampton. Leg.- son John land which came by his mother, known as Edward Penny's plantation; son Edward a lot in Hampton bought of John Cook; granddaughter Charity Chapman. Exs. sons John and Edward Face. D. September 7, 177-. R. November 17, 1774. Wit. William A. Bayley, John Massenburg. Original Will.

FAULKNER, Elizabeth. Leg.- grandson Thomas Faulkner my plantation between Newport News and Salters Creek, with reversion of bequest to William, son of Thomas Faulkner, reversion to next heir at law; to son John Faulkner and his children Thomas and Sarah Faulkner. D. February 28, 1742/43. R. May 18, 1743. Wit. John Bushell, Jr., Jane White, William Paton. Thomas Faulkner qualified, security-Thomas Massenburg and John Bushell, Jr. Book 1737-49, p. 166. Estate appraised by John Nelson, John White and Tucker Smith. June 15, 1743. Book 1737-49, p. 170.

FAULKNER, Thomas. Leg.- wife Alce; son John; grandson Thomas Faulkner. Extx. wife Alce Faulkner. D. October 10, 1726. R. January 18, 1726. Wit. John Green, John Ryland, John Standly. Book 1704-30, p. 59.

FENN, John. Appraisal ordered recorded. May 19, 1736. Order Book 1731-47, p. 115.

FENN, Thomas, Sr. Leg.- daughter Mary; son Thomas; daughter Martha Ribble; daughter Sarah; daughter Rosey; daughter Amey; land Mr. Robert Wallace was to pay me to son Thomas and daughters Martha Ribble, Sarah and Rosey; to daughters Frances and Ann a negro bought of John Gail; refers to money Mrs. Sarah Gail is to pay. Ex. son Thomas Fenn. D. December 28, 1787. R. October 28, 1788. Wit. Richard Williams, Thomas Fenn, Jr., John Boushell, Thomas Fenn, Jr. qualified, security-John Boushell. Original Will. Account of sale. October 24, 1799. Book 1787-1800, p. 503.

FIELD, John. Leg.- wife Rose, with reversion of estate to sons John and Robert when they come of age. Wife, Extx. D. June 18, 1787. R. January 24, 1788. Wit. John Perry, James Bray Armistead, Edward Delany. Rose Field qualified, security-George Booker and John Perry. Original Will.

FIELD, Leonard. Inventory recorded, January 18, 1689. Book 1689-1699, p. 118.

FIELD, Sarah. Leg.- to Charles Jenings in consideration of the loving care taken of me in my sickness, the estate of my father Thomas Field, decd. and of my brother Leonard Field decd., with the land which is to come to me at my sister-in-law's death, also all the land my father purchased of Colonel Leonard Yeo. Ex. Charles Jenings. April 1, 1689. R. May 18, 1689. Wit. William Bowles, Thomas Hawkins, Sebastien Perrin, Elizabeth Mares, William White, Jane Gunnell, John Overton. Book 1689-1699, p. 281. Charles Jenings qualified. Order Book 1689-1699, p. 81.

FINNEY, William. Administration granted the Extx. Mary, who

married William Tucker. August 16, 1732. Order Book 1731-47, p. 33.

FIVEASH, Peter. Late of the County of Norfolk. Whereas the estate of the late Captain Tabb is indebted to me for my part of the legacy left to my late mother by my grandmother, I instruct my Exs. to institute a suit against Mrs. Tabb, if recovered to be used for my wife and my child's education. Ex. friend Mr. William Latimer. D. July 30, 1799. R. January 23, 1800. Wit. John Shepard, Lawrence Haynes, Richard Routon. Book 1787-1800, p. 512.

FLOYD, William. Leg.- wife Martha, provision for an unborn child; sister Elizabeth Floyd with reversion to uncle Richard Floyd. Exs. wife Martha and Samuel Cade. D. February 19, 1726/27. R. June 21, 1727. Wit. Gerrard Young, Thomas Jones, Robert Tucker. Book 1704-30, p. 70. Inventory, signed Martha Floyd. July 18, 1727. Book 1704-30, p. 90.

FORGESON, Daniel. Leg.- eldest daughter Ann Whitfield, land adjoining John Forgeson and Shadrack Williams. Exs. wife Katherine and son John Forgeson. D. July 28, 1697. R. 20 of 7ber 1697. Wit. Thomas Bayly, Christopher Copeland, Mary Robinson, Mary Copeland. Probation granted John Forgison his son. September 20, 1697. Book 1689-1699, p. 217 & 272.

FORGISON, Katherine. Leg.- granddaughter Elizabeth Dunn when she is 17; daughter Ann the wife of William Dunn. Ex. son-in-law William Dunn. D. January 24, 1713/14. R. Wit. Thomas Needham, Charles Avera. Book 1715-21, p. 16.

FRASEY, Mary. Appraisal of estate by John Henry Rombough, Anthony Tucker, John Nelson. February 17, 1741. Book 1737-49, p. 117.

FRASIER, William. Account of estate recorded February 16, 1737. Book 1737-49, p. 39.

FRASER, William. Of the Town of Hampton. Leg.- unto master Robert Bowrey of Elizabeth City County, the negroes now in the hands of Richard Chapman of the County of Hanover, Parish of St. Paul, also money in the hands of Mr. John Webb of Hanover County. Ex. Captain Robert Bowrey. D. August 14, 1777. R. March 23, 1780. Wit. Samuel Allyne, Joseph Selden. Security for Robert Bowrey, William Brough and John Rogers. Original Will. Division of negroes between Mary Courtney Bowrey and Grace Elizabeth Bowrey received from Richard Chapman guardian of William Frazer. February 23, 1792. Wit. William Brough, Robert Brough, Richard Hurst. Book 1787-1800, p. 60.

FREEMAN, Samuel. Inventory. Indexed, but the page on which recorded has been destroyed. Book 1689-1699.

FREEMAN, William. Leg.- to Hannah Ridge; son Thomas all my land in Elizabeth City County; wife Mary. Extx. wife Mary Freeman. D. October 29, 1723. R. Wit. Anthony Armistead, Archibald Anderson. Book 1704-30, p. 16. Appraisal p. 20. Appraisers appointed, William Moore, John Merritt, William Parsons and Samuel Hunter. Appraisers, William Tucker, George Rogers, William Parsons and Samuel Hunter. August 19, 1724. Order Book 1723-29, p. 50.

FRY, Thomas. Appraisal of his estate in the possession of Mrs. Katherine Croft by Samuel Sweny and Joseph Banister. August

18, 1719. Book 1715-21, p. 216.

FYFE, Rev. William. Administration granted Rosanna Fyfe, security-Robert Brough. Appraisers appointed Walter McClurg, George Wray, George Wray, Jr., and Henry King. July 6, 1756. Order Book 1755-60, p. 60.

GEORGE, John. Estate appraised by John Lowry, Robert Bumpass and Francis Mallory. Ordered December 9, 1762. R. May 3, 1763. Book 1758-64, p. 453.

GEIRR, Andrew. Administration requested by wife Mary Geirr for Samuel Sweny the greatest creditor. Appraisers appointed, John Meredith, Alexander Kennedy, William Lyell, Nicholas Parker. February 19, 1723/24. Order Book 1723-29, p. 1.

GIGGOTT, see Jiggetts.

GIGLY, George. Probation granted to Frances Gigly, his relict. September 24, 1698. Book 1689-99, p. 217.

GILBERT, Henry. Account of sale. May 19, 1742. Book 1737-49, p. 130.

GILBERT, James. Estate appraised by Francis Ballard, James Ricketts and William Smelt. September 1, 1718. Book 1715-21, p. 225. Mary Gilbert Qualified, security-Joseph Wragg and William Winterton. August 20, 1718. Book 1715-21, p. 132 & 133. Mary Gilbert's bond was signed by Henry Robinson and William Sorrell. June 18, 1719. Book 1715-21, p. 206 & 285.

GILBURD (Gilbert), James. Leg.- son James; daughter Sidwell Proby Gilburd; wife Mary Gilburd. Extx. wife Mary Gilburd. D. November 15, 1745. R. January 15, 1745. Wit. Robert Brough, Thomas Allen, Minson Proby. Mary Gilbert being sick, appointed Robert Brough as Ex. December 15, 1745. Wit. Samuel Galt, Thomas Allen. Book 1737-49, p. 275.

GODDIN, William. Leg.- to Thomas Watts. Ex. Thomas Watts. D. December 26, 1795. R. April 27, 1797. Wit. B. Sheppard Morris, Samuel Watts, Jr., William Morris. Original Will. Book 1787-1800, p. 349.

GODFREE, Edward. Estate appraised by Thomas Wilson, William Davis and Thomas Balis. Ordered April 5, 1748. R. May 3, 1748. Book 1737-49, p. 283.

GODWIN, William. Account of sale returned by Robert Armistead, Sheriff. (From items he was obviously a schoolteacher). February Court 1798. Book 1787-1800, p. 391.

GOODWIN, Martin. Leg.- wife Elizabeth; son James; son Martin; daughter Elizabeth; son Robert; my wife to consult my good friend Mr. Merit Moore of York County. Extx. wife Elizabeth Goodwin. D. November 12, 1749. R. March 3, 1752. Wit. ----- Roberts, Merritt More, ------ Baynes, ---iam Young. Original Will. Account estate due from the estate of Mathew Barradell, decd., late administrator of the estate of Martin Goodwin. Paid James Goodwin, Martin Goodwin and Elizabeth Goodwin the same amount. Examined by John Parsons, John Lowry and Henry Allen. April 3, 1764. Book 1763-71, p. 8.

GOOCH, William. Leg.- wife Sarah; son William; daughter Polly and daughter Elizabeth the money due me for land in King

William County. Exs. wife Sarah and son William Gooch. D. February 18, 1792. R. October 25, 1792. Wit. Gerrard Seymour, Susannah Dunn. Security for Exs. John Minson and Thomas Humphlett. Book 1787-1800, p. 108. Original Will.

GOULD, -----. Will indexed, but the page on which it was recorded was destroyed. Book 1689-1699.

GOULD, Captain Samuel. Account of estate, among items a bill paid to Dr. Walter McClurg for medical attention to his spouse and child. Audited by Cary Michell, George Wray and H. King. Walter McClurg, Adm. November 1, 1763. Book 1758-64, p. 526.

GROVE, Samuel. Will indexed, but the page on which it was recorded has been destroyed. Book 1689-1699. Samuel Debery in right of Sarah Groves (or Gromes) his wife petitions for the estate of Samuel Groves from Joseph White. February 18, 1694/95. Order Book 1689-1699, p. 55.

GUILFORD ------. Will indexed, but the page on which it was recorded has been destroyed. Book 1689-1699.

GUTHERICK, Quintellian. Administration of his estate granted Ann his relict. November 18, 1689. R. April 21, 1690. Book 1689-1699, p. 84. Bond of Ann now the wife of Thomas Wythe as Admtx. of the estate of Quintellian Gutherick. Security, Thomas Wythe, Jr., Thomas Wythe, Sr. Wit. William Lowry and Pasco Curle. Book 1689-1699, p. 103. Suit brought against Thomas Wythe, Jr., who married the widow of Quintellian Gutherick. Elizabeth Gutherick orphan of Quintellian Gutherick was a niece of Baldwin Sheppard. William Gutherick the brother of Elizabeth Gutherick died young. February 20, 1692/93. Order Book 1689-1699, p. 15 and 59.

GUTHERICK, William. An infant. Administration of his estate was granted Ann his mother, now the wife of James Wallace, Clerk. August 18, 1696. Book 1689-1699, p. 156.

HALL, Mark. Leg.- wife and my two sons and two daughters. Ex. brother David Hall. D. April 18, 1793. R. February 27, 1794. Wit. Thomas Minson, Jr., William Kirby, Rebecca Russel. Book 1787-1800, p. 140. Original Will. Estate appraised by James M. Cooper and Thomas Minson. January 23, 1800. Book 1787-1800, p. 514.

HAM, Benjamin. Of the Town of Southampton. Leg.- son Joseph; son William; daughter Mary; daughter Anne; wife Mary Ham. Extx. wife Mary Ham. D. April 24, 1767. R. July 28, 1768. Wit. Robert Brough, John McLacklin, John Armstrong. Book 1763-71, p. 232. Original Will.

HAMILTON, Alexander. Merchant. Leg.- wife Mary whole estate. Exs. Wilson Curle, Miles Cary, Gent., Charles Jenings, Jr. and wife Mary Hamilton. D. February 18, 1745. R. July 16, 1746. Wit. William Fyfe, Walter McClurg, Ann Patterson. Book 1737-49, p. 222. Estate appraised by George Wray, W. Wager and Robert Armistead. September 17, 1746. Book 1737-49, p. 226.

HAND, Richard. William Lowry qualified as his administrator in right of Frances his relict, now the wife of the said Lowry. Bond signed by William Wilson and Edmund Sweeny. Book 1689-1699, p. 103. Estate of Richard Hand, William Lowry Adm. Paid Martha Hand's part of estate, paid her mother's part.

July 18, 1692. Book 1689-1699, p. 120.

HARRIS, Captain John. Receipt of James Drew McCave (or McCaw) to William Plume and William Brough for the estate of Captain John Harris. William Brough the guardian of his wife Sarah McCave. April 21, 1794. Wit. James Smith, Minson Proby, Benjamin Bryan, George Hope. Book 1787-1800, p. 144.

HARRIS, William. Leg.- rings to the following, Mr. Bertram Servant, George Walker, Madam Kelly, Madam Servant, Francis Servant and Mary Servant; wife Judah; to my daughter one third of my estate whose name is unknown. Ex. friend Mr. Bertram Servant. D. December 14, 1695. May 18, 1696. Wit. George Walker, William Leader (?), John Smith, William Price. Book 1689-1699, p. 209.

HARRONS, John. Probation granted Elizabeth Harron his relict. 18 of 8ber 1698. Order Book 1689-1699, p. 138.

HART, John. Anne, orphan of John Hart being of age, petitions for her estate in the hands of Mr. Stephen Howard of Newport News and wife Elizabeth, relict of Samuel Westoby. November 11, 1693. Order Book 1689-1699, p. 9 & 23.

HARVEY, Jane. Leg.- son Nehemiah Nicolls land adjoining William Merritt, reversion to grandson Thomas Nicholls; grandson Joseph Nicholls land adjoining Gerrard Roberts and Anthony Armistead; to grandchildren Jane and Elizabeth Nicholls. Ex. son Nehemiah Nicholls. D. August 11, 1742. R. December 19, 1744. Wit. John Tabb, Samuel Tompkins, William Wood. Book 1737-49, p. 194. (Nehemiah Nicholls was a Quaker.) Estate appraised by Johnson Mallory, William Mallory and William Coridon. February 20, 1744. Book 1737-49, p. 196.

HARVEY, Richard. Estate appraised by Edward Ward, Joseph Myhill, Samuel Tomkins and Daniel Marrow. Signed, Jane Harvey. Ordered February 19, 1723. R. June 17, 1724. Book 1704-30, p. 15.

HAWKINS, Anthony. Leg.- wife Uphan; son James; to my three youngest children, Anthony, John and Richard Hawkins; my wife to purchase the land of William Allen on which I hold mortgate at her death to belong to my son William. Extx. wife Uphan Hawkins. D. April 19, 1770. R. April 23, 1772. Wit. Edward Hurst, Philip Mallory. Uphan Hawkins qualified, security- William Mallory and John Smith. Original Will.

HAWKINS, John. Leg.- eldest son Thomas, with reversion to son John; daughters Sarah, Anne and Elizabeth Hawkins (under 18). Extx. wife. Trustees, friends Anthony Tucker and William Tucker. D. April 14, 1742. R. July 21, 1742. Wit. William Paton, James Allen. Ann Hawkins presented the will. Dower to be alloted by John Moore, Anthony Tucker, John Jenkins and Charles Jenings, Jr. Book 1737-49, p. 146. Original Will.

HAWKINS, James. Leg.- son William; brother William Hawkins to have the land on which he now lives during his and his wife's life or widowhood. Ex. brother William Hawkins, in case of his death John Smith. D. July 8, 1785. R. August 25, 1786. Wit. James Bullock, William Hawkins, Mille Smith. Original Will.

HAWKINS, Richard. Leg.- son Anthony; daughter Elizabeth Read; daughter Mary; daughter Phebe; wife Hannah Hawkins. Exs. friends Anthony Tucker and Thomas Read and my wife. June 12,

1737. R. September 21, 1737. Wit. John Hawkins, Anthony Tucker, Charles Jenings, Jr. Executorship refused by Tucker, Read and Charles Jenings, who married the Extx. of the said Hawkins. John Hawkins the next of kin also refused. The Sheriff ordered to sell the estate. Book 1737-49, p. 15. Original Will.

HAWKINS, Samuel. Estate appraised by John Brodie, John Hy Rombough and William Tucker. November 19, 1741. Book 1737-49, p. 108.

HAWKINS, Thomas, Sr. Planter. Leg.- son John land bought of John Bowles with reversion to his next brother; son James, with reversion to son Thomas; daughter Anne, daughter Mary; daughter Elizabeth Whitacher; daughter Phebe Parish; son Richard. Ex. son Thomas Hawkins. D. January 2, 1725/26. R. June 21, 1727. Wit. Richard Nusum, Elizabeth Nusum, Samuel Cade. Thomas Hawkins being dead, Elizabeth Hawkins qualified. Book 1704-30, p. 69. Administration granted Elizabeth Hawkins, security-Richard Hawkins. June 21, 1727. Order Book 1723-29, p. 12.

HAWKINS, Thomas, Jr. Administration requested by Robert Tenham and Elizabeth his wife. Security, Richard Nusum. June 21, 1727. Order Book 1723-29, p. 12. Appraisal of estate by John Howard, Christopher Davis, Allen Shaw and William Spicer. Ordered June 21, 1727. R. July 19, 1727. Book 1704-30, p. 84.

HAWKINS, William. Leg.- wife Sarah; son John; son Anthony; son Richard. Advice to be had concerning my right to the land whereon Willis Skinner now lives and if my right should appear good, I desire a suit may be brought to recover the same and if secured I give it to my son Anthony. Extx. wife Sarah Hawkins. D. November 15, 1785. R. July 27, 1786. Wit. Monsieuer Dissenis, James Bullock. Original Will.

HEAD, Ann. Administration granted to John Bean the next of kin. Security, William Mallory. February 18, 1694/95. Book 1689-1699, p. 155. Estate of Ann Head's in the hands of Mrs. Ann Hollier left by Mr. Thomas Hollier. 25 of Xber, 1694. Book 1689-1699, p. 203.

HENDERSON, Arthur. Leg.- wife Anne; to Ann Boutwell the daughter of my wife Ann Henderson; to Elizabeth Davis. Ex. friend Miles King. D. 1794. R. February 26, 1795. Wit. Samuel Selden, Thomas Latimer, Mary Black. Book 1787-1800, p. 226. Original Will.

HENDERSON, John. Estate appraised by Joseph Jegetts, John Moore, Anthony Tucker. Ordered January 21, 1746/47. R. February 18, 1746. Book 1737-49, p. 237.

HERBERT, John. Leg.- wife Judith; son Pasco; son Thomas; son Joshua Curle Herbert; daughter Margaret; daughter Rosea Tyler Herbert; my plantation on the Southern Branch in Norfolk County to be sold; son John ----(badly torn, probably the name of another child gone.). D. April 1, 1761. R. June 2, 1761. Wit. William King, Mary King, Rebecca Fitzpatrick. Book 1758-64, p. 252. Original Will.

HERBERT, Judith. Widow. Leg.- sons John and Pascow a plantation if son John comes to Virginia to claim his half, if not Pascow to pay the lawful son of John if he should have any at my death, reversion to John Herbert's oldest daughter; son Thomas;

son Joshua Curle Herbert land in the county of Norfolk, if said son should return to Virginia from beyond the sea; daughter Rosea Tyler Herbert; granddaughter Judith Curle Armistead and granddaughter Elizabeth Moseley Armistead. Exs. son Pascow Herbert and Mr. Milos King. D. February 16, 1779. R. Wit. Rose Boyce, Pheby Waters. Original Will.

HERBERT, Rosea Tyler. Leg.- daughter Judith Curle Herbert at 18 or marriage; son John Curle Herbert; son Richard at 21, reversion to my brothers Pascow and Thomas Herbert. I desire that my cousin Rosea Latimer have the bringing up of my daughter Judith Curle Herbert. Ex. brother Pascow Herbert. D. February 10, 1782. R. Wit. Benjamin Bryan, William King. Original Will.

HERON, John. Elizabeth Heron his wife and Extx. February 19, 1699/1700. Book 1689-1699, p. 268.

HILL, John. Appraisal of estate by Richard Joanes and William Bowles. Signed Charles Jenings. January 8, 1693. Book 1689-1699, p. 150. Thomas Dunston of York County gave bond as the guardian of Elizabeth Hill the daughter of John Hill. Signed William Bowles and Joseph White. Book 1689-1699, p. 151. Account of his estate. March 19, 1693/94. Book 1689-1699, p. 185.

HILL, Justinian. Justinian Hill the son and heir brings suit against James Scott for his right to 400 acres of land February 18, 1694/95. Order Book 1689-99, p. 52.

HILL, Thomas. His estate was settled by Joanna Michell August 17, 1738. Book 1737-49, p. 55.

HINDS, Thomas. Elizabeth Hinds his orphan, guardian Captain William Armistead. Her mother, Mrs. Hannah Powers relict of John Powers. 5 of Xber 1693. Order Book 1689-1699, p. 14, 21 & 27.

HINTON, Mary. Her son John Hinton granted probation of will. September 10, 1692. Book 1689-1699, p. 118.

HOLLIER, Edmond. Leg.- nephew Mary Stuckey with the reversion of the bequest to her sister Elizabeth Stuckey; nephew Edmond Stuckey with reversion to his brother Simon Stuckey; to my brother Penuel Crooke; to Abraham Pickett; to John Berry; to William Wilson, Jr., to William Flenn; to Florence Dreskell; to George Paine; nephew Simon Hollier; nephew Robert Crooke; nephew Pennuell Crooke, Jr., nephew Debra Crooke; nephew Martha Crooke. Exs. brothers Simon Hollier and Penuell Crooke. D. April 21, 1719. R. May 20, 1719. Wit. Thomas Wythe, Edward Tabb. Book 1715-21, p. 182. Simon Hollier qualified, security-Edward Tabb. May 19, 1719. Book 1715-21, p. 199. Estate appraised by William Lowry, Edward Tabb and William Tucker. Book 1715-21, p. 207. Account estate. September 3, 1721. Book 1704-30, p. 324.

HOLLIER, Simon. Will presented by Edmund Sweny, who was named Ex. D. July 18, 1698. R. October 23, 1690. Book 1689-1699, p. 82. Appraisal and division of Simon Hollier's estate. Paid each an equal share-Symon Hollier, Edmund Hollier, Alice Cole, Mary Hollier and Elise Cobbs. Appraised by William Marshall, William Lowry and Thomas Taylor. January 7, 1690. Book 1689-1699, p. 141 & 162.

HOLLIER, Simon, Jr. By will appointed Simon Hollier, Ex. Appraisers appointed, Mr. Lowry, Mr. Parsons, Mr. Smelt and Mr. Mallory. April 16, 1735. Mary Hollier renounced her part of estate. Will proved by Anthony Robinson and Thomas Tabb. Order Book 1731-47, p. 92, 93 and 97. Appraisal of estate of Captain Simon Hollier, by William Parsons, Thomas Smith and William Mallory. June 2, 1747. Book 1737-49, p. 247. Ordered the estate to be settled by George Wythe, John Lowry, William Parsons, Jr. and William Parsons, Sr. October 8, 1755. Order Book 1755-60, p. 27.

HOLLIER, Simon. Estate settled by Robert Brough, John Perry and F. Riddlehurst. Signed, Miles King, Adm. Ordered July 25, 1788. R. June 23, 1791. Book 1787-1900, p. 29.

HOLLIER, Thomas. Administration granted Ann Hollier his relict. February 18, 1691/92. R. April 29, 1692. Book 1689-1699, p. 88. Appraisal of estate by John Powers and Thomas Gray. Signed Ann Holliard. January 2, 1691/92. Book 1689-1699, p. 143.

HOLLYMAN, Nicholas. Will indexed, but the page upon which it was recorded has been destroyed. Book 1689-1699.

HOLLOWAY, James. Settlement of his estate. Among items, sundry goods taken out of the estate by Henry Wilson, same by Jane Holloway. The widow received one third, Henry Wilson one third and ----- Holloway one third. Signed Dunn Armistead, Sub Sheriff. D. 1743. R. June 20, 1744. Book 1737-49, p. 185.

HOLMES, Robert. Probation granted Ann Carrill and Ellynor Allen. March 18, 1697/98. Order Book 1689-1699, p. 128.

HOPKINS, Richard. Estate appraised by J. Ricketts, Thomas Howard and Jo. Banister. D. August 25, 1718. R. 21 of 8ber 1718. Joyce Hopkins, his widow qualified. Book 1715-21, p. 149 & 9.

HOPKINS, William. Leg.- to Henry Noblin; to Edward Jones; to Mary Bridge; nephew William Calecote; to James Calecote; to William Creek; to Mark Powell; to John Meredith. Exs. Mary Bridge and Myhill Roberts. D. May 20, 1717. R. June 18, 1718. Wit. Mark Powell, William Creek, Thomas Jones. Book 1715-21, p. 284. Appraisal of estate by Hind Armistead, William Spicer, Mark Powell and William Creek. August 15, 1718. Book 1715-21, p. 140.

HORSINGTON, Thomas. Thomas Wingfield and wife Katherine are granted administration of his estate. May 18, 1698. Order Book 1689-1699, p. 147.

HOUSE, John. Administration granted William Wilson and Mary House. April 28, 1691. Book 1689-1699, p. 80.

HOUSE, Thomas. Leg.- to sons John and William the land on which I live; daughter Mary Baylis; wife Elizabeth; son Anthony; daughters Elizabeth, Ann and Martha House. D. November 7, 1702. P. May 18, 1703. Wit. John Bushell, John Bushell, Jr., John Dunn. R. August 25, 1719 (?). Book 1715-21, p. 211.

HOWARD, Estance (written in another place Ustace). Estate appraised by Francis Riddlehurst, Thomas Wootten and Thomas Skinner. D. December 3, 1768. R. January 25, 1770. Book 1763-71, p. 319. The estate of Eustace Howard was audited by

George Wray, Jacob Wray and F. Riddlehurst. January 25, 1771. Book 1763-71, p. 412. John Jones, Administrator.

HOWARD, John. Leg.- daughter Rebacker Skinner land adjoining William Morehead, reversion to Howard Skinner; daughter Ann Smith, reversion to Howard Smith; daughter Martha Watkins, reversion to William Watkins; to Henry Bains, Sr.; to grand-daughter Mary Banes; to Joseph Jegetts; daughter Elizabeth Pool; daughter Sarah Morehead. Exs. Thomas Skinner, William Morehead, George Watkins. D. July 17, 1755. R. June 7, 1757. Wit. Joseph Jegetts, Thomas Hatton, Mark Parrish. Thomas Skinner and George Watkins qualified, security, Mark Parish and Cary Selden. Original Will. Order Book 1755-60, p. 135.

HOWARD, Thomas. Elizabeth Howard qualified on his will. Appraisers appointed were William Tucker, George Watts, John Henry and John Nelson. September 17, 1735. Order Book 1731-47, p. 97 & 99. Estate in account with John Salmon. Paid the widow's part, paid Thomas Howards part; paid Agnes Howard's part; paid Anne Howard's part. Robert Brough guardian to the heir. Settled by Alexander Hamilton, David O'Sheal and William Westwood. February 19, 1740. Book 1737-49, p. 100.

Humphlett, Umphlett.
UMPHLETT, Thomas. Estate appraised by Richard Nusum, John Howard, Charles Jenings, William Morehead. September 15, 1725. Book 1704-30, p. 42.

HUMPHLETT, Thomas. Leg.- whole estate to wife Elizabeth and her heirs. Extx. wife Elizabeth Humphlett. February 13, 1794. R. February 26, 1795. Wit. Francis Moss, John Minson, William Burgess. Book 1787-1800, p. 221. Original Will.

HUNDLEY, Robert. Appraisal of estate by H. King, Charles Cooper and Humphry Massenburg. Ordered January 1, 1765. R. February 5, 1765. Book 1763-71, p. 26. Estate audited by W. Wager and Jacob Wray. Signed by Walter McClurg, Adm. R. August 3, 1766. Book 1763-71, p. 85.

HUNT, William. Leg.- wife Ann Hunt. Extx. wife Ann Hunt. D. July 1, 1797. R. June 26, 1800. Wit. John Cooper, Richard Gilliam, J. Hardyman. Original Will.

HUNTER, John. Leg.- wife Susannah; daughter Mary Ann Barbary Hunter; son John; son William Jones Hunter; son Thomas Hunter. Exs. wife Susannah and son John Hunter. D. December 26, 1794. R. June 26, 1795. Codicil. I desire that the estate my wife shall be entitled to from her mother, Mrs. Barbara Jones shall be considered solely her own. January 6, 1795. Wit. Miles Cary, Thomas Jones, William Davenport. Book 1787-1800, p. 239. Estate of Captain John Hunter appraised by William Brough, William Kerby and William Smith. R. February 23, 1797. Book 1787-1800, p. 339.

HUNTER, Mary Ann. Leg.- daughter Mable; daughter Elizabeth; daughter Mary; daughter Roseanna. Exs. Mr. John Brodie and Mr. William Westwood. D. February 9, 1742/43. R. March 16, 1742. Wit. Mary Bordland, Martha Brodie, James Westwood. Exs. refused. Samuel Sweny qualified, security-John Brodie. Book 1737-49, p. 158. Appraisal of estate by Charles Pasteur, Alexander Kennedy, Isaac Rambow. May 19, 1743. Book 1737-49, p. 168.

HUNTER, William. Appraisal of estate. Large estate, evidently a merchant. Page missing. Book 1737-49, p. 83. Settlement of the estate. Wife Mary Ann one third of estate and remainder divided between six children. Signed, Jacob Walker and Robert Armistead. Petition of Samuel Sweny and Theophilus Field against Mary Ann Hunter Admtx. of William Hunter, Gent. decd. for counter security. She declared she was willing to accept her one third and was willing to deliver residue to petitioners for the use of children of said deceased. July 21, 1742. Book 1737-49, p. 135. Final settlement of estate. Mrs. Hunter paid one third, also one seventh being per part of a child's estate who is deceased, balance due six children. Audited by Alexander Hamilton, John Brodie and Robert Armistead. Signed, Samuel Sweny. July 18, 1744. Book 1737-49, p. 186.

HURST, Edward. Leg.- wife Phebe; son Richard Hawkins Hurst; daughter Elizabeth Parish; land in Warwick to be sold and money divided between the above three; granddaughter Elizabeth Parish; to wife the money due me from Thomas Minson; money due me from Locky Collier to be used to defray my debts. Exs. friend Miles King and son-in-law John Parish. D. October 1, 1785. Wit. Henry Jenkins, Samuel Healy, John Baylis. Original Will.

HUSON, John. Estate appraised by Nicholas Parker, George Waffe and William Robertson. March 19, 1728. Book 1704-30, p. 173.

JAMES, Elizabeth. Estate appraised by Thomas Faulkner, John Borland and Joseph Banister. Adm. granted Thomas Wilcox the greatest creditor. June 8, 1716. Book 1715-21, p. 33.

JARVIS, Thomas. Will dated April 6, 1684. Exs. wife Elizabeth, George Richards and Edmond Moss. Suit over his property to be sold to defray debts and the remainder to be divided between Elizabeth Hole his then wife and defendent Thomas Jarvis his son. March 5, 1692/93. Book 1689-1699, p. 76. Edward Hole the husband of Elizabeth and guardian of Thomas Jarvis, infant.

JARVIS, William. Leg.- Joseph White, Jr., my tract of land; to William White; to John Skinner; to Bridget Wethersby; to Christopher Goold; to Jeremiah Smith; to John Skally (?); to wife; to Thomas Faulkner; to John Ruggles. Exs. friends William Bowles and Joseph White. D. December 14, 1693. R. February 19, 1693/94. Wit. John Hill, Bartholomew Wethersby, William Smith. Book 1689-1699, p. 152.

Jeggitts, Jegits, Giggits, Geggetts etc.
(JEGGITTS) Giggots, Garden. Account of estate among items expenses for his wife's funeral and two coffins were paid for. Signed, Henry Lewis. 10 of 7ber 1692. Book 1689-1699, p. 128. Ordered Henry Lewis give an account of the estate of the orphans, John and Edward Giggots. September 11, 1693. Order Book 1689-1699, p. 23.

(JEGGITTS) Gigels, George. Nuncupative will. Leg.- cousin Elizabeth Ridge; to Mary Ridge; to William Ceely; to Robert Johnson. D. R. January 22, 1718. Wit. William Ceely, Charles Ceely. Administration granted to John Bordland. Book 1715-21, p. 158.

(JEGGITTS) Gigets, John. Leg.- to Ann Gigots at age or married; son Joseph. I desire that Thomas Umflet will continue upon my plantation until my son comes of age. John Howard to take my son. Exs. John Howard and wife Jane Gigets. D. December

15, 1721. R. June 20, 1722. Wit. Thomas Umflet, Thomas Weatherbie, Thomas Howard. Jane Gigets qualified, security- Thomas Weathersby and Mathew Small. Book 1721-28, p. 55. Estate appraised by Thomas Hawkins, John Skinner and Thomas Umphlet. Signed Jane Gigetts. August 15, 1722. Book 1721-28, p. 66.

JEGGITTS, Joseph. Leg.- wife Elizabeth; rest of estate to be divided between Gardeen, John, Joseph, William and Edward Roe Jeggitts and Elizabeth Allen my daughter. Exs. Gardeen, John and Joseph Jegitts. D. March 30, 1767. R. May 28, 1767. Wit. Lewis Meredith, William Allen. Security for Exs. William Allen. Book 1763-71, p. 158. Original Will. Appraisal of estate by Anthony Hawkins, King Humphlet, J. Casey and William Allen. June 25, 1767. Book 1763-71, p. 161.

JEGITTS, Joseph. Leg.- wife Martha, the land which formerly belonged to Howard Smith, reversion to daughter Mariar. Trustees, friends Signe Parrish and Richard Burt. D. October 5, 1778. Wit. Thomas Hatton, John Skinner, Howard Skinner. Original Will.

JEGGITTS, Thomas. Account of estate, John Gemmill, Adm. Among items, board for Elizabeth Jeggitts and expense for sending her to Norfolk County. Audited by Ro. Shields, William Garrow and Thomas Robinson. July 26, 1799. Book 1787-1800, p. 478.

JENKINS, Elizabeth. Appraisal of estate by John Harron and Nah. Parrish, at Mr. Batts. Ordered April 13, 1693. R. May 21, 1693. Book 1689-1699, p. 131. William Waterson, Adm. of Elizabeth Jenkins. March 19, 1693/94. Order Book 1689-1699, p. 31. Account of estate, signed Thomas Batts. June 16, 1693. Book 1689-1699, p. 165. Thomas Batts sued William Waterson as Adm. of Elizabeth Jenkins for payment of expenses during her sickness. February 19, 1693/94. Order Book 1689-1699, p. 28.

JENKINS, Henry. Leg.- brother Daniel Jenkins; sister Mary Jenkins, als. Lewis; my son Henry Jenkins; nephew Daniel son of brother Daniel Jenkins. Mourning rings to Mr. Richard Trotter, Mr. James Scott, Mr. John Moore and Mr. John Howard. Exs. son Henry Jenkins and nephew Daniel Jenkins. D. March 12, 1697/98. R. September 24, 1698. Wit. Thomas Hawkins, Francis Harlewit, William Mallory. Book 1689-1699, p. 279. Probation of will of Captain Henry Jenkins granted to Henry Jenkins and Daniel Jenkins. September 24, 1698. Mrs. Bridgett Jenkins petitions for her one third of estate. November 18, 1698. Order Book 1689-1699, p. 139.

JENKINS, Captain Henry. Bond of Mary Jenkins, his Admtx. signed by Thomas Wythe, Joshua Curle and John Bayley. Wit. Charles Jenings, William Westwood. Book 1715-21, p. 169. Appraisal of estate by John King, H. Irwin and Francis Ballard, Joseph Banister. August 17, 1719. Book 1715-21, p. 208.

JENKINS, Henry. Leg.- sister Bridget; sister Elizabeth; mother Mary Jenkins; brother John Jenkins and his heirs male; brother Lewis Jenkins. Ex. brother Lewis Jenkins. D. February 19, 1721. R. January 15, 1723. Wit. Elizabeth Powers, Thomas Fisher, W. Hopkins. Book 1721-28, p. 167. Estate appraised by J. Reiketts and Joseph Banister. February 19, 1723. Book 1721-28, p. 178.

JENKINS, John. Leg.- daughter Mary; son John; son James; son Henry; son Edward; wife Ann Jenkins. Exs. wife Ann Jenkins, friends James Dixson and Thomas Dixon. D. March 23, 1754. R. October 1, 1754. Wit. Charles Jenings, John Moore. Original Will. Estate account examined by Cary Selden, Charles Jenings, Henry King and George Wray, Jr. September 8, 1756. Order Book 1755-60, p. 78. Valuation of building done that the heir-at-law should be charged with, returned by Rt. Armistead, Charles Jenings and Rt. Armistead, Jr. Signed, Thomas Dixon. August 8, 1759. Book 1758-64, p. 81. Division of slaves, to Mrs. Cowper for her fifth part; to paid heir-at-law by Mr. Cowper. Examined by Rt. Armistead, Cary Selden and George Wray. Legacy due Mary Jenkins. Received of Edward and Ann Cowper. Thomas Dixon, acting Ex. September 6, 1763. Book 1758-64, p. 507.

Jenings and Jennings

JENINGS, Charles. Leg.- son Charles; son John, the house and land on which I live bought of Edward Parish; son Thomas land in Nansemond County; to daughter Mary, town land bought of Thomas Wilcox; daughter Ann a lot bought of Edward Ballard. Exs. sons John and Charles Jenings. D. June 14, 1745. R. August 2, 1748. Wit. Thomas Latimer, John Webb, James Naylor. Hannah Jenings renounced the will. John Jennings qualified, security-Thomas Latimer and James Baker. Book 1737-49, p. 302. Estate appraised by Robert Brough, Baldwin Shepard and John Selden. January 3, 1748. Book 1737-49, p. 307.

JENINGS, Charles. Account of estate with Mary Jenings, Administratrix. 1764. 513 acres in Lunenburg County; 400 acres in Dinwiddie County; 120 acres in Brunswick County; 100 acres in Prince George County; 100 acres in Elizabeth City County; one lot in Blandford and one lot in Hampton. Estate divided by H. King, John Riddlehurst and Jacob Wray, between Jane Jenings, Cary Selden, William Smith, William Jenings and Mary Jenings, with Mrs. Jenings receiving one-third. R. February 5, 1765. Book 1763-71, p. 29. Estate appraised September 3, 1762 by Thomas Dixon, John Moore and Curle Tucker. Book 1758-64, p. 500.

JENINGS, Thomas. Charles Jenings qualified as Administrator, his security Thomas Jones and John King. July 13, 1720. Book 1704-30, p. 324. Estate appraised by Edward Lattimore, John Lyell and James Baker. (One old gun at John Batts not appraised.) D. August 14, 1721. R. December 20, 1721. Book 1721-23, p. 20.

JENINGS, Thomas. Leg.- wife Elizabeth; son Charles; son John; son William; son Thomas; daughter Jean Robinson and her two children, Thomas and Henry Robinson; daughter Susanna Rudd; daughter Jenny (context shows her to be the same as Jean). Ex. son Thomas Jenings. D. July 20, 1791. R. July 24, 1794. Wit. John Parish, Jr., William Dobbins, Sally Parish. Book 1787-1800, p. 154. Original Will.

JOANES, see Jones

JOHNSON, Mark, Gentlemen. Leg.- wife Elizabeth, the plantation on which I live, adjoining Jacob Face; daughter Mary the land on which John Wilson and Charles Pierce live; daughters Jane and Elizabeth my lots in Hampton when sixteen; to William Allen; to my sister Elizabeth Walker. Extx. wife Elizabeth Johnson, with the request that my brother-in-law William Westwood see that my will is performed. D. February 10,

1717/18. R. February 18, 1718. Wit. Charles Jenings, Jacob Face, Elizabeth Jenings, Wil. Westwood. Book 1715-21, p. 168. Estate appraised by Thomas Wythe, Edward Tabb and Joseph Banister. R. August 22, 1719. Book 1715-21, p. 210. Account of estate. Slaves delivered to the children of Mark Johnson by Anthony Armistead, who married Elizabeth the widow of the said deceased. November 21, 1722. Book 1721-23, p. 84.

JOHNSON, Philip. Probation of will granted to Mark Johnson, his son. September 18, 1699. Book 1689-1699, p. 217.

JOHNSON, Robert. Leg.- to Charles Cely; to William Cely; son Thomas Johnson, with reversion of bequests to John Bordland of Hampton Town; to John Floyd of Warwick County. I request John Bordland to bring up my son Thomas. Exs. James Ricketts and John Bordland. D. March 27, 1718. R. May 22, 1718. Wit. Jo. Wragg, Catherine Whitticar, William Spicer. Book 1715-21, p. 112.

JONES, Ann. Leg.- brother Thomas Jones; to Mr. Miles Cary; sister Amelia Jones. D. February 7, 1796. R. April 28, 1796. Wit. Miles King, John Applewhite. Book 1787-1800, p. 296. Original Will.

JONES, Barbara. Leg.- whereas my deceased husband made certain bequests to his daughters, Susanna Hunter, Barbara King and Mary Herbert and her husband Pascow Herbert, I make the following provisions of my own estate in reference to above; daughter Amelia; daughter Anne; daughter Elizabeth; son Thomas Jones, when he becomes 21. Exs. John Hunter, Miles King and Pascow Herbert. D. R. January 22, 1795. Proved by John Applewhaite, George Hope and John Banks. Book 1787-1800, p. 214. Original Will. Estate appraised by Charles Jennings, William Kirby and William Brough. D. December 29, 1794. R. July 23, 1795. Book 1797-1800, p. 258.

JONES, Charles. Leg.- wife Elizabeth. Extx. wife Elizabeth Jones. D. July 14, 1781. R. May 27, 1785. Wit. John Paul, William Price. Elizabeth Jones refused the Executorship and Edward Cowper qualified, with Thomas Wootten and Richard Barron his security. Original Will.

JONES, David. May 4, 1714. Appraisal of two negroes seized for debt and now in the hands of William Coopland, by William Minson, Henry Dunn and James Naylor. William Copeland and Elizabeth Jones were granted the probation on the nuncupative will of David Jones. May 18, 1715. Book 1715-21, p. 9 and 223.

JOANES, Edward. Account of the estate of his orphans, William and Elizabeth Joanes returned by John Smith. September 11, 1693. Order Book 1689-1699, p. 23.

JONES, John. Jane Jones was granted the administration of his estate. Appraisers were Bertrand Proby, John Roe, George Minson and Edward Roe. February 17, 1735. Order Book 1731-47, p. 109 and 110. William King and William Copeland were the administrators of the estate of Jane Jones the Admtx. of John Jones, whose accounts were examined by Thomas Mingham and John Selden. September 15, 1738. Book 1736-53, p. 87.

JONES, John. Settlement of the estate by Thomas Everard and John Selden, in which the widow was paid one-third. April 20, 1743. Book 1737-49, p. 159.

JONES, Lidia. Leg.- brother Francis Jones; brother John Jones; brother Tingnal Jones; brothers Harwood Jones and Vinkler Jones; sister Margaret Thompson, with reversion of the bequest to nieces Elizabeth Harwood Thompson, Mary Shaw Thompson and Elizabeth Smith, cousin Mildred Smith, cousin Elizabeth Smith and nephew Starkey Armistead; to sister Elizabeth Armistead. Ex. brother Francis Jones. D. October 10, 1773. Wit. William Simmons, Abraham Parish. Original Will.

JONES, Morris. Leg.- wife Rachell; son Charles; daughter Susanna Pasteur Jones; daughter Mary; provision for unborn child. D. October 31, 1759. R. January 1, 1760. Wit. W. Wager, Charles Pasteur. Book 1758-64, p. 108. Original Will. Rachel Jones qualified as Extx. security, David Curle and Robert Hunley. Appraisers appointed, Francis Riddlehurst, John Riddlehurst, Thomas Dixon and Francis Ballard. January 1, 1760. Order Book 1755-60, p. 268. Rachell Jones was the daughter of Charles Pasteur. Book 1737-49, p. 347.

JOANES, Richard. Probation granted Thomas Hawkins, Ex. May 18, 1698. Order Book 1689-1699, p. 132.

JONES, Samuel, Pilot. Leg.- wife Hannah; son Cowper; son John; son William; daughter Ann Jones. Exs. wife Hannah Jones and her brother Charles Cowper. D. February 1, 1752. Wit. R. Brough, John Hobbs, Philip Cowper. Original Will. Ordered that the settlements of the estates of Samuel Jones and Hannah Jones be recorded. Order Book 1755-60, p. 36.

KELLY, Richard. Account of estate settled by Cary Selden, Samuel Watts and Thomas Lattimer. January 1, 1764. Book 1763-71, p. 20.

KENNEDY, Alexander. (Badly torn) -------- in Cork in the Kingdom of Ireland; to the Minister and Church Wardens of Christ Church Parish; to brother-in-law Adam Stevely's daughter Elizabeth; to cousin Michael Caisie's two sons; to cousin Alexander Kennedy; to Anne Hinson Wager, the daughter of my best friend, William Wager all the money due to me by bond from Mr. James Balfour; to cousin William ------, to Mrs. Dorothy Hurt, the widow of the Rev. Hurt; to Mrs. Rosanna Fyfe, widow of the Rev. William Fyfe; to Samuel Galt; to Patrick Mathews, butcher in York; to Thomas Adams and James Boyd when they are twenty-one; Francis Riddlehurst to continue on part of my lot as long as he shall think proper, also Mr. Abram Mains on the other part; to William the son of Charles Jennings; to Martha Gold, the daughter of Ann Gold; to Mr. Isaac Goldsmith, Dean of Cloyne and Rector of the Parish of Holy Trinity, otherwise Christ Church in the City of Cork; to Lettice Williams the house in which Laurence Baines now lives; Exs. friends Robert Brough, William Wager and Thomas Latimer. D. August 12, 1760. R. September 4, 1760. Wit. John Riddlehurst, William Patton. Heir-at-law of Alexander Kennedy not found and William Wager qualified as Executor. R. June 1, 1762. Book 1758-64, p. 184. Will proved by Roe Cowper and William Bennett. November 4, 1760. Appraisers appointed, Charles Cooper, Charles Pasteur, John Jones and Jacob Wray. Codicil proven by William Patton, who also saw John Riddlehurst sign. Order Book 1755-60, p. 311. Appraisal recorded, February 3, 1761. Book 1758-64, p. 198. Account of sales. William Wager, acting Executor. November 25, 1760. House and lot whereon Roe Cowper lived; the lot whereon John Nelson and Ab Mair lived; the lot whereon Francis Riddlehurst lived; the lot whereon William More lived, which included the square on which Mrs. Gould lived. Book 1758-64, p. 317.

Kerby and Kirby.
KERBY, John. Leg.- wife Martha, with reversion of bequest to son Thomas (not eighteen); reversion to John Kerby the son of Robert Kerby; reversion to Mary Tompkins the daughter of Benit Tompkins, Sr. Extx. wife Martha Kerby. D. December 2, 1734. R. November 21, 1739. Wit. Nicholas Bourden, John Chapple, Ann Parris. Book 1737-49, p. 70. Appraisal by William Mallory, William Parson and Samuel Tompkins. February 19, 1739/40. Book 1737-49, p. 80.

KERBY, John. Leg.- Thomas Kerby, to brother Robert Kerby. Exs. Martha Kerby and brother Robert Kerby. D. February 25, 1741. R. May 19, 1742. Wit. Merrit Sweny, Ann Paris, John Hunter. Book 1737-49, p. 120. Inventory, signed Martha Kerby. August 21, 1745. Book 1737-49, p. 208.

KERBY, Thomas. Leg.- wife Sarah; daughter Martha King; granddaughter Martha King, with reversion of the bequest to my son-in-law Miles King. Exs. wife Sarah, son-in-law Miles King and daughter Martha King. D. February 25, 1786. R. April 27, 1786. Wit. Mary Mallory, Johnson Tabb, James Tompkins. Original Will.

KERBY, Thomas. Leg.- brother William Kerby. Ex. brother William Kerby. D. October 28, 1796. R. April 27, 1797. Wit. Miles King, Charles Jenings. Book 1787-1800, p. 349. Original Will.

KERBY, Thomas. Account of estate presented by Mrs. Kerby. Audited by M.E. Chisman, George Wray and John S. Westwood. February 27, 1800. Book 1787-1800, p. 527.

KING, Armistead. Leg.- wife and children, Judith, Rebecca, Mary, Charles and Henry King. Exs. wife Mary King and nephew Henry King. D. December 15, 1761. R. January 5, 1762. Wit. Rt. Armistead, Joseph Selden. Book 1758-64, p. 303. Appraisal of estate by Josiah Massenburg, Robert Massenburg and Thomas Wootten. September 4, 1764. Book 1763-71, p. 18.

KING, Captain Charles. Settlement of estate, James Westwood, Administrator. Paid John King of Nansemond, one-sixth of the personal estate. By one-third part of Captain John King's legacy of two negroes. Division of estate, January 1, 1762 by Thomas Dixon, H. King and W. Wager, to James Westwood in right of his wife, to Mary King, to Miles King, to John King, to Hanah King, to Elizabeth King. January 5, 1762. Book 1758-64, p. 291. Account of the estate of Charles Kings' orphan in account with estate of James Westwood. To Mary King, Hannah King, Elizabeth King and John King. February 23, 1770. Audited by H. King, Francis Riddlehurst and W. Wager. Book 1763-71, p. 337.

KING, Hannah. Leg.- daughter Judith Curle King; granddaughter Elizabeth Owings; son Joshua C. King; son Henry Jenkins King; son John C. King; son William King. D. March 22, 1796. R. April 28, 1796. Wit. Henry Jenkins, Pascow Herbert. Book 1787-1800, p. 298. Original Will.

KING, Henry. Of the Town of Petersburg, in the County of Dinwiddie. Leg.- my two lots in Hampton, being part of "Little England" to be sold and money divided between my sisters Rebecca King and Mary Whitaker. My friend Miles King of Hampton is to make the sale of my property. Ex. friend John King. Wit. Thomas Armistead, Wm. Wright, John King. D.

June 21, 1780. R. April 26, 1787. Original Will.

KING, John. Inventory before 1718. Book 1715-21, p. 121.

KING, John. Leg.- son John land in the Upper Parish of Mansemond, on Sumerton Swamp and land in Albemarle County at head of Bennett's Creek in the Province of North Carolina if he pays William Folk of Nansemond the money I owe him; son William land in Chowan in the Province of North Carolina; to grandson Michael King, the son of Michael King, adjoining the land of Sarah Cox, Dorothy Wilson and Holmes' line, being the land formerly given to my said son by deed from his mother Jane King and to his brother; to sons Armistead and Charles King; my land in Nansemond, bought of William Perry to be sold to pay my debts; to wife Rebecca a looking glass which was Major Armistead's; to my daughter-in-law and her two sons; to my three sons, William, Armistead and Charles King. Wife Extx. and guardian to my two young sons, Armistead and Charles. Exs. sons John and William King. D. January 13, 1735. R. Wit. John Robinson, Jr., Miles Cary, William Armistead, Samuel Markham. Original Will. Will proven by Miles Cary, William Armistead and Samuel Markham. Ordered, the Executors, John King and William King be summoned. May 19, 1736. Order Book 1731-47, p. 112. Additional appraisal by William Smelt, William Parsons, Francis Mallory and Thomas Smith. September 2, 1738. Book 1737-49, p. 55. Settlement of the estate of Captain John King;-the amount of the legacy and slaves recovered by Riddlehurst; silver spoons and tankard belonging to the estate of Henry Royal claimed by Mrs. Taylor; paid Edward Armistead's decree; paid Judith Robinson's decree; to a legacy by Mr. M'k. King of Nansemond; to Charles and Armistead King in the hands of Mr. John King, decd.; suit of Robert Armistead against John King's estate for balance due to Moss Armistead's estate; negroes kept by William King; judgement against Mundell; judgement against Mrs. Rebecca King; tract of land sold in Nansemond to pay his debts; by cash received of Capt. Miles Cary, which was paid him more than legacy. Audited by Thomas Mingham, Wil. Westwood and John Selden. July 22, 1742. Book 1737-49, p. 137.

KING, John Curle. Leg.- wife Elizabeth; son John Curle King; daughter Hannah Herbert King. Exs. wife and friend Samuel Watts. D. January 20, 1800. R. February 27, 1800. Wit. Book 1787-1800, p. 521.

KING, Mary. Leg.- daughters Mary Hudson with reversion of bequest to her children; daughter Rosea Latimer, with reversion to her children; son William King; granddaughter Mary Curle ---- the daughter of William King, with reversion to her children if no such children reversion to my grandson John Curle King; to grandsons Thomas and William King. Exs. Mr. Miles King and Mr. Henry Jenkins. D. October 14, 1778. R. December 24, 1778. Wit. Robert Brough, Susanna Watts, Miles King. Miles King qualified, security, Francis Mallory. Original Will.

KING, Michael. Administration granted Jane King. Appraisers appointed, John Lowry, Merit Moore, William Parsons and William Armistead. June 16, 1736. Order Book 1731-47, p. 117. Settlement of estate by Jane Allen, wife of William Allen, the Admtx. of Michael King. Audited by John Lowry, John Tabb and W. Parsons. February 17, 1742. Book 1737-49, p. 154.

KING, Michael. Leg.- my property to be sold to pay my friend John Hunter, the money advanced for me to pay for my commission as Ensign; to brother Henry King. As witness my seal in Albany. D. November 5, 1757. Wit. John Hall, Thomas B--ley. Michael King now an Ensign in his Majesty's Royal American Regiment. Original Will. Administration granted Henry King, security, John Tabb, Jr. Appraisers appointed, George Wray, Jr., Robert Armistead, James Westwood and Jacob Wray. February 7, 1758. Order Book 1755-60, p. 165 & 167.

KING, Rebecca. Widow. Leg.- son Edward Armistead and his son William Armistead; daughter Judith Robinson; son Robert Armistead; granddaughter Mary King, the daughter of my son Charles King; to the children of my son Armistead King; to grandsons, John and Robert Cary;-if my sons Armistead King and Charles King sue to recover slaves belonging to my former husband William Armistead, my estate is to be divided into three equal parts and divided between Robert Armistead, Judith Robinson and John and Robert Cary. Exs. ------torn ------. D. February -- 1755. R. August 1, 1758. Wit. Booth Armistead, Robert Armistead, Jr., Starkey Robinson, Jr. Robert Armistead qualified, security, James Wallace. Book 1758-64, p. 3. Original Will. Estate in account with Robert Armistead. Paid the account of Elizabeth King. Audited by James Westwood, H. King and Richard Cary. October 1, 1765. Book 1763-71, p. 70.

KING, William. Appraisers appointed, John Moore, Miles Cary and John Jenkins. D. May 5, 1747. R. June 2, 1747. Book 1737-49, p. 243 & 250. Mary King, Admtx. of William King returned the account of his estate. Paid the orphans of Michael King, decd. Paid William King, the heir-at-law. Audited by John Riddlehurst, Francis Riddlehurst and Will Wager. D. July 3, 1750. R. February 7, 1764. Book 1758-64, p. 533.

KIRKPATRICK, Priscilla. Administration granted to Augustine Moore and Daniel Barraud, security, Samuel Curle and John Parsons. Appraisers appointed, Robert Armistead, Jr. George Wray, John Jones and James Westwood. November 2, 1756. Order Book 1755-60, p. 82. Account of estate of Mrs. Priscilla Kirkpatrick. Balance carried to the estate of Mrs. Jane Kirkpatrick. Audited by H. King, Jacob Wray and John Riddlehurst. D. 1757. R. August 28, 1768. Book 1763-71, p. 242.

KITE, William. Indexed. Book 1689-1699.

KITELY, Edward. Mary Ricketts his daughter qualified as Extx. October 1690. Book 1689-1699, p. 82.

KITTLEY, William. Indexed. Book 1689-1699.

KNIGHT, William. Appraisers appointed, Thomas Jones, John Howard and Richard Hawkins. February 21, 1727. Audited by Mr. Moore, Anthony Tucker and Richard Hawkins. March 18, 1735. Order Book 1731-47, p. 110. Book 1704-30, p. 84.

LANDRUM, Robert. Appraisers appointed, Michael King, Robert Marrow and William Armistead. January 26, 1797. R. February 2, 1797. Account of Sales. Signed by Mrs. Landrum, Admtx. October 24, 1799. Book 1787-1800, p. 508.

LANGSTON, William. Leg.- to Sarah Hurst as long as she remains single to bring up her daughter Mary Hurst; at her death or marriage to be divided between my son Thomas Langston and Mary Hurst. Exs. son Thomas Langston, brother Mathew Langston and William Reade. D. January 27, 1773. Wit. Ann Reade. Original Will.

LARRIMORE, ---------. Appraisal. Indexed. Book 1689-1699.

Latimer, Lattimer and Latimore

LATIMER, Ann. Leg.- grandson Thomas Haughton; grandson Thomas Latimer, the son of William Latimer; granddaughter Ann Latimer, daughter of Thomas Latimer; to son Thomas; to all my children. Exs. sons William and George Latimer. D. November 8, 1774. R. June 26, 1777. Wit. William Jones, Margaret Jones, Edward Latimer, Sr. George Latimer qualified, security, William Latimer. Original Will.

LATIMER, Edward. Leg.- wife Ann, with reversion at her death to my following children, William, Ann, Elizabeth, John, Thomas, James, George and Samuel Latimer. My Executors are to make a deed to Mr. Hope of the lot bought from the estate of John Nelson, decd. Exs. wife Ann and son William Latimer. D. July 7, 1774. Wit. William Armistead, Gerrard Seymour, Edward Yeargain. Original Will.

LATIMER, George. Appraisers appointed, John Dunn, Thomas Minson and James Manson. February 17, 1741. Book 1737-49, p. 116. Estate account returned by James Manson and wife Sarah, Admtx. The widow's dower allotted, to the child's part. Audited by James Wallace, Joseph Banister and John Selden. May 16, 1744. Book 1737-49, p. 183.

LATIMER, George, Sr. Leg.- wife Mary; son John at age; son Thomas; daughter Jane Watts; son George, the rest of my estate between my four children, Ann, Mary, Barbara and George Latimer. Exs. Mr. Thomas Watts and Mr. Joseph Cooper. D. November 13, 1789. R. July 22, 1790. Wit. Mark Hall, Joseph Cooper, Shelden Moss. Original Will. Book 1787-1800, p. 435.

LATIMER, James. Leg.- son James; son William Copeland; son Edward, land bought of Falvey Copeland, decd.; daughter Mary Latimer; -- son Roe; daughter Anne; daughter Peggy. Exs. son William Copeland and Mr. James Naylor. D. December 21, 1760. R. February 3, 1761. Wit. James Bullock, James Naylor, Thomas Latimer, Jr. Book 1758-64, p. 197. Original Will. Appraisers appointed, Banister Minson, John Sheppard and William Dunn. April 7, 1761. Account of estate. Among items, paid Dr. McClurg account against Jean Meredith; discounted in settlement of David Meredith's estate for Jane Meredith's funeral expense. Audited by Cary Selden, James Wallace and W. Wager. November 3, 1761. Book 1758-64, p. 207 & 284. Account of Roe Latimer, orphan of James Latimer. Signed, William Latimer. September 6, 1763. Book 1758-64, p. 503.

LATIMER, Mary. Leg.- son John at twenty-one, reversion to son George; son Thomas; daughter Jane Watts. Exs. Mr. Thomas Watts and John Cooper. D. April 8, 1794. R. September 25, 1794. Wit. Joseph Cooper, Sr., Joseph Cooper, Jr., George Latimer. Dept. this life Wednesday ye 16th day of April 1794. Book 1787-1800, p. 172. Original Will.

LATIMER, Rosea. Account of estate with George Latimer, decd., Administrator. Sundries furnished the children, paid William Hunt, the guardian of William Latimer and John Latimer. Audited by Joseph Cooper, Joseph Needham and Arthur Henderson. February 24, 1791. Book 1787-1800, p. 14.

LATIMER, Sarah. Leg.- daughter Frances Holstead; daughter Ann; granddaughter Sarah Holstead; cousin Andrew Bushell. Ex. son-in-law Drew Holstead. D. January 7, 1736/37. R. February 1736. Wit. Thomas Baylis, Sr., John Bushell, Sr. Book 1737-49, p. Inventory returned by Drew Holstead. February 21, 1738. Book 1737-49, p. 61.

LATIMER, Thomas. Leg.- son John my plantation in Dinwiddie County; son William my plantation in Foxhill, bought of my brother James Latimer; son Thomas the plantation at Scowne Dam; son George the plantation on Harris Creek, called Brittains, which I bought of Samuel Watts; daughter Ann Shepard; daughter Jean Naylor; daughter Uphan Minson; daughter Elizabeth Haughton; wife Ann; my great grandson John Cooper; grandson Thomas Haughton. Exs. wife Ann, son William Latimer, James Naylor and William Haughton. D. April 23, 1767. R. January 24, 1771. Wit. Charles Pasteur, Jr., George Johnson, Peter Puryear, Andrew Bushell, J. Wallace. Ann Latimer qualified, security, William and Thomas Latimer. Book 1763-71, p. 408. Original Will.

LAW, Andrew. Joyner. Leg.- son William, wife Ann Law. Extx. wife Ann Law. D. January 30, 1722. R. February 20, 1722/23. Wit. John Smith, William Price, William Fyfe. Book 1721-23, p. 94. Ann Law qualified, security, John Bordland and John Cook. Book 1721-23, p. 97.

LAYLESS, Stephen. Leg.- money left me by my son John in the hands of Catherine Norden ------ to my wife, son Thomas and my daughter; my personal estate to be divided between Mary Henderson and Catherine Norden. Exs. Catherine Norden and John Bordland. December 17, 171-. R. March 8, 1717. Wit. Nathaniel Parker, John Henry Rombough, Joseph Wragg. Book 1715-21, p. 108. Probation of the will of Stephen Lillis was granted Robert Norden. March 1717. Book 1715-21, p. 9.

LEE, John. Probation of will granted Edward Myhill, Ex. November 18, 1698. Order Book 1689-1699, p. 139.

LEWIS, ------. Appraisal. Indexed. Book 1689-1699.

LEWIS, John, Sr. Leg.- son Thomas; son Mathew, rest of my estate to be equally divided among my surviving children. D. December 24, 1785. R. December 28, 1786. Wit. James Williams, John Britain, William Bushell. Original Will.

LEWIS, William. Leg.- son William (not of age); daughters, Jane, Sarah, Elizabeth and Ann Lewis. Exs. friends Mark Hall and William Latimer. D. November 26, 1792. R. September 26, 1793. Wit. Mark Hall, Robert Brown, Richard Routon. Book 1787-1800, p. 136. Original Will.

LISTER, John. Of Abingdon Parish, County of Gloucester, Shipwright. Leg.- wife Margaret all the estate which is left of Mr. William Dalton's, decd., if she pays Michael Dalton, Margaret Dalton and Elizabeth Noden their portions; to Michael Dalton at twenty-one, the plantation called "Half Way House", between York and Hampton at the expiration of Captain Tabb's lease; to Mary Noden; to Benjamin Lister the son of Mary Daley land adjoining Gloucester Town also land bought of Capt. William Dalton; to Richard Ambler of York County, Esq. Ex. and guardian of Benjamin Lister, the aforesaid Ambler. D. January 10, 1734. R. January 23, 1734. Wit. Robert Bowis, John May, James Delpich. Original Will.

LIVINGSTONE, Edward. Of Pennsylvania. Died at the home of Dr. George Eland, the 18th day of 9ber, 1695 and was buried in his orchard. Nathaniel Hinson, Master of ye ship, who ye said Livingstone came with, said that he had married ye Governor's daughter of Pennsylvania and withall gave me ye said Eland a great charge of him, but it was so ordered he dyed. November 18, 1695. Signed, George Eland. Book 1689-1699, p. 177.

LOVE, Silas. Isabella Langley qualified as Administratrix, security, Dunn Armistead and William Chislom. Appraisers appointed, Edward Parish, Thomas Crook, Thomas Read and William Manson. September 17, 1746. Book 1737-49, p. 230. Order Book 1731-47, p. 507.

LOWRY, John, Sr. Leg.- son John; son Thomas land in Lunenburg County, bought of Samuel Wilson; son William tract in Lunenburg County bought of Benjamin Winsley, said William has now gone to sea and it is possible he may not come back, reversion of bequest to son Thomas; daughter Frances Stevenson; grandson William Stevenson; granddaughter Ann Stevenson; granddaughter Sarah Stevenson; granddaughter Frances Stevenson; granddaughter Mary Tabb; grandson John Tabb. Exs. son John Lowry and son-in-law William Stevenson. D. May 2, 1763. R. October 7, 1766. William Stevenson qualified, security, John Tabb and Richard Cary. Book 1763-71, p. 97. Original Will. Appraisal of estate of John Lowry. Among items, a negro left in will to his son Thomas, but as he died before his father, the said negro is claimed by John Lowry. Appraised by John Tabb, Augustine Moore and Will Mallory. May 28, 1767. Book 1763-71, p. 152. Account and division of estate. Each of the following received one-fourth of the estate; Thomas Lowry, William Lowry, Pascow Turner and William Stevenson. Audited by Nicholas Dickson, George Wilson and Lawrence Smith, Jr. Signed William Stevenson. May 26, 1768. Book 1763-71, p. 205.

LOWRY, John. Leg.- loving wife; son John the plantation which was formerly my brother William's; to son Thomas the residence which was formerly my brother Thomas'; the waste land between the two plantations in Lunenburg to be divided between the said John and Thomas; son Robert; son Edmund; daughter Nancy; daughter Frances; daughter Molly; daughter Jenny; oldest son William Lowry. Exs. wife, son William Lowry, Mr. George Booker and Mr. Richard Brown. D. January 29, 1786. R. February 17, 1790. Wit. Westwood Armistead, Benjamin Bryan. William Lowry qualified, security, William Booker and Miles King. Original Will. Estate appraised by Joseph Cooper, William Davis and Augustine Moore, Jr. February 7, 1791. R. July 26, 1792. Book 1787-1800, p. 88.

LOWRY, William. Leg.- my deceased daughter Ann Kirbie left five children, one has since died, to the foresaid children; son William my land in Essex and King and Queen Counties; daughter Margaret Booker; son William lot bought of Edmund Kerney; son-in-law Thomas Kirbie; grandson William Booker; grandson William Lowry and his sister Frances Lowry; son John Lowry; daughter-in-law Martha Tabb, daughter-in-law Mary Lowry, daughter-in-law Jane Lowry and daughter Margaret Booker all the money I have in England and Ireland; son-in-law Richard Booker; son-in-law Thomas Kirbie. Exs. Thomas Kirbie and son John Lowry. May 13, 1724. R. September 16, 1724. Wit. William Tucker, Susanna Tucker, Nicholas McKey. Book 1704-30, p. 17. Inventory. Book 1704-30, p. 25 & 89.

MALLORY, Diana. Leg.- grandson Augustine Moore; granddaughter Ann Collier; granddaughter Elizabeth Collier; grandson Francis Mallory, son of Edward Mallory; to William Moore; to Margaret Goodwin; to Mary Moore. Exs. son Edward Mallory and son-in-law William Moore. D. November 6, 1782. R. January 27, 1785. Wit. John Parsons, William Seymour. William Moore qualified, security, Michael King. Original Will.

MALLORY, Edward. Leg.- wife Rachel, with reversion of the bequest to son Johnson; son James Goodwin Mallory; son William Mallory; daughter Elizabeth Wallace, son Francis stones in the hands of Mr. James Goodwin. Exs. wife Rachel and son Johnson Mallory. D. April 10, 1789. R. September 23, 1789. Wit. Mark Hall, George Latimer, Joseph Cooper, Sheldon Moss. Security for Exs. Miles King and George Booker. Original Will.

MALLORY, Francis. Granddaughter Ann Mallory, reversion of the bequest to my son Johnson Mallory; cousin Elizabeth Read when she is twenty-one; to friend Captain John Tabb; to son Johnson my land in Elizabeth City and Warwick Counties and my reversion right to the Indian land in King William County. Ex. son Johnson Mallory. D. January 7, 1742. R. July 18, 1744. Wit. John Tabb, Margaret Tabb, William Bean. Security for Ex. John Tabb and William Mallory. Book 1737-40, p. 187. Estate appraised by Simon Hollier, John Lowry and W. Parsons. September 19, 1744. Book 1737-40, p. 191.

MALLORY, Colonel Francis. Account of estate, signed by Miles King. 1789. Sundries for Betsey, Mary and Charles Mallory. Betsey and Mary boarded with Col. Westwood and Charles Mallory with George Wray. Book 1787-1800, p. 102. Additional account of estate. Part allotted to Mrs. Mary Mallory, widow; to George Wray in right of wife Diana and three other parts to Elizabeth, Mary and Charles Mallory. Audited by John Cary, Sheldon Moss, William Moore. November 27, 1788. R. March 25, 1793. Book 1787-1800, p. 116. Additional account of estate, audited by Charles Jenings, George Hope and William Brough. Signed, Molly Mallory, 1789. Division of estates of Francis and Mary Mallory, decd. To John Page in right of wife Elizabeth; to M. G. Latues in right of wife Mary; to Charles Mallory. October 25, 1798. Book 1787-1800, p. 431, 432 and 438.

MALLORY, Johnson. Leg.- daughter Margaret; son Edward at twenty-one; daughter Mary; daughter Ann King; son Francis land on Back River, between Thomas Watts and the late Philip Allen; son Edward land on Harris Creek bought of John Massenburg, John Armistead and Gill Armistead; wife Diana; to Henry King a mourning ring, who I also appoint trustee for my son Francis. Exs. wife Diana and sons Francis and Edward Mallory. D. May 9, 1760. R. May 5, 1762. Wit. George Johnson, John Bayley, Francis Parker. Francis Mallory qualified, security, Henry King and John Bayley. Book 1758-64, p. 324. Estate appraised by John Lowry, Jr., John Bayley and Augustine Moore. January 4, 1763. Book 1758-64, p. 373.

MALLORY, Mary. Leg.- land entered with Mr. Robert Walker, surveyor to my son Charles King Mallory; to Mr. Merritt Moore; daughter Elizabeth King Mallory; daughter Mary King Mallory; daughter Diana Wray. Ex. brother Miles King. D. January 20, 1789. R. April 24, 1789. Wit. Martha King, Hannah Westwood. Original Will.

MALLORY, William. Leg.- son Francis the plantation on which I live adjoining Thomas Wythe and Anthony Armistead; son William (not sixteen); daughter Mary; daughter Anne Mallory. Exs. sons Francis and William Mallory. Overseer, Mr. Thomas Wythe. D. August 17, 1719. R. February 15, 1720. Wit. John Bean, Ann Bean. Book 1715-21, p. 289. Bond for Francis Mallory as Executor with Hugh Ross, security. Wit. John Thomas, John Fitzgerald, John Hicks and H. Irwin. May 18, 1721. Book 1704-30, p. 320. Estate appraised by William Moore, Lokey Myhill and William Tucker. July 18, 1722. Account estate. Book 1721-23, p. 57 and 74.

MANEY, William, Sr. Leg.- daughter Mary; son Alexander; daughter Isabella; daughter Catherine; son John; son Robert. Exs. sons John and Robert Maney. D. February 7, 1779. R. Wit. W. Seymour, George Jarvis. Original Will.

MANSON, James. Leg.- wife Sarah, my plantation adjoining Thomas Hawkins and Anthony Hawkins, if she takes care of my children, Sarah, Peter and James Manson; to son Chapman Manson. Exs. wife Sarah and Mr. William Armistead. D. December 12, 1761. R. March 2, 1761 (?). Wit. Hursley Carter, John Sheppard, Thomas Palmer, William Armistead. Book 1758-64, p. 315. Original Will. Estate appraised by James Naylor, William Carter and Thomas Jenings. July 6, 1762. Account of sale. Book 1758-64, p. 343 & 396. Division of estate by Henry King, John Riddlehurst and James Wallace Bayley. One-third of estate to Edward Parish; one-third to Peter Manson and one-third to James Manson. February 5, 1765. Book 1763-71, p. 28.

MANSON, John. Leg.- brother Robert Manson; brother-in-law John Patrick; sisters, Frances, Elizabeth and Hannah Manson. Exs. uncle James Manson, brother-in-law John Patrick and cousin William Houghton. D. January 1, 1758. Wit. Curle Tucker, Joseph Massenburg, John Armistead. Estate appraised by Henry Allen, J. Massenburg and John Bayley. February 7, 1758. Original Will. John Patrick qualified, security, Curle Tucker and Thomas Dixon. Appraisers appointed, Josiah Massenburg, John Bayley, Henry Allen, Thomas Webster and Anthony Hawkins. February 7, 1758. Order Book 1755-60, p. 165. Account of estate. John Patrick, Ex. To the hire of a negro belonging to the estate of Peter Manson, due to the five children of the said decedent from John Manson; due Robert Manson as a legacy received by John Manson; due Frances Manson. Audited by Robert Armistead, Booth Armistead and W. Wager. February 6, 1759. Book 1758-64, p. 40.

MANSON, Mary. Inventory to be recorded. March 3, 1756. Order Book 1755-60, p. 37.

MANSON, Peter. Leg.- son John; son Peter; son Robert; daughter Mary Patrick; daughter Frances; daughter Elizabeth; daughter Hannah Manson. Exs. son John Manson and friend Bennet Kerby. D. December 12, 1754. Wit. Rt. Armistead, Curle Tucker, Jonah Massenburg, Peter Houghton. Original Will. Auditors appointed, Francis Jones, Thomas Dixon, Robert Armistead, Jr., John Jones. August 3, 1756. Order Book 1755-60, p. 64.

MARLOW, Robert. Administration granted William Wilson. May 19, 1700/01. Book 1689-1699, p. 217.

MARROW, John Alias John Williams. Administration granted William Jones and wife Ann, Admtx. Appraisers appointed William Mallory, Samuel Tompkins, Francis Mallory and John Chapple.

April 16, 1735. Order Book 1731-47, p. 93.

MARSHALL, James. Estate appraised by Joseph Cooper, Charles Jennings and Joseph Needham. D. April 14, 1792. R. January 24, 1793. Book 1787-1800, p. 115.

MARSHALL, William. Appraisers appointed, Henry Royall, Mathew Watts, Robert Miller and Charles Jenings. 19th of Xber last past. R. January 12, 1692/93. Book 1689-1699, p. 87. Wife Hannah Marshall qualified. April 29, 1693. Book 1689-1699, p. 117. Appraisal, signed by Hannah Marshall. January 12, 1692/93. Book 1689-1699, p. 134. Bond of Richard Booker of the County of Gloucester, who married Hannah the relict of W William Marshall. Security, Henry Jenkins and William Lowry. March 19, 1694/95. Book 1689-1699, p. 186. Order Book 1689-99, p. 9 & 32.

MARSHALL, William. Leg.- son William; wife Elizabeth, with reversion of bequests to the child of my brother George Booker. Exs. wife and son William Marshall. October 14, 1734. Wit. Simon Hollier, John Lowry. Original Will. Elizabeth Marshall qualified, security, Richard Booker. Appraisers appointed, Augustine Moore, John Tabb, William Parsons and William Parsons, Jr. November 2, 1756. Order Book 1755-60, p. 82.

MASSENBURG, John. Leg.- son John land adjoining Samuel Dewbry; son Zachariah; son Robert; son Nicholas a tract known as "Sandifurs"; son Josiah; daughter Susannah; daughter Elizabeth; daughter Barbery; wife Barbery. Exs. wife Barbery and sons Nicholas and Josiah Massenburg. D. October 16, 1748. R. April 4, 1749. Wit. Charles King, Peter Manson. Book 1737-49, p. 324.

MASSENBURG, Robert. Leg.- wife Catherine to sell land adjoining widow Dewbre to defray my debts; son John; son Robert; son William; son Beverley; son Josiah; daughter Elizabeth Massenburg. Exs. wife and nephew Josiah Massenburg of Warwick County. D. R. July 26, 1787. Wit. Josiah Massenburg, Samuel Dewbry, Sarah Debry, William McHollan. Josiah Massenburg, Jr. qualified, security, Josiah Massenburg. Original Will.

MASSENBURG, Thomas. Estate appraised by William Tucker, Charles Pasteur and John Nelson. April 1, 1748. R. October 4, 1748. Book 1737-1749, p. 305.

MELYEN, Isaac. Inventory returned by Charles Jennings. May 19, 1693. Book 1689-1699, p. 146. Administration granted Mr. Pascho Curle in behalf of Ryderus Melyen son and heir of Isaac Melyen, decd. March 19, 1693/94. Book 1689-1699, p. 155. Order Book 1689-99, p. 14.

MEREDITH, David. Estate appraised by Charles Pasteur, John Henry Rombough and Samuel Walker. April 4, 1749. Book 1737-49, p. 322. Account of estate to James Latimer and wife Margaret, Admtx. One-half of estate due to James Latimer in right of his wife. Due to James Latimer's estate for Doctors and funeral expenses for Jean Meredith. November 3, 1761. Book 1758-64, p. 286. Audited by Cary Selden, James Wallace and W. Wager.

MEREDITH, John. Of the Town of Hampton. Leg.- wife Sarah; to Thomas Nell land adjoining John Ryland; son Joseph Meredith; son John Meredith. Extx., wife Sarah Meredith. D. January 8, 1727. R. March 19, 1728. Wit. John Standly, William

Smelt, Pas. Green. Book 1704-30, p. 127. Estate appraised by William Loyall, John McDowell and Nicholas Parker. August 21, 1728. Book 1704-30, p. 144.

MEREDITH, John. Of Hampton. Leg.- wife Elizabeth; son John; son Edward Roe; son DAvid; son Lewis; daughter Elizabeth; daughter Sarah Meredith. Extx. wife Elizabeth Meredith. D. January 28, 1748/49. R. May 2, 1749. Wit. Thomas Faulkner, Charles Avera Sr., Charles Avera, Jr. Security for Elizabeth Meredith, Dunn Armistead and Armistead King. Book 1737-49, p. 330. Account estate presented by Joseph Jegitts and wife Elizabeth, Extx. Audited by Thomas Dixon, George Wray and W. Wager. Paid John Webb's expenses for going twice to Charles City County.

MEREDITH, Jean. Leg.- sister Ann Latimer; sister Peggy Latimer. Ex., father-in-law James Latimer. D. May 24, 1760. R. January 4, 1763. Wit. Sarah Cowper, Lucy Loyall, Thomas Latimer. Original Will. David Meredith, heir at law to be summoned to contest validity of will. Book 1758-64, p. 380.

MEREDITH, John. Estate appraised by John Henry Rombough, William Tucker and Charles Pasteur. April 1, 1749. Book 1737-49, p. 346.

MEREDITH, John. Estate appraised by Francis Riddlehurst, Jacob Wray and Will Armistead. January 6, 1767. Book 1763-71, p. 106.

MEREDITH, Captain John. Estate appraised by M.E. Chisman, William Kerby, John L. Westwood and George Wray. Extx. Elizabeth M. Meredith. April 20, 1798. R. February 27, 1800. Book 1787-1800, p. 526.

MEREDITH, Joseph. Leg.- wife Elizabeth Margaret; son Joseph; daughter Elizabeth Margaret. Extx. wife Elizabeth Margaret Meredith. March 12, 1797. R. January Court 1798. Wit. John Z. Spooner, Minson I. Proby, Ann Toomer, Mary Proby, Elizabeth Bean. Book 1787-1800, p. 383. Original Will. Estate appraised by Charles Jennings, George Hope, ----- Minson and T. Proby. Book 1798-1800, p. 416.

MEREDITH, Mary. Leg.- father John Allen, my entire estate. Ex. father John Allen. D. July 10, 1766. R. November 26, 1767. Wit. William Smelt, Elizabeth Smith. Book 1763-71, p. 187. Original Will.

Merritt, Merit, Merrit.

MERRIT, John. Leg.- son William, a tract of land bought of Edward Tabb of York County, with reversion of bequest to son John; my land to be divided by Mr. Edward Tabb, Mr. William Moore, Mr. Merrit Sweny and Mr. William Tucker; my son John a certain bequest if he will pay my three children, William, Mary and Frances Merrit. (Son John not twenty-one). Ex. son William Merrit. D. July 23, 1725. R. June 21, 1727. Wit. Samuel Bland, Martha Bland, Miles Cary. Book 1704-30, p. 71. Estate appraised by Henry Cock, Samuel Tompkins and Lockey Myhile. Signed, William Merrit. July 19, 1727. Book 1704-30, p. 87.

MERRITT, William. Administration granted Captain Daniel Taylor of York County in behalf of Elizabeth, the orphan of the said William Merritt. Appraisers of the estate, Robert Creek, Augustine Moore and Mr. Lowry. September 18, 1695. Book

1689-1699, p. 73, 156 and 199.

MERRY, John. Estate appraised by Samuel Hawkins, Charles Pasteur and William Henry. July 20, 1738. Book 1737-49, p. 54.

MERRY, Thomas. Leg.- son Prettyman; son Thomas; son John; daughter Elizabeth; daughter Mary; cousin William Brasey; cousin Mary Brasey. Exs. friend and Kinsman William Tucker, if he should die, friend Samuel Roberts. D. May 12, 1718. R. June 18, 1718. Wit. Simon Hollier, Plane Ward, John Wilson. Bequest to the poor of Elizabeth City County at the disposing of Mr. William Lowry and the Executors. Book 1715-21, p. 111. William Tucker qualified. Estate appraised by Simon Hollier, Edmond Hollier, John King and Edward Tabb. Book 1715-21, p. 119. Account of estate. May 1718. Paid Henry Burkey, legatee, paid Margaret Hatton, legatee, paid Thomas Hatton, legatee, paid Elizabeth Merry as per will, paid Thomas Merry as per will, paid Philip Saunders and Mary his wife their legacy. At the time of death of Thomas Merry the eldest child was nine years old and the youngest fifteen months (five children). Signed, William Tucker and audited by And. Giles and David O'Sheale. September 17, 1730. Book 1704-30, p. 193.

MICHELL, Thomas, Esq. Estate appraised by William Tucker, George Wray and Lawrence Dent. June 6, 1749. R. July 4, 1749. Book 1737-49, p. 339.

MILBY, Joseph. Estate appraised by George Eland and Mark Parrish. March 19, 1693-94. Ordered that Thomas Curle, Cordw'r., who married Ann the relict of Joseph Milby, do give to the Richard Milby, the younger, certain cattle. Order Book 1689-1699, p. 33 & 42.

MILBY, Mary. Account of estate, returned by Thomas Latimer and ordered record. August 3, 1756. Order Book 1756-60, p. 69.

MILBY, (MILBEE), Richard. Administration of estate granted to Bridget Milbee. Appraisers appointed Leonard Whiting, Charles Needham, John Cooper and James Baker. May 19, 1736. Order Book 1731-47, p. 115. Account of estate, March 22, 1738/39. To balance due Milby's children. Audited by Joseph Banister and John Selden. Book 1737-49, p. 61. Additional inventory signed by Thomas Bully. September 19, 1744. Book 1737-49, p. 190. Division of estate to widow's share, to Bridget Milby, to Mary Milby, funeral expenses for children that died. Examined by Joseph Banister and John Selden. Signed Thomas Bully, Administrator. July 17, 1745. Book 1737-49, p. 206.

Miles, Myles

MILES, Thomas. Inventory signed by William Corneck. January 17, 1688. R. October 25, 1689. Book 1689-1699, p. 78 & 105. Administration granted William Myles the brother of Thomas Myles. September 18, 1700. Book 1689-1699, p. 217.

MILLER, John. Leg.- my two eldest sons, James and John Miller; daughter Margaret; to my three youngest children. Exs. Mr. William Wilson and daughter Margaret Miller. D. November 4, 1688/89. R. Xber 18, 1689. Wit. William Corneck, George Digells, George Elyand. Book 1689-1699, p. 109. Margaret Miller his daughter qualified. April 24, 1690. Order Book 1689-1699, p. 83. Estate appraised by Thomas Morgan, Robert Tucker and George Giggles. Paid to the following, Margaret's share, Elizabeth's share, William's share, John's share and

Robert's share. Signed Margaret Miller. June 3, 1690. Book 1689-1699, p. 132.

MILLER, Robert. Of Back River. Leg.- wife Ephica, God-daughter Margaret Lowry; to friend Will Lowry; to God-son Augustine Moore, Jr.; to Mrs. Hannah Marshall and Frances Marshall rings; rest of estate to be divided between wife Ephica Miller and Ephica and Thomasin Prettyman. Extx. wife Ephica Miller. D. January 25, 1693. R. May 21, 1695. Wit. William Marshall, John Phells (?). Book 1689-1699, p. 182. Inventory signed by Aphia Miller. Estate appraised by Mathew Watts, Thomas Marwood, Philip Johnson and Robert Crooke. April 14, 1696. Book 1689-1699, p. 226.

MINGHAM, Anne. Leg.- sister Elizabeth Mingham; sister Chivers Elliot and nephews William and Henry Elliot, when they are twenty-one; the debt which Nathan Yancy owes me to be paid Nathan Jenks; I desire that the three children that John Gooch of York County had at one birth may each have one years schooling at my expense. Ex. William Russell of Warwick County. D. November 9, 1778. R. October 28, 1779. Wit. Elizabeth Garton, Nathan Jenks. Will proved by Martha Elliot, who relinquished the legacy left her in the said will. William and Nathan Yancey and Elizabeth Mingham qualified. Original Will.

MINGHAM, Ann. Ordered that William Westwood, George Wray, Sr., James Westwood and George Wray, Jr. settle the estate. September 2, 1755. Order Book 1755-60, p. 10.

MINGHAM, Henry Howard. Leg.- sister Elizabeth; sister Ann; to Nathan Yancey; to sister Chivers Elliott's children when they are twenty-one. I am security for a bond for John Broyde, Jr., which I wish to be paid. Ex. Nathan Yancey. D. December 26, 1777. R. June 25, 1778. Wit. Samuel Watts, Jr., Lodowick Brodie. Original Will.

MINGHAM, Thomas. Leg.- daughter Margaret; daughter Elizabeth; daughter Anne; daughter Chivers; daughter Sarah; daughter Mary; son Thomas Townshend Mingham; son Henry Howard Mingham. Debts to be paid Mr. Samuel Sweny and Mr. Jenings. Exs. wife Anne, John Howard, Jr., and John Tabb. D. September 17, 1748. R. February 7, 1748. Wit. John Selden, John Cooper, Jr., Christopher Needham. Codicil. Mr. Samuel Sweny appointed as Executor. Estate appraised by John Selden, John Allen and Thomas Smith. May 2, 1749. Book 1737-49, p. 308 and 331. Account of the estate of Thomas Townshend Mingham, orphan of Thomas Mingham decd. Signed Elizabeth Howard of Warwick County and sworn before Hinde Russell. June 21, 1768. Book 1763-71, p. 225.

MINSON, Bannister. Leg.- son Thomas; daughter Whiten Armistead; daughter Ann Dowsing; daughter Afphia; daughter Euphan; daughter Susanna Bannister Minson; wife Euphan; to William Armistead, the son of Moseley Armistead and Whiten his wife. Exs. wife, Moseley Armistead and George Latimer. D. June 11, 1777. R. Wit. -------. Original Will.

MINSON, Frances. Leg.- son John; to John Armstrong; negroes to be sold to pay the debt due Mr. George Minson estate; daughter Mary Scott, the money in the hands of James Wood; daughter Ann; daughter Sarah Randolph; grandsons George and William Randolph; to daughter Armstrong. Exs. Jacob Wray and Ann Minson. D. October 9, 1767. R. February 25, 1768. Wit. John Bennett,

William Bennett, William Harper. Book 1763-71, p. 189. Probation granted Ann Minson, security, William Morris and William Randolph. Estate appraised by Samuel Watts, John Bennett and Philip Cowper. June 23, 1769. Book 1763-71, p. 298.

MINSON, George. Leg.- wife Frances; daughters Mary, Ann, Sarah and Lucy Minson. Extx. wife Frances Minson. D. August 21, 1752. R. November 7, 1752. Wit. R. Brough, William Williams, Joan Robertson. Original Will.

MINSON, John. January 18, 1699/1700. Order Book 1689-1699, p. 165.

MINSON, Robert. Of Hampton. Leg.- to Servant John Proby son of Bartrand Proby, a lot in Hampton; with reversion of bequest to his sister Mary Proby; reversion to Bartrand Proby. Ex. Bertrand Proby. D. February 25, 1718/19. Codicil. Morning rings to Mary Servant and her daughters, Lucy, Mary and Sidwell. April 15, 1719. Wit. Robert Tennoch, Benjamin Rolfe, Joseph Wragg. Security for Bertrand Proby, James Ricketts and William Copeland. Book 1715-21, p. 177. Bond for Bartrand Proby, with James Ricketts, William Copeland and Charles Jenings. April 20, 1719. Wit. John Smith, William Riddouch. Book 1715-21, p. 200. Estate appraised by Joseph Banister, Samuel Sweny and Thomas Howard. October 6, 1719. Book 1715-21, p. 233.

MINSON, Thomas. Administration granted Apphia Minson, security Joseph Banister and John Cooper. Appraisers appointed Baldwin Shepard, James Manson, Abram Cooper and James Baker. June 2, 1747. R. July 7, 1747. Order Book 1731-47, p. 540. Book 1737-49, p. 243.

MINSON, William. Leg.- son Thomas; oldest son William; wife Hester. Extx. wife Hester Minson. D. December 12, 1717. R. February 18, 1718. Wit. Samuel Selden, John Bushell, Thomas Jones. Bond for Easter Minson, with Joshua Curle and John Bailey as security. Wit. Charles Jenings. February 18, 1718. Book 1715-21, p. 171 and 173.

MINSON, William. Estate appraised by John White, Angus McKoy and H. Irwin. Signed Thomas Minson, Administrator. April 16, 1737. Book 1737-49, p. 6.

MINSON, William. Leg.- wife Mary; son Thomas; son John; daughter Elizabeth; son William. Extx. wife Mary Minson. D. December 17, 1773. R. March 24, 1774. Wit. Claus'l Clausel, John Sheppard, Sr., John Sheppard, Jr. Original Will.

Mitchell and Michell

MITCHELL, Ross. Leg.- wife Elennor to have my part of my father's estate with reversion at her death to my three children, Edward, Ann and Elennor Mitchell. Exs. wife Elennor and friend Adam Boutwell. D. November 14, 1750. R.   1750. Wit. John Ryland, John White, James Wallace. Original Will.

MITCHELL, William. Leg.- to son Nazareth Ansey Mitchell, lot purchased of Mr. James Wallace Bayley, land I live on also, bought of Colonel Selden if he pays his brother and sister and my unborn child ten pounds each. Extx. wife Mary Mitchell. D. September 26, 1768. R. November 25, 1768. Wit. W. Wager, John Jones, John Riddlehurst, James Bullock. Book 1763-71, p. 270. Original Will. Estate appraised by W. Wager, Francis

Riddlehurst, Thomas Younghusband. January 25, 1770. Book 1763-71, p. 317.

MOORE, Ann. Leg.- sister Lucy Loyall; nephew Lewis Meredith; niece Jenny Barron, -- reversion of bequest to her son Archibald Bordland; sister Mary Ballard; niece Sarah Webb; sister Sarah Cowper; sister Elizabeth Jeggitts; to Anne Armistead, the daughter of James Armistead the money he owes me. Exs. Lewis Meredith and Lucy Loyall. D. December 27, 1767. R. January 29, 1768. Wit. James Cunningham, Mary Tarrant. Book 1763-71, p. 187. Original Will. Lewis Meredith qualified, security, Roe Cowper.

MOORE, (MORE) Augustine. Leg.- to brother John More the tract on which he now lives; nephew Augustine, the son of my brother William Moore, decd. a tract of fifty acres bought of James Toomer, when he is twenty; reversion of this bequest to my brother Merritt More; to niece Elizabeth, the daughter of my brother William Moore decd.; to nephew Augustine More, my seal ring; sister Martha Dixon; brother Daniel More. Ex. brother Merritt More. D. March 24, 1736. R. May 18, 1737. Wit. John Tabb, Thomas Tabb, William Merritt. Book 1737-49, p. 10. Original Will.

MOORE, Augustine. Appraisal of the negroes to be delivered to John Moore when he comes to age, the son of Augustine Moore and Elizabeth his wife, both decd. Appraised by William Wilson, Pascho Dunn, Edmond Swaney, William Lowry. November 23, 1688. Book 1689-1699, p. 119.

MOORE, Augustine. Leg.- wife Ann, with reversion to son William; son Augustine; son Merritt; son John; daughter Ann King; daughter Jane Sweny; son-in-law George Booker. Exs. wife Ann and sons William and Merritt Moore. D. November 9, 1793. R. June 26, 1795. Wit. Roscow Parsons, Jenny Parsons, Mary Parsons. Book 1787-1800, p. 237. Original Will.

MOORE, John. Nuncupative will proven by Coleman Brough. Dr. George Eland appointed Administrator. Charles Jenings, clerk to take an inventory of the estate. February 20, 1692/93. Order Book 1689-1699, p. 16.

MOORE, (MORE) John. Leg.- to nephew John More, land adjoining Thomas Jennings; nephew Edward Moore, land adjoining William Creeke; nephew Merrit More, the plantation on which John Merritt lives; nephew Daniel More; niece Martha More; niece Ann More; niece Rachell Wise, widow; niece Susanna Goodwyn; sister Elizabeth Goodwyn, widow; nephew William More; uncle William Lowry and Aunt Rachell Lowry; cousin John Lowry. Exs. sister Elizabeth Goodwyn and nephew William More. D. December 11, 1715. P. January 18, 1715. Wit. Thomas Kerby, Charles Rowin, William Lowry. R. February 4, 1715/16. Book 1715-21, p. 17. Inventory signed by Elizabeth Goodwyn and William Moore. Book 1715-21, p. 283.

MOORE, John. Leg.- daughter Elizabeth land in Cooper's Neck on which Daniel Sieley now lives; wife Ann; nephew Augustine More, son of William Moore; to Ann Armistead, the wife of James Armistead. Exs. wife, nephew Augustine Moore, James Armistead and John Riddlehurst. D. September 13, 1762. R. October 5, 1762. Wit. Sarah Cowper, John Riddlehurst, James Armistead. Probation granted John Riddlehurst and Augustine Moore, security Thomas Kerby and Roe Cowper. Book 1758-64, p. 364. Original Will. Ordered John Moore Bayley and Elizabeth

Moore, heirs-at-law to be summoned to contest the validity of said will. Book 1758-64, p. 364. Account of estate, audited by H. King, John Jones and Roe Cowper. February 23, 1769. Book 1763-71, p. 282.

MOORE, Merritt. Leg.- to my Mother, the property on my plantation rented to Mary Wise for the support of herself and children; brother William Moore; brother John Moore. D. April 25, 1798. R. December 27, 1798. Wit. Augustine Moore, Jr., Ann Mallory Moore. Book 1787-1800, p. 448. Original Will.

MOORE? William. Account of estate, audited by Charles King, John Tabb and John Lowry. D. January 27, 1747. R. February 2, 1747. Book 1737-49, p. 267.

MOREHEAD, William. Leg.- wife Sarah; daughter Rebecca; daughter Martha Morehead. Exs. wife and daughters. D. June 11, 1772. R. March 24, 1774. Wit. Mark Parrish, Mary Jegitts, James Bullock. Original Will.

MORES, Elizabeth. Inventory. Indexed. Book 1689-1699.

MORGAN, Edward. Account estate to be audited by Robert Armstead, Jr. Thomas Dixon, John Jones and Francis Jones. May 5, 1756. Order Book 1755-60, p. 51.

MORGAN, Elizabeth. Account estate and sale. Signed, Henry Allen Deputy Sheriff. To goods bought for the orphans August 25, 1768. Book 1763-71, p. 237.

MORGAN, John. Estate appraised by John Cook, John Nixon and Edward Parish. May 21, 1729. Book 1704-30, p. 168.

MORGAN, Mark. Will Indexed. Book 1689-1699.

MORGAN, Thomas. Administration granted to Mary the relict. August 19, 1695. Book 1689-1699, p. 156. Estate appraised by George Griggley, Ruthe Joanes, William Spicer and William Bowles. November 18, 1695. Mary the relict of Thomas Morgan, decd., also the relict of Thomas Dolby to be summoned to the next court to show what claims she has to the land of the said Dolby. Order Book 1689-1699, p. 77 & 93.

MORGAN, William. Bond for Thomas Gray as guardian of Mary and Rebecca Morgan the children of William Morgan. Signed, Thomas Gray and William Mallory. Wit. September 10, 1689. Wit. Charles Jenings, Clerk, Robert Taylor. Book 1689-1699, p. 103.

MORRIS, Baldwin Sheppard. Leg.- wife Ann; daughter Mary Bridgford, with reversion of the bequest to her children. Exs. friends, Thomas Watts and Samuel Watts. D. June 3, 1799. R. July 26, 1799. Wit. John Dewbre, Daniel Webb. Book 1787-1800, p. 477. Original Will.

MORRIS, William. Estate appraised by John Bennett, Philip Cooper and John Minson. April 8, 1761. Account of estate signed by William Morris, Jr., Administrator. Item, paid for coffin for my Mother. Each of the following paid a proportional part of the estate, Giles Morris, Elizabeth Morris, Daniel Simson in right of his wife, John Morris and my own part. Audited by Cary Selden, Samuel Watts and William Naylor. R. November 1, 1763. Book 1758-64, p. 248 & 527.

MORRYSON, Charles. Leg.- my funeral sermon to be penned and sent to my wife Rebecca, for which I request Mr. Rooke to answer satisfaction to my wife and if my wife should die before this my will reaches Virginia, then my former will to stand in full force. Exs. wife and her assistant my friend Col. Philip Ludwell. D. November 28, 1688. R. July 18, 1689. Wit. Drury Smith, Merchant, Edward Folwell, Merchant. Will proved by Captain John Brunskill, Master of the Ship Margaret. Ejectment suit proves that the widow Rebecca married Colonel John Lear and that Rebecca, who married Samuel Selden was the cousin and heir-at-law to Rebecca the widow and devisee of Charles Morryson. Book 1734-70, Ejectment Suits, p. 63.

MORRYSON, Richard. Leg.- wife Winifred; remainder of my estate to be divided between my children; to son Richard when he becomes of age. Exs. wife Winifred and friends John Chandler and Richard Hull, Overseers. D. September 9, 1626. P. September 27, 1748. Wit. William Wilkinson, William South, Thomas Lorryman. Book 1734-70, Ejectment Suits, p. 62.

Mullin and Mullen
MULLEN, John. Leg.- son James; friend Thomas Williams to take care of my estate and son until he is eighteen. D. October 13, 1738. R. May 19, 1742. Wit. Robert Tucker, John Hawkins. Thomas Williams refused Executorship, Robert Cross qualified. (John Hawkins was dead when will was probated.) Estate appraised by John Moore and Joseph Jeggitts. May 18, 1743. Book 1737-49, p. 124 & 167. Account of estate inaccount with Robert Cross, decd. Audited by Miles Cary, Anthony Tucker and Thomas Everard. June 19, 1745. Book 1737-49, p. 198.

MYHAN, Terrence. Estate appraised by W. Wager, Charles Pasteur, Richard Bickerdick and Charles White. June 6, 1749. Book 1737-49, p. 334.

Myhill, Myhile
MYHILL, Edward. Leg.- liberation of slaves; daughter Elizabeth with reversion of bequest to my cousin Edward Myhill, the son of cousin Lockey Myhill, with reversion to my cousin Joshua Myhill; to cousin Lockey Myhill; my wife Ann did some years past elope and has lately borne a child, the said child and my wife are disbarred from inheriting any part of my estate. Exs. Cousins Lockey and Joshua Myhill, who are also appointed guardians to my daughter Elizabeth. D. October 23, 1718. R. May 17, 1719. Wit. Edward Ward, Pasco Ward, Edward Ward, Jr., Gerard Roberts. Bond for Lockey and Joseph Myhill, signed by Samuel Sweny and William Marshall. June 17, 1719. Book 1715-21, p. 199. Estate appraised by Simon Hollier, John Lowry, Edward Tabb and Merritt Sweny. Book 1715-21, p. 214. Administration of estate granted Anne Myhill, with Francis Mallory, security. June 21, 1727. Order Book 1723-29, p. 12.

MYHILL, (Myhile) Joshua. Leg.- sister Anne Ellyson; niece Judith Collier; niece Lucy Dowling. Ex. sister Ann Ellyson. D. January 30, 1727. R. June 21, 1727 (?). Wit. Edward Ward, Humphrey Ward. Ann Ellyson, the Extx. named being dead, Lockey Myhill qualified. Book 1704-30, p. 68. Lockey Myhill qualified, security, Francis Mallory. Order Book 1723-29, p. 12.

MYHILL, Lockey. Sarah Latimer, the widow of said Myhill qualified. Thomas Latimer petitions to be appointed as the guardian of Elizabeth Myhill. November 15, 1732. The will of Lockey Myhill was proven by Samuel Tompkins, William Mallory and Ann Mallory. Wit. to codicil, John Langhorne, Martha Rumley. Sarah Myhill and John Langhorne qualified as Executors. Appraisers appointed, Samuel Tompkins, Michael King, Francis Mallory and William Mallory. Order Book 1731-47, p. 39 & 40.

McCLURG, Walter. Leg.- wife Rachel all the estate which I received from her former husband, Henry King; daughter Barbara Vance McClurg my lot in Norfolk, formerly the property of William McCaa decd.; to son James McClurg. Exs. son James and friends Jacob Wray and George Wray. D. October 24, 1783. R. March 25, 1784. Wit. Robert Brough, Thomas Kerby, Joseph Needham. James McClurg qualified, security, Cary Selden. Original Will.

McCREEST, Mathew. Leg.- to John Armistead, Sr.; to John Riddlehurst. Ex. John Riddlehurst. D. October 17, 1766. R. March 4, 1767. Wit. Moseley Armistead, Westwood Armistead, John Armistead. John Riddlehurst qualified, security, Robert Wallace. Book 1763-71, p. 122. Original Will.

McHOLLAND, John. Estate appraised by Edward Lattimer, William Reade and John Yeargain. D. July 1, 1766. R. August 2, 1766. Book 1763-71, p. 84. Account of estate returned by John Armistead, Administrator. January 28, 1768. Book 1763-71, p. 185.

McHOLLAND, William. Leg.- wife Mary; to my three children, John, Mary and Allen McHolland. Exs. wife Mary and Thomas Minson on Scoan Dam. D. January 29, 1789. R. January 28, 1790. Wit. Richard Young, Samuel Dewbre, Mary Sanderfur. Mary Mc Holland qualified, security, George Booker, Gent. Original Will. Account estate signed by Miles King. Audited by Charles Jenings, Joseph Needham and John Perry. October 26, 1796. Book 1787-1800, p. 417.

McKENZIE, William. Administration granted Samuel Curle with John Brodie, security. Appraisers appointed, Thomas Smith, Thomas Watts, Thomas Webster and Curle Tucker. December 13, 1755. Order Book 1755-60, p. 36.

McNAMARA, Florence. Leg.- wife Sarah; daughter Charollette. Regers to money in the hands of Jacob Wray and a bond due him from Henry Robertson and Thomas Gordon. D. January 22, 1771. R. June 27, 1771. Wit. Robert Bright, Ann Hundley, Rachael Jones. Exs. wife and Mr. Francis Jones of Warwick. John Brodie security for the Extx. Book 1763-71-433. Original Will.

NAYLOR, James. Settlement of estate ordered by Leonard Whiting, Charles Jenings, Thomas Latimer and Baldwin Sheppard. February 21, 1732. Order Book 1731-47, p. 48.

NAYLOR, James. Leg.- daughter Ann Cooper; daughter Susanna; daughter Euphan; daughter Mary; daughter Sary; granddaughter Ann Buxton with the reversion of the bequest to her two brothers Josiah and James Buxton; to grandson James Naylor Cooper; to my wife. Exs. wife, George Latimer and Joseph Cooper. D. February 7, 1776. Wit. W. Coltart, George Latimer, William Latimer. Original Will.

NAYLOR, John. Leg.- son Thomas land bought of Col. John Lear, adjoining my father's land; daughter Ann; daughter Sarah land on which William Williams now lives; daughter Elizabeth with reversion of bequest to youngest daughter Mary Naylor; wife Sarah; son James; my sister Westwood cattle at Richard Thursleys; to Godson John Hous; to Thomas and William Sorrell; balance to my wife and five children. Exs. wife Sarah and son Thomas Naylor. Overseer, Major William Wilson. September 27, 1694. R. October 10, 1694. Wit. Christopher Copeland, Thomas House, Thomas Francis, Baldwin Sheppard. Book 1689-1699, p. 195. Appraisal and division of estate by Baldwin Shepperd, Thomas Bayly, Christopher Copeland and Thomas Francis. April 3, 1696. Book 1689-1699, p. 227.

NAYLOR, John. Estate appraised by Thomas Minson, James Manson and Baldwin Shepard. February 17, 1741. Book 1737-49, p. 117. Settlement of the estate. Paid Falvy Copeland the guardian of William Naylor; paid Mr. John Selden for James Naylor's part; paid Ann Naylor her part of her father's estate. John Webb, Administrator. July 20, 1743. Book 1737-49, p. 170.

NAYLOR, Thomas. Leg.- son William when he is sixteen; wife Elizabeth Naylor, daughter Mary Naylor. D. March 30, 1717. R. May 15, 1717. Wit. Charles Jenings, William Westwood, Elizabeth Jenings. Book 1715-21, p. 72. John More having married the widow Elizabeth Naylor, qualified as Executor. Security, Henry Robinson and Brian Penny. July 16, 1718. Book 1715-21, p. 129.

NAYLOR, William. Leg.- grandson Thomas Naylor; daughter Elizabeth Westwood, with reversion to my grandsons Thomas and James Naylor; granddaughter Sarah Naylor; granddaughter Ann House; granddaughter Mary Westwood; wife Mary, with reversion to grandson Thomas Naylor. Exs. wife and grandson Thomas Naylor. Son Thomas House, Sr. to be an aid and trustee to my Executors. D. February 15, 1695. R. March 18, 1696/97. Wit. Christopher Copeland, Edward Latymore, George Cooper. Book 1689-1699, p. 230.

NEAL, Thomas. Estate appraised by William Patten, Charles Avera and William Face. May 25, 1743. R. July 20, 1743. Book 1737-49, p. 172. Estate settled by John Selden and Robert Brough. June 18, 1746. Book 1737-49, p. 219.

NEEDHAM, Sarah. Leg.- son Joseph; daughter Ann; daughter Sarah; son John (not twenty-one); daughter Susanna Lenard. Ex. son Joseph Needham. D. October 2, 1766. R. May 25, 1769. Wit. Afphia Tompkins, Mary Selden, Joseph Selden. George Latimer was security for the Executor. Book 1763-71, p. 294. Original Will. Estate appraised by Thomas Fenn, Thomas B. Armistead and William Latimer. July 27, 1769. Book 1763-71, p. 300.

NEEDHAM, Thomas. Leg.-(torn from book) ----to my wife; son Thomas, if either of my said children should die their part to be equally divided between the survivors. Wife, Extx. March 29, 1690, R. March 18, 1690/91. Wit. Thomas House, Edward Lattimore, George Cooper. Book 1689-1699, p. 75.

NELSON, Hannah. Leg.- brother John Nelson Adams; sister ------- Fields, with reversion of the bequest to cousin Robert Fields; to cousin John Fields. Ex. John Fields. D. October 23, 1781. R. January 24, 1782. Wit. Shelden Moss, Baker Armistead, Mary Heverlin. Security for Executor, Worlich Westwood and Thomas Wootten. Original Will.

NELSON, John. Leg.- Mary Adams; to Rose Adams the daughter of Mary Adams the land bought of Henry Allen; to Hannah the daughter of Mary Adams, with reversion to her brother John Adams; to Jeremiah the son of Mary Adams; to Thomas the son of Mary Adams. If said Mary Adams marries the reversion of bequests made her to her five children. D. July 4, 1769. R. February 28, 1772. Wit. John Brodie, Francis Mallory, James Bray Armistead, Philip Mallory. Original Will.

NICHOLS, (Niccols), Nehemiah. Administration granted Jane Nichols, security, Joseph Nichols and Thomas Nichols. Appraisers appointed, Edward Latimer, William Tompkins, John Pressie and John Buck. January 1, 1760. Order Book 1755-60, p. 268. Book 1758-64, p. 136. Estate settled by William Reade, Edward Armistead and Robert Sandefur. Book 1763-71, p. 107.

NIXON, Thomas. Administration granted to Mary Nixon, security William Allen and Edward Parish. June 21, 1727. Order Book 1723-29, p. 12.

NOBLIN, Henry. Inventory signed by T. Ballard. Book 1715-21, p. 205. June 9, 1719.

OLDIS, ------. Inventory. Indexed. Book 1689-1699.

ORSON, John. By last will and testament appointed John Barnes as his Executor. February 18, 1689/99. Book 1689-1699, p. 85.

PAGE, John. Of Buck Roe. Leg.- brother William Byrd Page of Fairfax County; Dr. Wilson Cary Selden; wife Elizabeth King Page; sister Mary Mason Page; to Edward, Mary and Thomas Swann; to my reputed son John Page Barron of Hampton. May 1, 1800. R. June 1800. Wit. Charles King Mallory, Charles King, John Smith, George Wray. Marriage Indenture between John Page of Elizabeth City and Miles King and Elizabeth King Mallory, the daughter of Colonel Francis Mallory decd. April 15, 1795. Williamsburg Wills.

Parish and Parrish

PARISH, Edward. Estate appraised by Thomas Smith, Phill Allen and Henry Allen. June 28, 1748. Book 1737-49, p. 296.

PARRISH, Mark. Leg.- wife Temperance; son Abraham; grandson Mark Parish; grandson Edward Parish. Ex. son Abraham Parish. D. June 9, 1717. R. March 19, 1717. Wit. Henry Jenkins, John Bayley, John Curle. Book 1715-21, p. 107.

PARRISH, Mark. Leg.- wife Martha; son Signe; daughter Anne Baines; son William; son Mark; son John Parrish. Ex. son Signe Parrish. D. November 11, 1777. Wit. Barth'w Lightfoot, John Smelly, Jr., Joseph Chapman, H. Baylis, John Skinner. Original Will.

PARISH, Mark. Leg.- wife Mary; daughter Polly; daughter Lidea; daughter Nancy Parish; provision for an unborn child. Extx. wife Mary Parish. D. November 26, 1781. Wit. Westwood Armistead, John Field, Henry Baines. Original Will.

PARRISH, William. Leg.- wife Sarah; daughter Elizabeth; son John; son William; son Mark Parrish. D. October 26, 1781. Wit. William Bennett, William Parrish. Original Will.

PARSONS, John. Leg.- son William ap Thomas Parsons, the land recovered in England of William Parsons, decd., lying in the County of Elizabeth City; daughter Jenny; daughter Priscilla; daughter Mary; son Edmund Sweny Parsons; son Roscow Parsons; son Thomas Parsons; son Samuel Parsons; my debt to the estate of Edward Ambler, decd., to be paid; to wife Mary the land bought by William ap Thomas of John Armistead, with reversion at her death to my son James Parsons. Exs. son William ap Thomas Parsons and friend George Booker. D. April 6, 1787. R. February 25, 1790. Wit. William Brown, Henry Tabb, Robert Presson. William ap Thomas Parson qualified, security, Worlich Westwood and Michael King. Book 1787-1800. Account of estate audited by George Booker, William Lowry and John Randle. September 26, 1799. Book 1787-1800, p.

PARSON, William. Leg.- My plantation and negroes to be kept together until grandson Thomas Parsons is twenty-one; granddaughter Nancy Parsons, with reversion to James Parsons of Charles Parish in York County. Exs. Captain John Tabb and Mr. Starkey Robinson. D. May 18, 1761. R. June 2, 1761. Wit. William Smelt, Sr., Walter McClurg, Mary Blade. Starkey Robinson qualified, security, Walter McClurg and Cary Selden. Book 1758-64, p. 254. Original Will. Estate appraised by William Smelt, Sr., Augustine Moore, John Allen. July 7, 1761. Book 1758-64, p. 258. Estate account audited by John Lowry, John Tabb and Augustine Moore. Signed, Mrs. Judith Robinson. Cash paid Mrs. Parsons for sundries. November 24, 1768. Book 1763-71, p. 260.

PARSONS, William. The Younger. Leg.- son Thomas at twenty-one land I bought of Mrs. Thomasine Rogers, reversion to my daughter Nancy; to my wife; friend and relative Starkey Robinson, Jr., Godfather of my son I make guardian of my son Thomas Parsons. Exs. father, Starkey Robinson, Jr. and wife. Wit. Starkey Robinson, John Tabb, Jr., John Brodie, Curle Tucker. D. January 29, 1760. R. May 6, 1760. Security for Exs. John Bayley, William Wager and Curle Tucker. Book 1758-64, p. 151. Original Will. Estate appraised by Augustine Moore, John Tabb, Jr., John Armistead. Estate appraised in Northampton County by William Burton. Edward Robins, John Wilkins. July 7, 1761. Book 1758-64, p. 230. Will of William Parsons, Jr., was proved by John Brodie and Curle Tucker, William Parsons, Starkey Robinson and Sarah Parsons. Exs. qualified, security, John Bayley, William Wager and Curle Tucker. May 6, 1760. Appraisers appointed, John Tabb, William Smelt, John Armistead, Augustine Moore. Appraisers appointed in Northampton County, William Buxton, Edward Robins, Nathaniel Savage and John Wilkins. Order Book 1755-60, p. 283. Part of the estate administered by William Parson, Sr., audited by John Tabb, John Lowry and Augustine Moore. Part of the estate administered by Mrs. Judith Robinson audited by John Tabb, John Lowry and Augustine Moore. November 24, 1768. Estate at the Eastern Shore was audited, with Sarah Parsons, administratrix. Book 1763-71, p. 258.

PASTEUR, Charles. Now in North Carolina. Leg.- son Charles; daughter Mary; daughter Elizabeth; daughter Rachel. Extx. daughter Rachel Pasteur. D. August 8, 1726. R. January 18, 1726. Wit. Hugh Jones, William Lane. James Vaughan and Robert Brough testified that the will was in the handwriting of the testator. Book 1704-30, p. 75. Estate appraised by Thomas Howard and John McDowell. Book 1704-30, p. 97.

PASTEUR, Charles, Sr. Leg.- I have already given my children their proportional part of my estate with the exception of son Blouet and daughter Elizabeth Pasteur. Extx. wife Elizabeth Pasteur. D. February 6, 1772. R. June 25, 1772. Wit. Mary Latimore, W. Wager, Robert Bright. John Pasteur qualified, security Roe Cowper and Worlich Westwood. Original Will.

PEART, Major Griffin. Of the County of Goochland. Leg.- wife Elizabeth the slaves that fell to her at the death of her mother, Grace Brough of Elizabeth City; to my three children, Francis Peart; Sarah Griffin Peart and Leroy Griffin Peart. Exs. wife and friend John Tayloe Griffin of Goochland County. D. January 12, 1784. R. March 25, 1784. Wit. Elizabeth Brough, Robert Brough, John Swann. Original Will.

Peirce and Pierce

PEIRCE, Elizabeth. Leg.- niece Maxey Peirce Leonard at eighteen, with reversion of the bequest to her mother Elizabeth Peirce and at her death to niece Ann Boush Peirce. Exs. brother Thomas Peirce and Edward Blaney. D. May 4, 1786. R. July 27, 1786. Wit. Ann Thomas, Mary Hicks, Robert Brough. Original Will.

PIERCE, Christopher. Estate appraised by John Sheppard, Thomas Fenn, William Dunn. October 6, 1762. Book 1758-64, p. 431.

PIERCE, Michael. Administration granted to William Copeland, with consent of the widow. Appraised by Charles Jenings, Edward Lattimer, Leonard Whiting and James Naylor. Order Book 1723-29, p. 129. September 15, 1725. Book 1704-30, p. 35.

PEIRCE, Peter. Will Indexed. Book 1689-1699.

PENDER, Barbara. Appraisal of her estate ordered recorded June 16, 1736. Order Book 1731-47, p. 117.

PENDER, Rev. Thomas. Estate appraised by John Henry, Samuel Hawkins, John McDonicke and William Tucker. Barbara Pender granted administration. April 16, 1735. Order Book 1731-47, p. 92. Account of estate audited by James Wallace and William Westwood. Account made out by John Brodie. March 21, 1743. Book 1737-49, p. 181.

PENNY, Edward. Leg.- daughter Susannah; wife Elizabeth and children; provision for unborn child; to Mary Husk. Extx. wife Elizabeth Penny. D. March 31, 1714. R. September 15, 1715. Wit. Robert Armistead, Thomas Read, William Williams. Book 1715-21, p. 12.

PENNE, Penuel. Leg.- wife Phillis; son Penuel; daughter Ann; daughter Mary Penne. Exs. wife and Morris Jones. D. January 4, 1755. R. Wit. Anth'o Tucker, Joseph Meredith, John Jones. Original Will. (Two copies in one place Ann is written Ann Powers and the following paragraph she is called Ann Penne.) Estate audited by Charles Jenings, Anthony Tucker and John Moore. July 6, 1756. Order Book 1755-60, p. 62.

PERRIN, Sebastian. Leg.- wife Easter; cousin William Wass and I wish Captain William Wilson to bring him up. Extx. wife Easter Perrin, Trustee, Capt. William Wilson. D. March 5, 1691/92. Xber 19, 1692. Wit. Henry Turner, John Heyward.

Book 1689-1699, p. 78. Thomas Taylor married the Extx. of Sebastian Perrin. p. 79. Bond for Easter Perrin as Extx. security, Pascho Curle. August 17, 1696. Book 1689-1699, p. 224.

PETTER, Katherine. Leg.- to Katherine Shaw; to granddaughter Mary ------; to John Tanner; to Anthony King. Ex. friend Anthony King. D. February 20, 1688. R. July 8, 1690. Wit. Mark Parrish, Bennett Parrish. Book 1689-1699, p. 113.

Petts or Pitts
PETTS, John. Estate appraised by Joseph Wragg, John Smith, Sr., and John Bordland. May 18, 1721. Book 1704-30, p. 321. Bond for Thomas Skinner as Administrator, security, Bryan Penne and Hugh Ross. February 21, 1722/23. Book 1721-23, p. Appraisal of the remaining part of estate. Mr. Smelt appeared and informed the Court that the persons formerly ordered to appraise the estate refused. May 18, 1721. Book 1715-21, p. 307. Appraisers appointed July 25, 1718, were Robert Armistead, Thomas Allen, Thomas Read and Francis Rogers. William Smelt qualified as Adm. Book 1715-21, p. 9 & 136.

PHILLIPS, Margrat. Leg.- to Robert Kiplin Brown, with reversion of bequest to Sephey Bell. D. P. April 6, 1762. R. February 1, 1763. Wit. Andrew Bushell, Thomas Bulley. Book 1758-64, p. 465.

PICKET, Abraham. Estate appraised by Francis Mallory, Merrit More, William Parsons and William Mallory. Administration granted to Miles Cary. August 19, 1736. Order Book 1731-47, p. 125.

PICKET, Mary. Leg.- grandson John Picket; son Samuel Picket; to all my loving grandchildren. Ex. grandson John Picket. D. April 4, 1735. R. May 21, 1741. Wit. John Tabb, Nicholas Bourden. Book 1737-49, p. 103.

POLLARD, John. Administration granted to William Mallory his greatest creditor. September 18, 1695. Book 1689-1699, p. 156 & 223.

POOLE, ------. Probation of will. Indexed Book 1689-1699.

POOLE, Alexander. Leg.- son Samuel, the plantation given me by my father's will; wife Mary Poole. Extx. wife Mary Poole. D. June 13, 1742. R. March 21, 1743. Wit. Thomas Poole, John Poole, William Poole. Samuel Poole chose the Clerk of the Court as his guardian. Mary Poole qualified, security, Thomas Everard. Book 1737-49, p. 184. Estate appraised by Thomas Latimer, John Bushell and William Poole. July 18, 1744. Book 1737-49, p. 186.

POOLE, Ann. Estate appraised by Thomas Latimer, Thomas Baylis and Thomas Wootten. February 2, 1747. Book 1737-49, p. 268. Settlement of estate by Thomas Latimer, Baldwin Shephard and John Bushell. Signed William Poole, Adm. Among items, paid John Poole. Book 1737-49, p. 281.

POOLE, Francis. Account of estate, George Booker, Administrator. September 28, 1797. Book 1787-1800, p. 360.

POOLE, John. Will recorded March 16, 1667, recited in a suit. Order Book 1715-21, p. 67.

POOLE, John. Leg.- oldest son Thomas, next son John, land known as "Pooles Ridge"; oldest daughter Anne Robburtson; daughter Joan Lewis; daughter Mary; daughter Elizabeth; daughter Sarah; son Humphrey; son Christopher; son William; wife Ann. (three last named sons not twenty-one). Exs. wife Ann Poole and son Thomas Poole. D. January 22, 1730/40. R. May 21, 1740. Wit. John Baylis, And. Bully, Thomas Latimer. Book 1737-49, p. 91. Inventory, p. 104.

POOLE, Middleton. Leg.- son William my place called "The Points," adjoining the land of Thomas Poole; after the death of my wife, reversion to daughter Ann Poole; with reversion to my cousin Alexander, son of Alexander Poole. Extx. wife Elizabeth Poole. D. July 16, 1740. R. May 19, 1742. Wit. Thomas Poole, Catron Dunn, John Britain. Book 1737-49, p. 128. Estate appraised by Thomas Lattimer, Thomas Baylis, Jr., and John Bushell. July 21, 1742. Book 1737-49, p. 139. Original Will.

POOLE, Samuel. Leg.- Mother Mary Poole; brother James the money in the hands of Jacob Walker, with reversion to brothers, Alexander, Nicholas and David Poole. Ex. Mr. John Selden. D. January 5, 1748. R. October 1752. Wit. Jacob Walker, W. Bushell, Alex'er Robertson. Original Will.

POOLE, Thomas. Leg.- eldest son John; son William; son Thomas; son Alexander; son Middleton the tract given by my Mother, Jane Avera to her son John Poole; to my daughters, Jane, Ann and Mary Poole. Exs. sons John and Thomas Poole. D. January 27, 1725/26. R. July 20, 1727. Wit. Thomas Latimer, John Whitfield, John Bushell, Sr. Book 1704-30, p. 77.

POOLE, Thomas. Leg.- to my three youngest sons, Howard, Thomas and Robert; son John; to my three daughters, Sarah, Marthew and Elizabeth Poole. Extx. wife. (Will presented by Eliza-beth Poole.) D. September 8, 1750. R. April 2, 1751. Wit. William Bushell, John Lewis. Original Will. Estate audited by Thomas Lattimer, Samuel Watts, Baldwin Shephard and Thomas Baylis, Sr. December 2, 1755. Order Book 1755-60, p. 31.

POULSON, Captain Edward. Administration granted Captain Willis Wilson in behalf of John Poulson his son. February 18, 1695/96. Book 1689-1699, p. 156. Estate appraised by Bertrand Servant and Mathew Watts. Adms. Coleman Brough and Robert Taylor. Order Book 1689-1699, p. 81.

POWELL, -------. Probation of will. Indexed. Book 1689-1699.

POWELL, John. Estate appraised by Simon Hollier, John Lowry and William Marshall. March 18, 1740. Book 1737-49, p. 100. Account of estate. To balance due from the estate of Robert Phillipson, administrator of the estate of Thomas Powell. Settled and audited by John Tabb, Thomas Wythe and Robert Armistead. December 3, 1747. Book 1737-49, p. 270.

POWELL, Mark. Estate appraised by Richard Hawkins, John Moore, Anthony Tucker and Isaac Rumbow. Administrator, William Creek. June 19, 1734 Order Book 1731-47, p. 78. Account of estate, to nursing his child, to nursing the youngest child, balance due the two older children. July 18, 1739. Audited by Wil. Westwood, John Brodie, Rt. Armistead. Book 1737-49, p. 69.

POWELL, Mark. Leg.- wife Martha with reversion of bequest to son William Powell; reversion to my sister's children; to sister Rebecca Weymouth's sons, William and James Weymouth. Exs. wife Martha and William Weymouth. D. December 17, 1761. R. May 4, 1762. Wit. Samuel Roland, John Casey, Thomas Skinner. Security for Martha Powell, William Read and Thomas Skinner. Book 1758-64, p. 320. Estate appraised by Samuel Roland, Anthony Hawkins and Henry Humflet. May 4, 1762. Book 1758-64, p. 355.

POWELL, Mary. Leg.- to my uncle and aunt, Francis and Elizabeth Riddlehurst; cousin Catherine Armistead; cousin May Carleton, Jr.; cousin Priscilla Mitchell. Exs. uncle Francis Riddlehurst and friend John Perry. D. June 20, 1792. R. July 26, 1792. Wit. Anne Jones, John Perry. Original Will. Book 1787-1800, p. 126.

POWELL, Thomas. Leg.- daughter Hannah; brother Mark Powell. Ex. brother Mathew Powell. D. R. January 22, 1718. Wit. John Howard, Mich'l Roberts, Mark Powell. Book 1715-21, p. 157. Mark Powell qualified, security, William Spicer and Hind Armistead. Estate appraised by Hind Armistead, William Spiers and Mathew Small. May 21, 1719, Book 1715-21, p. 172 & 205.

POWERS, John. Estate appraised by Pascho Dunn, William Mallory, Captain Anthony Armistead and Mr. Edmund Swany. Estate of Elizabeth Hinds to be first taken out. Captain William Armistead is appointed guardian to Elizabeth Hinds, the orphan of Thomas Hinds. November 20, 1693. Order Book 1689-1699, p. 21. Appraisal signed by Hannah Powers. Book 1689-1699, p. 136 & 152. Estate divided by Mr. Edward Myhill and Mr. William Mallory in behalf of the widow, Mr. Pascho Dunn and Mr. Robert Crooke in behalf of the orphan. Robert Groomes of Warwick County appointed guardian of Edward and Mary Powers the orphans of John Powers. Darby Daniel, his security. August 20, 1694. Order Book 1689-1699, p. 27, 29 and 186.

PREEDY, -------. Will Indexed. Book 1689-1699.

PREEDY, Robert. Will dated March 1, 1667. Stated in deed. Book 1715-21, p. 299.

PREDY, John. Estate appraised by William Tucker, John Nelson and John Henry Rombough. November 19, 1741. Book 1737-49, p. 110.

PREDY, William. Estate appraised by John Henry Rombough, William Waff and George Waff. November 14, 1743. Book 1737-49, p. 176.

PRIEST, James. Will dated December 9, 1713. Margaret Priest was his widow and his daughter Dorothy married John Wilson. Order Book 1723-29, p. 117.

PRIEST, Margaret. Leg.- son James Priest; son Thomas; daughter Anfilody; daughter Martha; son Hugh Ross, furniture bought of Selva Langman; son William Ross; granddaughter Ann Ross; son Francis Ross. Ex. Hugh Ross. D. March 19, 1718/19. R. May 20, 1719. Wit. Edmond Hollier, Thomas Parris, Ann Picketts. Book 1715-21, p. 181. Security for Ex. Francis Ross and Francis Mallory. Wit. Charles Jenings. June 5, 1719. Estate appraised by Simon Hollier, Edward Tabb, Anthony Armistead, Jr. August 17, 1719. Book 1715-21, p. 189 & 209.

PRIEST, Thomas. Leg.- my plantation at Newport News to my wife, reversion to son James; son Thomas; son James plantation adjoining Booth Armistead; daughter Martha Priest. (children not of age). Exs. Mr. Thomas Watts, Sr., Mr. Thomas Smith and Mr. Francis Jones. D. February 23, 1752. R. March 3, 1752. Wit. Rt. Armistead, Anthony Armistead, John Ross. Thomas Watts and Thomas Smith qualified, security, Francis Jones, Mathew Watts and Charles King. Original Will. Account of estate audited by Robert Armistead, Charles Jenings, John Allen and John Manson. August 3, 1756. Book 1755-60, p. 68.

PRESCOTT, Elizabeth. Estate appraised by James Ricketts and Joseph Banister. July 15, 1719. Book 1715-21, p. 213.

PRETTYMAN, Thomas. Account of estate audited by William Lowry and Philip Johnson. Signed, Robert Miller. D. July 15, 1689. R. 9ber 18, 1690. Book 1689-1699, p. 120.

PRICE, Thomas. Administration of estate granted to Henry Royall. D. July 18, 1691. R. October 20, 1691. Book 1689-1699, p. 89. Estate appraised and divided by Richard Joanes, George Eland, Thomas Morgan and Robert Tucker. Each of the following received an equal share, Mary, Rebecca, Ann, Thomas, Edward, Margaret, Elizabeth and Ruth Price. March 10, 1690/91. Book 1689-1699, p. 146.

PRICKET, Miles. Of the Parish of Holy Cross, near and without the walls of the city of Canterbury, Baker. November 30, 1626. Proved June 30, 1627. Money due me in consideration of my adventuring into Virginia, under the worshipful Captain Pryn his charge; unto brother John Prickett and by him to be divided between my brethren; to brother William's two children, now in the hands of my brother Thomas; brother John money in the hands of sister Jane Prickett; to Edward Hollett; to brother John 200 acres lying in Elizabeth City in Virginia near Salford's Creek. Ex. brother John Pricket. Wit. William Brooke, John Slade, Thomas Boudler, Edward Turfitt. Waters Gleanings, p. 206.

PRIGS, -----. Inventory. Indexed. Book 1689-1699.

PRINCE, Edward. Bond of Joyce Simons as guardian to Susanna Prince, orphan of Edward Prince, security, Mathew Small. February 19, 1719. Wit. C. Jenings, George Lewis. Book 1715-21, p. 245.

PROBY, Bertrand. Leg.- wife Sidwell; son Servant John Proby, with reversion to son Minson Turner Proby; son Bertrand; son Thomas; son Peter; daughter Mary Gilbert; daughter Rebecca; daughter Elizabeth; daughter Jane; to my wife and my six small children. Exs. wife Sidwell and son Servant John Proby. D. November 4, 1736. R. May 18, 1737. Wit. James Gilbert, Servant Ballard. Book 1737-49, p. 12. Original Will. Estate appraised by William Copeland, John Roe and Robert Brough. February 15, 1737. Book 1737-49, p. 33.

PROBY, John. Of Newport in the Colony of Rhode Island. By his last will and testament he left Henry Pequet his Executor who refused to serve; Philip Johnson qualified in right of Winifred, his wife, sister of the deceased and his greatest legatee. January 18, 1699/1700. Order Book 1689-1699, p. 165.

PROBY, Minson Turner. Estate appraised by Charles Pasteur, Francis Ballard and John Langley. Robert Armistead, Administrator. January 5, 1761. Book 1758-64, p. 287.

Estate account examined by R. Brough, John Riddlehurst, H. King. April 5, 1763. Book 1758-64, p. 428.

PROBY, Peter. Administration granted to Jane his relict. Appraisers for the widow, Philip Johnson and Peter Johnson; appraisers for orphans, Robert Taylor and Walter Bayley. D. December 18, 1693. Book 1689-1699, Orders, p. 24. Security for Jane Proby was Bertrand Servant. Inventory Book 1689-1699, p. 139 & 148. Estate appraised by Philip Johnson, Robert Taylor, Walter Bayley and John Trimble, Sr. November 18, 1695. Order Book 1689-1699, p. 75.

PROBY, Peter. Administration of estate granted to his brother Bartrand Proby. June 15, 1715. Book 1715-21, p. 9.

PROBY, Thomas. Administration granted to his brother Bartrand Proby. February 20, 1716. Book 1715-21, p. 9.

PURVIS, Robert. Nuncupative will proven by Robert Hamilton and Anne Hamilton. Administration granted to Leonard Whiting. May 15, 1734. Order Book 1731-47, p. 76.

RANDLE, Mary. Leg.- brother John Randle; niece Elizabeth Randle; niece Ann Randle; remainder of my estate between my brothers and sisters and their children. Ex. brother John Randle. D. October 22, 1794. R. February 26, 1795. Wit. Henry Tabb. Book 1787-1800, p. 220. Original Will.

RANDOLPH, Lucy. Widow. Leg.- daughter Ann Carter; granddaughter Lucy Cook; daughter Elizabeth West; daughter Sarah Masters; grandson Thomas Cook. Ex. son-in-law Samuel Skinner. D. Xber 11, 1728. R. February 20, 1728. Wit. John Miller, Charles Jenings, Charles Jenings, Jr. Estate appraised by Leonard Whiting, James Naylor and John Batts. May 21, 1729 Book 1704-30, p. 181.

READE, John. Leg.- wife Anne; son Robert Sandefur Reade land bought of Clausel Clausell; son John land bought of Thomas Skinner; reversion of bequest to sons to my brothers William and Hawkins Reade; to the three children of my sister Mary Hurst; viz.- Elizabeth, Mary and Richard Hawkins Hurst. Exs. wife Anne and brothers William and Hawkins Hurst. D. December 30, 1773. R. Wit. John Brodie, Edward Hurst, George Jarvis and Peter Sandefur. Original Will. Account of estate presented by Hawkins Reade. Among items, paid William Read; paid John Dunn for schooling Robert Sandefur Russell; paid Richard Cary's tickets against Ann Russell. Audited by George Wray, Robert Armistead and Charles Jenings. D. January 12, 1774. R. June 26, 1795. Book 1787-1800, p. 227.

READE, Thomas. Planter. Leg.- son John; son Thomas; son William; beloved wife; daughter Hannah. Sons Thomas and William to be placed under care of their uncle William Allen. Exs. wife and son John Reade. D. October 18, 1721. R. December 20, 1721. Wit. Thomas Curle, Judith Predy, John Mason. Will presented by Ann Reade, security, William Allen and John Cook. Book 1721-23, p. 25, 31 & 42. Account of estate, among items paid Anne Reade for keeping William Reade seven months. September 16, 1724. Book 1704-30, p. 19.

RICKETTS, (Rickets), Henry. Estate appraised by Edward Ruddils, Peter Hobson, Robert Taylor and John Smyth. D. September 22, 1690. R. November 14, 1690. Book 1689-1699, p. 106.

RICKETTS, James. Estate appraised by John King, Charles Jenings and Edward Latimer. March 24, 1724/25. Book 1704-30, p. 36. Additional appraisal by Simon Holier, John Lowry, William Loyall and H. Irwin. January 18, 1726. Account of estate. July 19, 1727. Book 1704-30, p. 89. Estate account presented by Major Merritt Sweny. Audited by Joseph Banister, Jacob Walker and William Westwood. (See account also of the estate of Nicholas Curle for further information.). Book 1737-49, p. 207.

RIDDLEHURST, Francis. Leg.- wife Ann; son Francis; son John; son Richard; grandson Francis Bright; grandson William Powel; daughter Martha; daughter Ann; granddaughter Mary Tarrant. Exs. wife Ann and sons Francis and John Riddlehurst. D. October 16, 1756. R. Wit. Thomas Tabb, Carter Tarrant, John Bright. Original Will. Security for Executors, Carter Tarrant and Thomas Tabb. Estate appraised by Joseph Selden, James Wallace, James Naylor and William Latimore. December 7, 1756. Order Book 1755-60, p. 84.

RIDDLEHURST, Francis. Leg.- Francis Riddlehurst Bright, son of Robert and Mary Bright at twenty-one; with reversion of bequest to his brother John Bright; reversion to Frances Tarrants then eldest son; to Ann Toomer, daughter of Thomas Butts and wife Ann, as long as she remains a widow; to Susanna Selden, wife of Samuel Selden; to Hannah Drew, the widow of William Drew; rest of my estate to be equally divided between Samuel Selden, Priscilla Johnson and Mary Carleton. Exs. George Hope, Sr. and Pascow Herbert. D. May 7, 1796. R. July 28, 1796. Wit. Wilson C. Wallace, I. Hardeman, James Cunningham. Codicil in which a provision is made to fulfill a contract with William Armistead, Sr. Samuel Selden qualified as Executor. Book 1787-1800, p. 311. Original Will.

RIDDLEHURST, (Ridlehurst) John. Nuncupative will in which he leaves whole estate to brother Francis Riddlehurst. November 1761. Proved by William Ballard. Original Will.

RIDGE, Benjamin. Administration of estate granted to John Ridge and Robert Johnson. February 28, 1700/1701. Book 1689-1699, p. 217.

RIVERS, John. Will Indexed. Book 1689-1699, p. 99. Estate now in the hands of William Mallory, appraised by George Waffe, John Smith and Thomas Batts. September 2, 1694. Book 1689-1699, p. 185. Appraisal of estate in the hands of Henry Royall by George Waffe, John Cooper, John Smith and Thomas Batts. D. July 18, 1694. R. August 1, 1694. Book 1689-1699, p. 187. Samuel Rallyson, sued as marrying Hannah the relict of John Rivers. September 18, 1692. Ann and William Rivers orphans of John Rivers. Ordered that John, William and Hannah Rivers be apprenticed. Order Book 1689-1699, p. 17 & 42.

ROBERTS, Mrs. Mary. Estate appraised by Starkey Robinson, Augustine Moore and John Parsons. D. February 1760. R. November 4, 1760. Book 1758-64, p. 182. Administration granted to John Allen, security, Johnson Mallory and Henry Allen. Estate appraised by Augustine Moore, Starkey Robinson, John Parsons and John Tabb, Jr. February 5, 1760. Order Book 1755-60, p. 273. Estate audited by John Tabb, William Smelt, Augustine Moore and John Parsons. October 6, 1762. Book 1758-64, p. 364.

ROBERTS, Michael. Nuncupative will proven by Francis Williams, Elizabeth Creek and Elizabeth Hazelgrove at the house of Mary Bridge, the daughter of said Roberts. Depositions prove that he left his negro to daughter Mary Bridge during her life with reversion to his grandson John Roberts. November 26, 1718. Book 1715-21, p. 155. Security for Mary Bridge, Thomas Jones, Cordwinder. May 5, 1719. Book 1715-21, p. 202.

ROBERTSON, Deborah. Estate appraised by William Tucker, John Henry Rombough and Charles Pasteur. February 7, 1748. Book 1737-49, p. 309.

ROBERTSON, John. Leg.- daughter-in-law Jane Robertson; kinsman James, the son of my brother James Robertson, decd., with reversion to his sister Jane Robertson; my sister Rebeckah Relph (Rolph?) land adjoining Major Sweney; my son Henry at twenty-one, with reversion to my kinsman William Roberson, William Milbey and Samuel Robertson Harris, if he be living, the son of Elinor Harris, decd. Exs. Mr. William Westwood, Mr. John Selden and Robert Brough. D. December 19, 1747. R. January 5, 1747. Wit. Minson Proby, John Harris and Elizabeth Antony. Book 1737-49, p. 264

ROBERTSON, William. Estate appraised by John Henry Rombough, William Henry and John McDowell. May 17, 1737. Book 1737-49, p. 48.

ROBERTSON, William. Leg.- sister Rebecca; sister Mary. Exs. sisters Rebecca and Mary Robertson and William Wager. D. February 18, 1752. R. April 7, 1752. Wit. William Wager, Priscilla Michell and Ann Pennill (?). Original Will.

ROBINS, John. Will dated November 22, 1655. In said will he devised land to son Thomas and his heirs forever. The said Thomas Robins had a son John, who died seized thereof of the said land and the said Thomas had also the following issue, Thomas, Benjamin and William Robins; and that Thomas the younger died without issue and that Benjamin Robins is heir-at-law to the said Thomas Robins. Ejectments, 1736-70, p. 30.

ROBINSON, Anne. Widow. Leg.- son John Parsons; grandson John, son of John Parsons; granddaughter Mary, daughter of John Parsons; son William Parsons; daughter Elizabeth Thrift; daughter Ann Moore; grandson John, son of Samuel Hawkins; grandson Samuel, son of Samuel Hawkins; granddaughter Anne, daughter of Samuel Hawkins; grandson William, son of William Parsons; granddaughter Ann Moore. Exs. sons John and William Parsons. D. July 23, 1736. R. November 19, 1741. Wit. Henry Wilson, John Moore, William Smelt. Book 1737-49, p. 108.

ROBINSON, Henry. Leg.- wife Jane; daughter Mary; cousin Henry Robinson with reversion of bequest to wife and daughter and my brother's children. Extx. wife Jane Robinson. Overseer, brother-in-law Charles Jenings. D. December 14, 1719. R. August 15, 1722. Wit. Charles Jenings, Judith Bayley, Henry Dunn. Book 1721-23, p. 67. Inventory, p. 70. Security for Extx., Charles Jenings and Will Westwood. Book 1721-23, p. 96.

ROBINSON, (Robertson, will written under this name, but signed Henry Robinson) Henry. Leg.- son John at twenty-one; reversion to uncle William Poole, Sr., the land adjoining Mr. Bright and to aunt Jane Lewis the wife of John Lewis, with reversion to aunt Lewis' children; provision for unborn child; to loving wife. Ex. Cary Selden, who is also appointed guardian to my son John Robinson. D. December 30, 1758. R. February 6, 1759. Wit. Robert Brough, William Baker, Cary Selden. Book 1758-64, p. 31. Original Will. Cary Selden qualified, security, Robert Brough. Appraisers of estate, Carter Tarrant, Charles Cooper, Henry Batts and Charles Pasteur. February 6, 1759. Order Book 1755-60, p. 209.

ROBINSON, James. Estate appraised by John Meredith, John H.J. Rombough, Alexander Kenedy and Samuel Galt. January 17, 1737. Book 1737-49, p. 22.

ROBINSON, John. Leg.- wife Jean; son John; son Thomas; son Henry Robinson. (none of age). Exs. wife Jean Robinson and Charles Jennings. D. February 24, 1789. R. June 25, 1789. Wit. Charles Jennings, William Jennings, W. Durbin (?). Jean Robinson qualified, security, Thomas Jennings and Charles Jennings. Original Will. Estate appraised by Samuel Selden, Richard Williams and Arthur Henderson. October 2, 1794. Book 1797-1800, p. 304.

ROBINSON, Judith. Leg.- nephew John Cary; niece Mary King; to Judith, daughter of my nephew William Armistead; sister Cary's children, viz - Rebecca Selden, Elizabeth Watkins and Robert Cary; to Ann, daughter of my nephew James Armistead; brother Edward Armistead, with reversion for his four children, William, Anne, Samuel and Rebecca Armistead; niece Hannah King. Exs. brother Edward Armistead and nephews, John and Robert Cary. D. March 16, 1768. R. January 27, 1769. Wit. Augustine Moore, Clausel Clausell, William Maney. Will presented by John and Robert Cary, security, Richard Cary. Robert Armistead heir-at-law declared he would not contest the validity of the will. Book 1763-71, p. 276. Division of her negroes to Edward Armistead, Miles Selden, Benjamin Watkins, Robert Cary and Ann Armistead, daughter of James Armistead. August 23, 1770. Divided by John Tabb, Augustine Moore and William Reade. Division of slaves among claiments-to the following orphans, Rebecca, William, Ann and Samuel Armistead, made by John Tabb, Augustine Moore and John Parsons. May 23, 1771. Book 1763-71, p. 378 & 433.

ROBINSON, Mary. Estate appraised at the house of Mr. Joseph Banister by Thomas Wythe, James Wallace and Charles Cooper. D. February 11, 1726/27. R. June 21, 1727. Book 1704-30, p. 90. Account of the estate returned by Joseph Banister, who married Jane Robinson, the Admtx. of Mary Robinson. Xber 19, 1728. Book 1704-30, p. 162.

ROBINSON, Starkey. Leg.- Mother Judith Robinson. Exs. Judith Robinson and Richard Cary. D. November 13, 1761. R. March 5, 1762. Wit. Walter McClurg, William Armistead, Jr., John Cary. Security for Judith Robinson, James Westwood and John Parsons. Book 1758-64, p. 322. Original Will. Estate appraised by John Allen, William Latimer and John Bayley. April 5, 1763. Book 1758-64, p. 425.

ROBLY, (Rably ?) Jane. William Mallyward acknowledged a judgement to her Executor, Joseph Toppin. May 20, 1689. Book 1689-1699, p. 78.

ROE, Ann. Leg.- daughter Grisel; daughter Mary Ballard; daughter Ann Moore; daughter Sarah Cooper; daughter Elizabeth Merriday; daughter Cathrin Boutwell; daughter Margaret Merriday; daughter Ellenner Mitchel; daughter Luce Loyal. Exs. Mr. John Moore and Abraham Cooper. October 31, 1747. R. June 8, 1748. Wit. Robert Brough, John Bennett. Abraham Cooper qualified, security, Samuel Jones and Adam Boutwell. Book 1737-49, p. 292.

ROE, Daniel. Estate appraised by Miles Cary, John Moore and Joseph Jegitts. January 15, 1745/46. Book 1737-49, p. 213.

ROE, Edward. Leg.- wife Bathia; mother Ann Roe; eldest daughter Anne Roe; daughter Elizabeth Roe; provision for an unborn child. Extx. wife Bathia Roe. D. February 3, 1736/37. R. December 21, 1737. Wit. John Bennett, James Allen. William Allen, who married Bathia, the widow of Edward Roe qualified as Executor. Book 1737-49, p. 21. Estate appraised by Robert Brough, Angus McKay and William Ballard. July 20, 1738. Book 1737-49, p. 55.

ROE, Edward. Estate appraised by James Servant, Leonard Whiting and Robert Brough. Administration granted Ann Roe. Order Book 1731-47, p. 59 & 61. July 18, 1733. Estate appraised by Jacob Walker, James Servant and Rt. Brough. D. September 17, 1733. Among items, paid by Edward Roe, Jr. account of estate audited by John Selden, Cary Selden and Robert Brough. July 5, 1748. Book 1737-49, p. 295.

ROE, Jane. Leg.- Mother Ann Roe a negro given me in the will of Penuel (Pennywell) Crook; to my sisters, my part of my father's estate after the death of my Mother. Extx. Mother Ann Roe. D. March 1, 1741. R. May 19, 1742. Wit. D. Mossom, Mary Roe, Ann Mellens (?). Book 1737-49, p. 128. Original Will.

ROE, John. Leg.- grandson William Roe Cunningham, the land adjoining the land of Colonel Charles Morrison with reversion to Susaner Cunningham; to daughter Margaret Mossom the land given William Roe Cunningham until he is twenty-one; daughter Elizabeth Pasteur with reversion of bequest to Margaret Mossom. D. December 18, 1761. R. July 6, 1762. Wit. Philip Cowper, George Watkins, William Ballard. Book 1758-64, p. 348. Original Will.

ROGERS, Elizabeth. Leg.- son Francis; daughter Anne; daughter Bethiah; rest of my estate to John Cook to see that my children are brought up. Ex. John Cook. D. April 7, 1721. R. September 21, 1721. Wit. John Roe, Eleanor (Rooe) Roe. Security for John Cook, James Ricketts and John Roe. Book 1721-23, p. 8 & 29. Appraisal of the estate of Widow Rogers (Elizabeth), by William Allen, Hugh Rose (Ross ?) and Abraham Parrish. January 17, 1721. Book 1721-23, p. 37.

ROGERS, Francis. Leg.- son Francis the plantation bought of Thomas Reade and his wife, with reversion of bequest to daughters Ann and Bathia; to my loving wife's daughter Martha. Extx. wife Elizabeth Rogers. D. February 13, 1717. R. May 17, 1719. Wit. Robert Armistead, Brien Penne, Henry Cumblin. Security for Elizabeth Rogers, Penuell Crook and John Cook. Wit. Charles Jenings, Will Westwood. Book 1715-21, p. 195 & 201. Estate appraised by Thomas Read, Charles Tucker, John Roe. August 15, 1719. Book 1715-21, p. 204 & 255.

ROGERS, George. Petition of Agnes Rogers for her proportional part of her father's estate. Ordered that William Lowry, John Tabb, Thomas Tabb and ------ Hollier settle the said estate. July 18, 1733. Order Book 1731-47, p. 60.

ROGERS, Thomasine. Widow. Leg.- son Thomas; to my three grandchildren, Elizabeth, Mary and Ann Smith. Exs. son Thomas Rogers and Tucker Smith. D. December 25, 1753. R. November 4, 1760. Wit. W. Parsons, William Parsons, Jr., Martha Smith. Book 1758-64, p. 180. Original Will. Estate appraised by Robert Weymouth, Mallory Ross and Robert Bumpass. March 2, 1762. Book 1758-64, p. 316.

ROMBOUGH, John Henry. Leg.- son John Henry Rombough; daughter Barbary Warff; daughter Sarah Massenburg; daughter Frances Rombough. Ex. Humphrey Massenburgh. D. April 5, 1754. R. Wit. R. Brough, Edmund Kelly. Original Will.

ROSCOW, Wilson. Died February 2, 1713 without issue. Order Book 1704-30, p. 18. Ejectments, 1736-70, p. 19.

ROSS, Elizabeth. Leg.- son-in-law Anthony Hawkins the title to a legacy left me by my uncle John Mallory living in England; daughter Ann Beam; grandson Mallory Ross; grandson William Bean. Ex. son-in-law Anthony Hawkins. D. September 20, 1756. R. October 5, 1756. Wit. Curle Tucker, Thomas Dixon, Owin Dayley. Security for Executor, Thomas Tabb. Original Will. Order Book 1755-60, p. 81 & 85.

ROSS, Francis. Administration granted Elizabeth Ross, security, Francis Mallory. Appraisers appointed, Thomas Tabb, A'm. Parsons, Locky Myhill and William Marshall. June 16, 1731. Order Book 1731-47, p. 1.

ROSS, Hugh. Estate appraised by Mark Parish, Joseph Jegitts and Robert Tucker. September 17, 1742. Book 1737-49, p. 175. Settlement of estate by Robert Armistead, Charles Jenings, John Casey. August 7, 1759. Book 1758-64, p. 79. Paid John Ross his one-fifth part. Ordered that Robert Armistead, Charles Jenings, Joseph Jegetts and John Casey to settle the estate. August 1, 1758. Order Book 1755-60, p. 192.

ROSS, James. Leg.- cousin Mallory Ross, Jr., my plantation on Saltford Creek, adjoining John Weymouth and a lot in Hampton adjoining Charles Miniss. Exs. John Seymour and cousin Mallory Ross. D. (torn). R. September 28, 1780. Wit. Mary Seymour, Alexander Brodie, Mallory Ross, Jr. Mallory Ross, Jr. qualified, security, William Hauton and Johnson Mallory Ross. Original Will.

ROSS, John. Leg.- wife Sarah; son James with reversion to my brother James Ross. Wife, Extx. D. May 25, 1758. R. May 1, 1759. Wit. William Weymouth, Ruth Leyton (another place Keyton), Charles Jenings. Joseph Jegitts, guardian to James Ross, orphan. Book 1758-64, p. 49. Administration granted John Brodie, security, John Herbert and Thomas Dixon. Appraisers appointed, Anthony Hawkins, Curle Tucker, John Casey and King Humphlet. April 3, 1759. Order Book 1755-60, p. 218. Book 1758-64, p. 65.

ROSS, Johnson. Leg.- sister Dyannah; brother Chealy; sister Ufan; sister Elizabeth; brother Frank; brother Thomas; brother Mallory Ross. Ex. brother Mallory Ross. D. October 22, 1794. R. February 26, 1795. Wit. Richard Smith, Samuel Rowland, William Rowland. Book 1787-1800, p. 222. Original Will.

ROSS, Martha. Leg.- daughter Dianah; daughter Elizabeth; daughter Euphan; son Cheely; son Johnson Mallory Ross. Exs. George Booker and Johnson Tabb. D. September 12, 1787. R. July 24, 1794. Wit. Johnson Tabb, William ap Thomas Parsons.

ROSSIER, Samuel. Account of estate signed by George Eland. 1690. Book 1689-1699, p. 118.

ROUTON, Richard. Estate appraised by George Minson, John Dunn and Thomas Minson. Estate signed by Dorothy Routon. September 7, 1742. Book 1737-49, p. 142.

ROWE, Daniel. Balance of estate in the hands of Mr. James Smith. Audited by John Moore, Miles Cary and Francis Jones. June 6, 1747. Book 1737-49, p. 291.

RUDDLE, Edward. Administration granted to Samuel Rallyson in right of Hannah his wife, the Admtx. of Edward Ruddle. February 19, 1693/94. Order Book 1689-1699, p. 26.

RUDDLE, Mary. Leg.- daughter Hannah Rallison. D. January 14, 1693/94. R. February 19, 1693/94. Wit. Mary Price, William Price, John Minson. Book 1689-1699, p. 152.

RUFFE, William. Estate appraised by Augustine Moore and Samuel Peirce. March 7, 1688. Book 1689-1699, p. 77. John Power granted Administration, being his greatest creditor. April 20, 1689. Book 1689-1699, p. 84.

RUSSELL, Agness. Leg.- Goddaughter Sarah Brough; Goddaughter Elizabeth Richards. Ex. Robert Brough. D. August 17, 1747. R. August 2, 1748. Wit. John Nobs, Nathaniel Wootten. Book 1737-49, p. 298.

RUSSELL, Elizabeth. Account of sale. D. March 9, 1792. R. February 24, 1796. Book 1787-1800, p. 289.

RUSSELL, Penuel. Leg.- wife Elizabeth; son Thomas; son Penuel Russell. Exs. wife Elizabeth and Curtis Patrick. D. R. May 23, 1782. Wit. James Russell, Alexander Lewelling, Daniel Marrow, Benjamin Hennis. Original Will.

RUSSELL, Robert Sandefur. Leg.- to my housekeeper Mary Saunders with the proviso that neither of her brothers live with her; with reversion of the bequest to my relations Penuel Russell and Peter Garrow; to relation Frances Garrow; to Richard Morris; friend Everard Robinson. Exs. friends Everard Robinson and George Purdie. D. November 5, 1798. R. July 27, 1799. Wit. Thomas Robinson, William Allen, John Weymouth. Codicil. to William Allen living near Tompkins Ordinary. Book 1787-1800, p. 481.

RUSSELL, Thomas. His co-heirs were William Morris, Thomas Hill and Elizabeth Dunn. May 21, 1687. Book 1689-1699, p. 107.

RYLAND, John. Grissel Ryland appointed Administratix. Security, William Naylor and Philip Cowper. Appraisers appointed, Charles Pasteur, Willis Scott, George Johnson and William Ballard. October 7, 1755. Order Book 1755-60, p. 26.

SALMON, John. Leg.- to Thomas Salmon the son of Elizabeth Picket; to Mrs. Selden the wife of John Selden; to the woman in England, who is supposed to be my wife, provided she comes to this country within one year after my death; with reversion to aforesaid Thomas Salmon; to Thomas Howard; to Andrew Bully; to Joseph Selden, to Mr. John Selden; to my boy John Smith. Ex. Mr. John Selden. D. March 19, 1741/42. R. May 19, 1742. Wit. Richard Bickardick, John Nelson. Book 1737-49, p. 129. Paid Elizabeth Picket for nursing Salmon's child. Estate settled by James Wallace and Joseph Banister. March 20, 1743. Book 1737-49, p. 179 & 180.

SANDEFUR, John. Deed of gift to his sons Robert, William and Peter Sandefur. D. February 16, 1742/43. R. February 16, 1742. Wit. William Davis, William Williams, Samuel Markoom. Book 1737-49, p. 155.

SANDEFUR, Peter. Leg.- son John at twenty-one; son Peter land adjoining my brother Robert Sandefur; reversion of bequests to my brother James Sandefur and my cousins, representatives of Elizabeth Morris, Gerrard Sandefur, Elizabeth Patrick and Mary Young; reversion of the bequest to brother James to his son John Sandefur, with reversion to his two brothers, Joseph and Abraham; my wife to have the guardianship of my two younger children; refers to all my children. Exs. wife, friends Richard Cary and Hinde Russell. D. March 7, 1774. R. March 13, 1777. Wit. Sarah Russell, Anne Reade, Margaret Hurst. He had three children, John, Franky and Peter. The widow died soon after the testator and the son John died an infant. A suit filed for the division of the negroes between Samuel Armistead, who married Franky and Peter Sandefur.

SANDEFUR, Robert. Leg.- to my natural son Robert Sandefur Russell, the son of Ann Russell the land adjoining Robert Bumpass and Edward Armistead with reversion to my daughter Ann Sandefur; reversion to brother William Sandefur; to nephew John, son of brother James Sandefur; to Anne Russel, daughter of Anne Hurst; to cousin Robert, son of my nephew John Sandefur. Exs. friends Francis Jones and John Tabb. D. December 28, 1769. R. Wit. Thomas Russell, Hinde Russell, Sarah Russell. Original Will.

SANDEFUR, Samuel. The Younger. Leg.- all the money due me for my services as a soldier to my father Samuel Sandefur in case he should survive me; with reversion to my sister Mary Sandefur. Ex. father Samuel Sandefur. D. November 27, 1783. Wit. Alexander Lewelling, William Langley. Original Will.

SANDEFUR, William. Leg.- wife Elizabeth; son James Nixson Sandefur; son William; son Robert; daughter Mollea; son Richard; daughter Patsea Sandefur. Exs. wife, son James Nixson Sandefur and Nathaniel Bell. D. March 19, 1782. R. October 28, 1784. Wit. John Drewry, Elizabeth Drewry. Nathaniel Bell qualified, security, John Skinner. Original Will. Account of estate audited by John Hunter, Joseph Needham and Charles Jenings. September 27, 1792. Book 1787-1800, p. 101.

SANDS, Penuel. Leg.- wife Margaret; daughter Sarah; son William; son Penuel; son John Skinner Sands; son Thomas Sands. Exs. wife Margaret and friend John Skinner. D. July 10, 1776. R. Wit. Westwood Armistead, Elizabeth Simmons, Mary Skinner. Original Will.

Saunders and Sanders

SAUNDERS, James. Leg.- wife Judith, with reversion of bequest to son William; son John; son Wilson; son James; daughter Judith; daughter Mary; daughter Ann; daughter Elizabeth Saunders; provision for an unborn child. Exs. with Judith and George Booker. D. August 30, 1781. Wit. William Jennings, John Wilson. Original Will.

SAUNDERS, Judy. Leg.- son Robert; daughter Mary; daughter Ann; granddaughter Mary Saunders; grandson James Saunders Wilson;

granddaughter Ann Wilson; daughter Elizabeth Saunders; son James Saunders. Ex. friend George Booker. D. July 2, 1794. R. July 23, 1795. Wit. William Davis, Ann Booker. Book 1787-1800, p. 246. Original Will. Account of the sale of James and Judy Sanders. September 28, 1797. Book 1787-1800, p. 362.

SAUNDERS, David. Account of estate audited by William Allen, R. Armistead and W. Armistead. February 27, 1800. Signed, William Saunders. Book 1787-1800, p. 530.

SAUNDERS, (Sanders) William. Leg.- son David; grandson William Sanders and his Mother Ann Sanders. Ex. son David Sanders. D. November 16, 1762. R. March 1, 1763. Wit. Edward Latimer, Nathaniel Bell. David Sanders qualified, security, Edward Latimer. Book 1758-64, p. 437. Estate appraised by William Cross, Richard Wilson and John Presson. April 5, 1763. Book 1758-64, p. 466.

SAWYER, ------. Inventory Indexed. Book 1689-1699.

SCOTSELL, James. Estate appraised by Henry Waterson and Walter Bayly. Signed Richard Street. September 8, 1696. Book 1689-1699, p. 225.

SEAMORE, William. Will. Indexed. Book 1689-1699.

SELDEN, Bartholomew. Extract from will: to beloved wife and my unborn child; with reversion to brother John Selden. Will proved before 1743. William Edwards married Sarah the widow of the said Bartholomew Selden. Ejectment Suits, 1734-70, p. 73.

SELDEN, Eleoner. Estate appraised by Cary Selden, John Jones and H. King. June 3, 1760. Book 1758-64, p. 206. Estate signed by Joseph Selden, Administrator. Among items, by receipt of her father's estate. Audited by James Wallace, John Jones, H. King and W. Wager. October 7, 1761. Book 1758-64, p. 282.

SELDEN, John. Settlement of estate, paid ----beth Selden; paid Elener Selden; paid -------rt Armistead in discharge, etc.; paid the master of the College for William Selden's schooling; by John Selden as a tax, which he was to pay agreeable to his father's will; by Richard Selden the same tax; by Joseph Selden the same tax. Audited by W. Wager, George Wray and ------ King. D. July 1, 1760. R. February 3, 1761 (badly torn). Book 1758-64, p. 189.

SELDEN, Joseph. Leg.- son Samuel, land on the Potomac in Stafford County when he is twenty-one; son Miles, when he is twenty-one; mother Rebecca; son Cary; brother John Selden; guardianship of my three sons to Mr. Wilson Cary and Mr. Miles Cary, their uncles. Exs. wife Mary, Mr. Wilson Cary and Mr. Miles Cary. D. F. June 21, 1727. Wit. John Brodie, R. Brough, Samuel White. Book 1704-30, p. 73. Estate appraised by James Wallace, Charles Jenings and William Loyal. November 15, 1727. Book 1704-30, p. 116. Mary Cary (Selden ?) produced the settlement of estate, which was ordered recorded. May 8, 1732. Order Book 1731-47, p. 24.

SELDEN, Joseph. Leg.- wife Mary; daughter Euphan; son John; daughter Ann A------; son Robert, land in Hampton facing Colonel Cary; son Joseph; son William; son Samuel. Exs.

brother -------- Selden and friend William Armistead. D. August 3, 1774. R. March 28, 1776. Wit. Original Will.

SELDEN, Mary. Wife of Captain Joseph Selden. Leg.- agreeable to the sense of our marriage contract, to my two daughters Priscilla and Mary Curle. Exs. friend William Roscow Wilson Curle. D. November 24, 1770. R. January 24, 1782. Wit. William Selden, John Selden. Joseph Selden consents to the above will, provided it shall not in any manner affect my right or title to the money recovered or expected to be recovered of a certain Edward Munford in the Province of North Carolina. Original Will.

SELDEN, Mary. Widow of Joseph Selden. Leg.- son Cary; son Samuel; son Miles my plantation at Fort Fields. D. October 5, 1723. R. March 25, 1775. Wit. Thomas Palmer, Elizabeth Deparks, William Selden, Mary Ann Selden. Original Will.

SELDEN, Rebecca. Leg.- daughter Elizabeth; grandson ------- Milner at twenty-one; grandson Samuel Milner at twenty-one a ring which was his mother's; grandson Cary Selden; grandson Samuel Selden; grandson Miles Selden; grandson Richard Selden; grandson Joseph Selden; granddaughter Elizabeth Selden; cousin George Yeo; son John Selden. Extx. daughter Elizabeth Selden. D. April 23, 1736. R. Wit. John Predy, Samuel Skinner. Memo: The money due me from Mr. Fortesque to be divided between daughter Elizabeth and son John Selden. D. July 14, 1737. R. January 17, 1737. Wit. Robert Brough, John Naylor. Book 1737-49, p. 24. Original Will.

SELDEN, Samuel. Leg.- wife Rebecca, plantation called "Buckrow"; son Joseph my plantation on Potomack Creek; son John, two plantation, one called "Back River" lately in the occupation of Leonard Yeo and "Old Field", being the tract I have on Hampton River, lately in the tenure of one Thomas Batts; son Bartholomew in case he gains none of his wife Ashley's negroes; daughter Elizabeth; daughter Mary Milner. Exs. wife and son Joseph Selden. D. May 29, 1720. R. June Court 1720. Wit. George Yeo, William Brough, Margaret M. Welch. Book 1715-21, p. 268. Bond for Rebecca and Joseph Selden, security, George Yeo and John Selden. July 19, 1720. Wit. Francis Mallory, Godfrey Pole. Book 1715-21, p. 285 & 306.

SELDEN, William. Leg.- son John Hancock Selden; wife Mary Ann; my slaves to be divided among my children. D. June 8, 1783. Exs. friend John Hancock and wife. Wit. Richard E. Lee, John Boggess. Original Will.

SERVANT, Bartrand. Gent. Leg.- daughter Frances George; daughter Mary Ballard; son James at twenty; son-in-law Francis Ballard to go to the charge of recovering the plantation that Samuel Selden has called the "strawberry Banks"; to Elizabeth Massenburg; to Peter Proby; to Bartrand Proby; to Thomas Proby; to Rebecca Long; grandchildren, servant Ballard, Francis Ballard and Frances George. Exs. son James, Francis Ballard, friend James Burtell and John George. D. November 1, 1707. P. November 18, 1707. Wit. Joshua Curle, James Howard, Thomas Faulkner. Ejectment Suits, 1734-70, p. 80.

SERVANT, Bartrand. Leg.- loving wife; son Samuel; son Richard Servant. Wife, Extx. D. November 19, 1758. R. December 5, 1758. Wit. Judith Barron, Richard Taylor, R. Brough. Book 1758-64, p. 29. Original Will. Elizabeth Servant refused, Robert Brough qualified, security, Cary Selden. Appraisers appointed, Cary Selden, Peter Purryear, John Bennet and John

Minson. Order Book 1755-60, p. 208-209. Book 1758-64, p. 59 & 157. Estate settled by Cary Selden, H. King and W. Wager. August 6, 1760. Paid the Sheriff for summoning the heir-at-law to contest the validity of father's will. Book 1758-64, p. 171.

SEYMOUR, Gerrard. Estate appraised by James Smith, William Guy and William Smith. July 24, 1794. Book 1787-1800, p. 241.

SHARPLESS, Courtney. Leg.- son William Sealy Lane; son John McCarty Lane; adopted daughter Courtney Brough; to dear little relation Mary Bradley Brough; relation Courtney Brough, reversion to relation Amelia Brough; relation Robert Brough. Ex. relation Robert Brough, who is to keep the estate given to my sons in his hands until he knows whether my children be dead or not, if so bequest to be used for the education of Mary Bradley Brough. D. September 19, 1788. R. October 28, 1790. Wit. William Kirby, James Banks, John Perry. Original Will.

SHAW, Allen. Appraisers appointed, John Howard, William Morehead and Richard Nusum. May 16, 1728. Book 1704-30, p. 124.

Sheppard, Shepard, Shepherd
SHEPPARD, Baldwin. Leg.- daughter Elizabeth Cofield; son John; wife Elizabeth Sheppard; Elizabeth Guthrye to be paid. Exs. son John and wife Elizabeth Sheppard. D. February 27, 1696/97. R. 20 of 7ber 1697. Wit. Henry Robison, Thomas Francis, George Cooper. Book 1689-1699, p. 231.

SHEPPARD, (Shepard) Baldwin. Nuncupative Will. To daughter Susanna; daughter Sarah Shepard. Proved by Sarah Jones, Elizabeth Bushell, John Sheppard, Sarah Whetheridge, Susanna Sheppard and John Bushell. September 11, 1757. Original Will. Administration granted Affiah Shepard, security, Banister Minson and Samuel Watts. Appraisers appointed, Thomas Lattimer, James Naylor, Ursley Carter and William Carter. October 4, 1757. Order Book 1755-60, p. 151. Ordered that the estate be settled by George Walker, Sr., James Wallace, William Wager and Thomas Lattimer. January 2, 1760. Order Book 1755-60, p. 271. Account of estate. Among items, paid John Shepherd, Jr. an account. Book 1758-64, p. 143.

SHEPPARD, Jean. Leg.- Mother Ann Sheppard; sister Sarah; brother Johney Sheppard. D. November 8, 1779. Wit. Joseph Cooper, Euphan Pears. Original Will.

SHEPPARD, (Shepherd) John. Leonard Whiting was appointed the guardian of his orphan Baldwin Shepherd. Security, John King and Charles Jenings. January 17, 1721. Book 1721-23, p. 38.

SHEPPARD, John. Leg.- wife Ann; son Baldwin; son John; daughter Ann Smelt; daughter Elizabeth Sikes; daughter Sarah; daughter Jean; I lend to John Smelt the tract bought of Peter Pearce, with reversion of bequest to granddaughter Elizabeth Smelt, reversion to son John Sheppard. Exs. wife Ann and Joseph Cooper. D. November 15, 1777. R. March 25, 1779. Wit. John Curle, James Williams, Baldwin Sheppard. Ann Sheppard qualified, security, William Latimer, George Latimer. Original Will.

SHERLEY, Richard. Leg.- to Susana Cain; to Keziah Cane; to Margaret, wife of Joshua Cain; remainder of estate to my Mother if alive, reversion to all my brothers and sisters. Ex. Miles King. D. December 17, 1778. Wit. Charles Jenings, Bosill

Smith. Original Will.

SHERWIN, John. Account of estate in which it states Mrs. Jane Sherwin sold household goods and that Thomas Michell, Esq. was on her bond. Estate appraised by George Wray, Robert Armistead and William Tucker. June 18, 1746. Book 1737-49, p. 220. Settlement of estate by George Wray, William Tucker and W. Wager. Paid one-third to the widow, remaining two-thirds due to John and Mary Sherwin. October 3, 1749. Book 1737-49, p. 349.

SHORT, William. Appraisal of goods, produced by John Boardland by Joshua Curle, Samuel Ricketts and Joseph Wragg. July 13, 1721. Order Book 1704-30, p. 315.

SHORTRIDGE, --------. Administration. Indexed. Book 1689-1699.

SILVERTHORN, Thomas. Leg.- son Sebastian bequest in the hands of Elijah Jervis; son John; son George; daughter Susanna Jervis. Ex. son John Silverthorn. D. March 16, 1798. R. June 28, 1798. Wit. John Nicholson, Thomas L. Nicholson, James Malaway. Book 1787-1800, p. 407. Original Will.

SIMPSON, Daniel. Will Indexed. Book 1689-1699. Richard Routen in right of his wife, who was the daughter of Daniel Simpson brings suit against George Burtenhead as marrying Elizabeth, the daughter of Thomas Tabb, decd. for trespass. February 19, 1693/94. Order Book 1689-1699, p. 28.

SKINNER, Anne. Leg.- son Thomas; daughter Rosey Skinner. Ex. Mark Hall. D. January 4, 1793. R. January 24, 1793. Wit. Mark Hall, John Been. Book 1787-1800, p. 114. Original Will.

SKINNER, John. Leg.- daughter Rebecca Cross; daughter Elizabeth Wilson; wife Jane, decd.; son Thomas; my daughter-in-law Ursula Berry, formerly the wife of my son Charles Skinner; son William; son John; son Henry; son Nicholas; grandson Charles Skinner. Exs. sons-in-law Robert Cross and Thomas Wilson. D. April 14, 1737. R. February 15, 1737. Wit. Charles Jenings, Joseph Jegits. Book 1737-49, p. 31. Original Will. Estate appraised by John Moore, John Howard and Joseph Jegits. March 16, 1737. Book 1737-49, p. 41 & 87.

SKINNER, John. Leg.- son John, after Mrs. Lively's estate has been settled; to all my children. Exs. wife and George Booker. Wit. A.B. Dissens (?), Thomas P. Roberts, Rebecca Russell. D. November 21, 1799. R. February --, 1800. Book 1785-1800, p. 522. Original Will.

SKINNER, Joseph. Estate appraised by William King, Henry Walker, Charles Jenings and Francis Riddlehurst. Signed, Hanah Skinner. March 18, 1735. Order Book 1731-47, p. 109.

SKINNER, Samuel. Planter. Leg.- wife Elizabeth; son William; daughter Loosea; daughter Elizabeth, son Samuel when of age; provision for unborn child. D. August 1, 1737. R. November 16, 1737. Wit. George Morgan, John Ridlehurst. Book 1737-49, p. 19. Original Will. Estate appraised by Samuel Galt, Alexander Kenedy, William Henry, Francis Riddlehurst. May 17, 1738. Book 1737-49, p. 47.

SKINNER, Thomas. Estate ordered appraised, December 18, 1723/24. Estate appraised by Edward Latimer, George Cooper, Charles Cooper and Charles Jenings. Among items, to legacies left by Ann Daniel to Skinner's children. Book 1704-30, p. 13.

Account of charges expended at my father and Mother's funerals. Signed, John Skinner. January 15, 1723/24. Book 1721-23, p. 175.

SKINNER, Thomas. Leg.- to my wife plantation bought of Mr. James Baker; daughter Frankey; son Thomas; my plantation at "Fox Hill" to be equally divided between my son John, son Thomas and daughter Mary Skinner after the death of Penuel Saunders; to my daughter Margaret Saunders. Exs. wife and John Skinner. D. May 23, 1776. R. October 25, 1776. Wit. Henry Howard Mingham, John Powell, Fanny Baines. John Skinner protested the filing of will, his security, Thomas Wootten, Sr., Thomas Wootten, Jr. Original Will (bad condition). Account of estate. 1776. Paid to Abia Clay, the husband of Sally Skinner, the amount of property delivered to Thomas Skinner as her guardian; paid to William Powell an orphan. Examined by John Hunter, Miles King and Robert Brough. Signed, John King, Ex. R. June 23, 1791. Book 1787-1800, p. 31.

SMELT, John. Leg.- daughter Sarah; daughter Jane; son Miles; daughter Elizabeth; reversion of my estate if all my children should die without heirs, to the children of my brother David Smelt. Ex. Mr. George Booker. D. December 11, 1787. R. February 28, 1788. Wit. Gerrard Seymour, William Armistead, Thomas B. Armistead, Sheldon Moss. George Booker qualified, security, Augustine Moore, Jr. Original Will. Account of estate: Legacy paid to David Smelt, left him by his father; paid board for Jenney and Sarah Smelt; paid David Smelt for three children; paid Robert Smelt for board for Miles Smelt. Audited by Shelden Moss, Thomas Allen and John Skinner. January 27, 1791. Book 1787-1800, p. 7.

SMELT, Joseph. Leg.- my whole estate to my two children Elizabeth and Mary Smelt, when they are eighteen or married. Ex. Mr. George Booker. D. January 12, 1790. R. January 28, 1790. Wit. William Seymour, Augustine Moore, Jr. George Booker, qualified, security, Miles King. Original Will.

SMELT, Robert. Leg.- loving wife and all my unmarried children; daughter Mary Tomkins. Exs. wife and friend George Booker, William ap Thomas Parsons. D. May 3, 1795. R. June 26, 1795. Wit. William ap Thomas Parsons, Robert Marrow, James Saunders. Original Will. Book 1787-1800, p. 220. Account of estate, Robert Marrow, Ex. Appraised by William ap Thomas Parsons, Michel King and Henry Tabb. Estate divided between nine legatees and audited by George Booker, William Lowry and John Randle. October 1799. Book 1787-1800, p. 505. Sales, p. 515.

SMELT, William. Of Hampton. Leg.- son William; daughter Mary; Godson John Pitt at twenty-one; Godson Thomas Falkner; God-daughter Mary Anderson. Exs. son William Smelt and friend Joseph Banister. D. July 1, 1720. R. October 18, 1721. Wit. Evan Alkin, Dunn Armistead, Godfrey Pole. Book 1721-23, p. 9. Estate appraised by H. Irwin, John Bordland and William Loyall. December 20, 1721. Book 1721-23, p. 16 & 41 & 76. Account estate, among items, suit land cause against Mr. King; the Executor is ordered to meet Mr. Holdcraft, Ex. of the estate of Randal Plat, to settle Mr. Smelt's account against him to the balance of John Pitt's estate, in William Smelt's, his Administrator's hands. The following subscribers have met at the house of Mr. Joseph Banister and audited the accounts, J. Ricketts, Samuel Sweny and Charles Jennings. January 13, 1723/24. Book 1721-23, p. 171.

SMELT, William, Sr. Leg.- daughter Elizabeth; son David; son John Smelt. Ex. Westwood Armistead. D. March 16, 1773. Wit. Westwood Armistead, Samuel Sandefur, William Sandefur. Original Will. Robert Smelt, Administrator summoned to Court to answer a plea of trespass brought by David Smelt and Elizabeth Smelt. October 9, 1782. Original paper.

Smith and Smyth
SMITH, -------. Will probated. Indexed. Book 1689-1699.

SMITH, Benjamin. Administration granted Susanna Smith, his widow. Inventory of estate, signed Susanna Barber. D. June 6, 1719. R. August 15, 1719. Book 1715-21, p. 9 & 204.

SMITH, Fanny. Leg.- sister Mary Smith. D. March 19, 1797. R. January Court 1798. Wit. Samuel Rowland, John Douglass, John Simpson. Book 1797-1800, p. 383. Original Will.

SMITH, Henry. Inventory. Indexed. Book 1689-1699.

SMITH, James. The bond of Martha Smith as Admtx. of her two husbands' estates, viz.: Daniel Row (ROE) and the aforesaid James Smith. Security, Maurice Langhorne. D. November 16, 1753. R. June 27, 1767. Wit. Thomas Tabb, Anthony Hawkins. Book 1763-71, p. 165.

SMITH, (Smyth) Joan. Leg.- granddaughter Jane, the eldest daughter of Thomas Bacchus; granddaughter Elizabeth Bacchus; daughter Amy, wife of Thomas Bacchus. Ex. friend Thomas Howard, Cordwainder. D. August 12, 1714. R. July 20, 1715. Wit. Joseph Wragg, Nathaniel Parker, Peter (?) Phillipson. Book 1715-21, p. 142. Account of estate. Paid Joan and Elizabeth Backhouse, their part of the estate. Audited by William Smelt and William Loyall. Book 1715-21, p. 34.

SMITH, John. Leg.- estate to William Creeke after all my debts are paid. Exs. George Elyand and William Spicer. D. August 11, 1690. Wit. Thomas Bennett, William Bowles. Administration on the estate granted to George Eland. Book 1689-1699, p. 83 & 109. Recorded twice. Appraisers of the estate of John Smythe, Silversmith, were Samuel Curle and Thomas Morgan. July 18, 1692. Signed, George Eland. Book 1689-1699, p. 121.

SMITH, John, Sr. Leg.- grandson John, son of Thomas Ryland, decd., the lot formerly belonging to Peter Hopson, adjoining John Meredith. Ex. son-in-law John Meredith. D. February 3, 1723. R. February 19, 1723/24. Wit. Samuel Sweny, William Fyfe, Richard Thomson. Book 1721-23, p. 177. Appraisers appointed, Samuel Sweny, Joseph Banister, William Lyell and William Brough. February 19, 1723/24. Order Book 1723-29, p. 2. Book 1704-30, p. 2.

SMITH, Mary. Leg.- son Richard H. Smith and his sisters Hannah Simpson, Mary, Fanny and Elizabeth Smith; daughter Ann Davis; son William Smith. Ex. son Richard Smith. D. November 9, 1792. R. April 25, 1793. Wit. Gerrard Seymour, Johnson Ross, Samuel Rowland. Security for Ex. James Burke and Thomas C. Amory. Book 1787-1800, p. 120. Original Will.

SMITH, Sarah. Bond for the administrators, William Barber and wife Susanna was signed by Robert Armistead. June 18, 1719. Book 1715-21, p. 198.

SMITH, (Smyth) William. Nuncupative will, proven by Thomas

Wythe, Jr. aged twenty-three and Mary Felts aged twenty-two. After all debts are paid, whole estate to mother, Mrs. Ann Wythe. Xber 18, 1693. Probation of will granted Thomas Wythe, Sr., security, Thomas Wythe, Jr. and William Mallory. December 18, 1693. Book 1689-1699, p. 138 & 154. Order Book p. 24.

SORRELL, William. Inventory of estate signed by Sarah Sorrell. December 18, 1689. Book 1689-1699, p. 119 & 124. Division of the estate gives a part to Sarah Sorrell, widow; to John Sorrell at Mr. Needhams; to George Sorrell at Edward Lattimores; to Elizabeth Sorrell at Mr. Johnsons; to William and Thomas Sorrell at John Naylors. Book 1689-1699, p. 129. John Naylor and Edward Lattymore ordered to return an account of the estates of the orphans of William Sorrell. September 11, 1693. Order Book 1689-1699, p. 9.

SORRELL, William. Administration of the estate granted to James Holloway. Appraisers appointed, Simon Hollier, William Marshall, William Dunn and William Copeland. November 17, 1725. Order Book 1723-29, p. 136. Appraisal by William Copeland, William Marshall, John Dunn. March 15, 1725. Account of estate, audited by Robert Armistead and Charles Jenings. November 22, 1728. Book 1704-30, p. 30 & 149.

SOUMAINE, Simon. Estate appraised by William Loyall and George Waffe. (Among items, a parcel of French Books) February 20, 1728. Book 1704-30, p. 165.

SPICER, Thomas. Nuncupative Will, proven by Robert Tucker, Penuel Penny and William Rowland. Leg.- sister Mary Spicer, plantation on Salters Creek; reversion to brother-in-law James Mullen; with reversion to nearest kindred; to Jane Block; to Mary DAvis. Extx. Mary Davis. March 1, 1747. Book 1737-49, p. 274.

SPICER, William. By will appointed Jane Cornelius, Extx., Appraisers appointed, Richard Hawkins, John Hawkins, John Moore and Robert Cross. January 21, 1735. Order Book 1731-47, p. 105.

SPICER, William. William Spicer qualified as Administrator. Appraisers appointed, John Howard, William Creek, Mark Powel and Thomas Morehead. June 20, 1733. Order Book 1731-47, p. 56.

SPILMAN, (SPELMAN) Thomas. Gent of Kecoughton in the Corporation of Elizabeth City. Received fifty acres as an "Ancient Planter". Declared his will that his daughter Mary should have all that he had here in England and what he made in Virginia his wife should have; in the presence of Jane Bridges, Mary Rowe and Fran. Spelman. Letter of administration was granted April 24, 1627 to Francis Spelman, natural and lawful brother of the said Thomas Spelman of Truro in County of Cornwall etc., and during the absence of Hannah Spelman, the relict of the said deceased in the parts of Virginia then dwelling. Water's Gleanings, p. 72.

SPINK, ------. William Robinson married Rebecca Spink. John Winterton, Administrator of estate. Appraised by Edward Ruddel and John Smith. May 25, 1689. Book 1689-1699, p. 79.

STAMBEE, ------. Probate of will. Indexed. Book 1689-1699.

STANELY, Thomas. Will. Indexed. Book 1689-1699.

STORES, Frazier. Leg.- to my housekeeper Martha Marshall; daughter Jane Ross and her surviving children; to my grandchildren Elizabeth Frazier Randle, Ann Randle, John Randle and James Randle. Ex. son-in-law John Randle. D. March 15, 1790. R. April 25, 1793. Wit. Marh Hall, Andrew Bulley, Baldwin S. Morris. Ex. qualified, security, George Booker. Book 1787-1800, p. 119. Original Will. Estate appraised by Joseph Cooper, Thomas Watts and James N. Cooper. September 26, 1793. Book 1787-1800, p. 134. Division of estate, to John Randle in behalf of his children; to Mrs. Jane Ross and her husband, Francis Ross, made by Joseph Cooper, James N. Cooper and Thomas Watts. March 27, 1799. Book 1787-1800, p. 141 & 392.

STORES, James. Account of his estate, filed by the Sheriff. March 1791. Book 1787-1800, p. 291.

STORES, John, Sr. Estate appraised by Samuel Watts, Banister Minson and John Sheppard. March 1, 1769. Book 1763-71, p. 299.

STORES, John. Leg.- brother Charles Stores. D. December 26, 1795. R. February 24, 1796. Wit. Joseph Cooper, James N. Cooper, Thomas Minson. Book 1787-1800, p. 287. Original Will.

STREET, Elizabeth. Nuncupative Will. She died at the house of Mrs. Elizabeth Jenings as proven by Mary Jenings, aged forty-five and Ann White, aged seventeen. Leg.- daughter Elizabeth Jenings; granddaughter Elynor Allainby all that I have except my land and desire her said daughter to call Mrs. Jenings and Nicholas Street her son to witness. February 12, 1695/96. Ordered probation of will of Elizabeth Street be granted to Elizabeth Innis, her daughter. May 18, 1696. Book 1689-1699, p. 213. Order Book 1689-1699, p. 86.

STREET, Richard. Indexed. Book 1689-1699.

STRINGER, John. Leg.- son John; son David; sister Elizabeth Wethersby; son Daniel; friend Michael Draper; friend William Allen. Sister Elizabeth to have son John until he is sixteen. D. April 12, 1718. R. May 21, 1718. Wit. Francis Rogers, John Crook, John Curle. William Allen, qualified. Book 1715-21, p. 120.

SULLEY, Adam. Will. Indexed. Book 1689-1699.

Sweny and Swany

SWENY, Edmund, Gent. Leg.- eldest son Edmund, land bought of Mr. Thomas Ceely; wife Martha; ring to Euphan Wallace; ring to Mr. Augustine Moore; discharge of all debts due me from Alice Cole; discharge of all debts due me from Mr. Simon Hollier; Goddaughter Martha Crook; brother-in-law Mr. Augustine Moore to manage the money in the hands of Mr. Edward Lemon, Merchant in London for the advantage of my children; wife the money in the hands of Mr. John Cooper, Merchant in London. Exs. wife Martha with overseers, Mr. Augustine Moore, Mr. James Wallace, Mr. Simon Hollier and Mr. Thomas Tabb. D. 19th of Xber 1696. R. May 18, 1697. Wit. James Wallace, Augustine More, Robert Crooke. Book 1689-1699, p. 273. Estate appraised by Thomas Harwood, Robert Crooke, Mathew Watts and Charles Jennings. October 6, 1697. Book 1689-1699, p. 276.

SWENY, Jane. Leg.- son Roscow; granddaughter Jane Sweny; the negroes which belonged to my husband Merrit Sweny's estate to son Roscow's children; daughter Elizabeth Cullington. Ex. son-in-law George Walker. D. July 31, 1757. Wit. David Curle, John Parsons. Original Will. George Walker, Sr., refused and Augustine Moore qualified as Executor, security, Thomas Dixon. Appraisers, Jacob Wray, George Wray, Jr., Francis Riddlehurst, Thomas Dixon. Order Book 1755-60, p. 160.

SWENY, (Swany) Martha. Probation granted to Thomas Tabb and John Tabb. March 18, 1700/01. Order Book 1689-1699, p. 217.

SWENY, Martha. Leg.- brother-in-law Augustine Moore; to the children of my brother Roscow Sweny at eighteen or marriage, my part of the estate of my late sister Priscilla Kirkpatrick. Ex. brother-in-law George Walker. D. May 30, 1757. Wit. Elizabeth Curle, Catherine Barraud, Daniel Barraud. Original Will. Book 1758-64, p. 381. Security for Executor, John Parsons. Appraisers appointed, Jacob Wray, George Wray, Jr., Francis Riddlehurst, Thomas Dixon. Order Book 1755-60, p. 137 & 161.

SWENY, Merritt. Leg.- son Roscow; daughter Priscilla Kirkpatrick; daughter Ann Moore; daughter Sarah Westwood; daughter Martha, my right to any part of the estate of Pascow Curle; daughter Mary; daughter Sarah Sweny; wife Jane, my mortgate on the land on which Mrs. Judith Bayley now lives. I desire that the money Mr. James Kirkpatrick paid Mr. Wm. Bowden in London for my son Roscow be repaid him out of my estate. D. December 28, 1751. R. October 3, 1752. Wit. W. Westwood, George Johnson, Ann Johnson. Original Will. Account of estate unadministered by Jane Sweny, decd., by Augustine Moore, Administrator. Paid Cary Michell's account; paid decree against Walker and als.; negroes recovered of Augustine Moore by Walker and als., negroes recovered of Priscilla Kirkpatrick, decd. The following paid an equal share, Augustine Moore, Martha Sweny, Roscow Sweny and John Parsons. Estate audited by George Wray, Will Smith and W. Wager. December 4, 1764. Attached note: As Mr. Moore will produce all accounts necessary to a settlement and I have no objections to accounts, I hope you'll proceed for a settlement without my attendance as I cannot conveniently attend. I am, Gentlemen, George Walker, Sr. April 29, 1765. Augustine Moore, Administrator of Jane Sweny, decd., who was the Extx and wife of Merrit Sweny against George Walker, Sr., Ex. of Martha Sweny, decd. Ordered that George Wray, W. Wager, William Smith and Henry King resettle the estates of Merritt Sweny and Jane Sweny. May 7, 1765. Book 1763-71, p. 42. Ordered that the following settle the estate of Merritt Sweny; Charles Jenings, George Wray, Jr., George Wythe and William Wager. August 4, 1756. Order Book 1755-60, p. 72. Provation granted Augustine Moore on the estate unadministered by Jane Sweny decd. Security, George Walker, Sr., Roscow Sweny, John Parson and James Westwood. May 2, 1758. Order Book 1755-60, p. 178.

SYMES, Benjamin. Leg.- my land and cattle to establish a free school; to George Thompson, son of Roger Thompson, late of Barstable in the County of Devonshire, also a bond from Thomas Worth of Perrine in the County of Cornwall in the hands of Wassell Webbing of Baeching in the County of Essex, with reversion of the bequest to Argell Thompson the son of Roger Thompson; to the said Argell Thompson, 250 acres due me for transporting five servants; to the church and its minister. Overseers of will, Mr. Thomas Oldis and John Snode to whom as a remembrance I give tobacco etc., at the house of John Branch at Back River. D. February 10, 1634. R. Wit. Henry Poole, Robert Spood. State Archives, Elizabeth City Petitions.

SYMONS, Anthony. Leg.- wife Mary, land adjoining Giles du Beryes and Moses Baker; brother Richard Symons land bought by my father from Thomas Hollier; brother Samuel Watts; provision for my unborn child. Ex. brother Richard Symons. D. June 18, 1698. R. July 18, 1698. Wit. William Armistead, Daniel Preedy, Margaret Preedy. Book 1689-1699, p. 238. Probation granted Richard Symons. Mathew Watts and wife Ann to be summoned to declare what estate they have in their custody. July 18, 1698. Order Book 1689-1699, p. 134 & 217.

SYMONS, John. Leg.- brother Richard the land on which my father-in-law, Mr. Mathew Watts now lives; brother Anthony Symons; cancels debts due from Moses Baker; uncle Daniel Preedy and each of his daughters. Ex. Mr. Mathew Watts. D. April 13, 1697. R. October 18, 1698. Wit. William Armistead, Mathew Watts, Sr., Mathew Watts, Jr. Book 1689-1699, p. 239.

TABB, Elizabeth. Bond for guardianship of her children granted her. Children, Edward Tabb and Martha Tabb. Security, Anthony Armistead, Robert Armistead and Merritt Sweny. May 20, 1719. Wit. F. Hayward, Will Westwood. Book 1715-21, p. 198.

TABB, Humphrey. Indexed. Book 1689-1699. Probation of estate granted Captain Anthony Armistead, security, Mathew Watts and Charles Jenings. July 18, 1694. Book 1689-1699, p. 155. Thomas Humphrey the father of Thomas Tabb, both deceased. Stated in a deed. August 28, 1695. Book 1689-1699, p. 200. Anthony Armistead, Ex. was sued by William Armistead for land left him by the last will and testament of Humphrey Tabb. July 18, 1694. Order Book 1689-1699, p. 45.

TABB, John. Receipt to William Lowry, Administrator of Richard Hand, decd., for estate of his wife Martha, the daughter of the said Richard Hand. December 16, 1698. Wit. William Marshall, Robert Ellis. Book 1689-1699, p. 239.

TABB, John. Leg.- wife; grandson John, son of Thomas Tabb; daughter Elizabeth; son William my plantation in Brunswick County on Wagua Creek; son John my plantation in Dinwiddie on Sappony Creek also the plantation in Dinwiddie on Stony Creek bought of William Tucker of Hampton and William Cary of York County; grandson John, son of Thomas Tabb; daughter Elizabeth; daughter Johana; daughter Sarah-the aforesaid daughters to live on my Stony Creek Plantation until their marriage; to daughter-in-law Mary Tabb, my son's widow an interest in my estate until she remarries; daughter Diana; granddaughter Mary, daughter of my son William; to each of my children born of my first wife the part of their grandmother's and grandfather's estates; son William, cousin John Tabb, John Robinson and Mr. Henry King, guardians of my children Diana and John Tabb; daughter Diana to be brought up by my daughter Johana or Elizabeth or by one of my daughter-in-laws, Mary or Diana Tabb. Extx. wife, with Capt. John Tabb. D. February 8, 1760. R. March 2, 1762. Wit. George Wray, Richard Cary, Daniel Sweny. John Tabb qualified, security, Henry Allen and Henry King. Book 1758-64, p. 309. Original Will. Appraisers of estate, John Allen, Henry Allen, Augustine Moore. March 2, 1762. Further appraisal by John Allen, Augustine Moore and John Parsons. Book 1758-64, p. 440. Estate audited by John Allen, William Armistead and Augustine Moore. August 6, 1765. Book 1763-71, p. 59.

TABB, John Jr. Orphan of Colonel Tabb. Audited by Cary Selden, George Wray and F. Riddlehurst. Captain John Tabb, Administrator. June 28, 1770. Book 1763-71, p. 362.

TABB, John. Leg.- son Johnson; son Henry; to wife; refers to land bought of Capt. John Parsons in York County and of Moseley Armistead, decd.; daughter Sarah Kendall; careful provision for support of son Thomas for life. Wife, extx. D. September 12, 1785. R. March 23, 1786. Original Will.

TABB, Johnson. Leg.- brother Henry; my said brother guardian to my two daughters, Mary Harwood Tabb and a little infant in arms. Ex. brother Henry Tabb. D. January 6, 1795. R. September 24, 1795. Wit. William Smith, Mary Tabb. Book 1787-1800, p. 250. Original Will.

TABB, Mary, Sr. Leg.- granddaughter Mary Jones; grandson Bourbin Jones; daughter Mary Lowry; son Simon Hollier. Ex. my son-in-law Mr. John Lowry. D. January 27, 1783. R. December 25, 1783. Wit. John Tabb. Original Will.

TABB, Mary. Leg.- daughter Priscilla; daughter Mary; refers to property which her deceased husband, John Tabb willed to his sons Johnson and Henry Tabb; to heirs of my deceased son Thomas Tabb. Extx. Priscilla Tabb. D. December 17, 1795. R. October 27, 1796. Wit. Miles King, Jenny Parsons. Book 1787-1800, p. 325. Original Will.

TABB, Thomas. Suit brought against George Burtenhead as marrying Elizabeth the daughter of Thomas Tabb. February 19, 1693/94. Order Book 1689-1699, p. 28.

TABB, Thomas. Leg.- son John; son Henry; son Thomas; to wife a slave given her by her father Moss and negroes left her by her former husband; son Edward; daughter Diana; daughter Mary; daughter Rachel; daughter Martha; son-in-law Francis Hayward; daughter-in-law Elizabeth. Ex. brother Edward Tabb. D. September 20, 1717. R. October 16, 1717. Wit. Henry Hayward, William Tabb, Richard Slater. Book 1715-21, p. 90. Wife named Elizabeth Tabb, p. 92. Edward Tabb qualified, security, Simon Hollier, Samuel Sweny.

TABB, Thomas. Leg.- son Thomas the plantation adjoining William Smelt, being the land I lately sold and repurchased of Mr. Francis Mallory; son John; to my wife and six children. Exs. wife and brother John Tabb. D. May 17, 1739. R. November 21, 1739. Book 1737-49, p. 71. Mary Tabb presented will. Account of estate audited by John Lowry, John Brodie and John Selden. July 21, 1742. Book 1737-49, p. 136.

TABB, Thomas. Administration of estate granted to Mary Tabb, security John Tabb and Westwood Armistead. Appraisers, James Wallace, Joseph Selden, John Allen and Thomas Lattimer. August 7, 1759. Order Book 1755-60, p. 237. Book 1758-64, p. 84. Account of estate returned by Thomas Talbot. Among items, stock returned to Elizabeth Howard belonging to the estate of Thomas Mingham. Examined by Jacob Wray, H. King, John Riddlehurst. November 24, 1768. Book 1763-71, p. 263.

TALLANT, John. Of James City County, whose wife married Doctor William Ellis. March 18, 1695/96. Order Book 1689-1699, p. 83.

TARRANT, Caesar. Of Hampton. Leg.- wife, my money to be applied to the purchase of my daughter Leddy's freedom; daughter Nancy; son Sampson Tarrant. Ex. William Brough. D. February 19, 1797. R. September Court 1797. Wit. John Hicks, David Hicks, Thomas Chisman, John Russell. (A slave who won his freedom for his bravery during the Revolutionary War.) Book 1797-1800, p. 387. Original Will.

TARRANT, Carter. Leg.- wife Mary; son Leonard; son Francis; daughter Jane Talbot, daughter Mary Carlton; daughter Kitty, debt due me from the estate of John Riddlehurst. Exs. friend William Ballard and son Francis Tarrant. D. July 28, 1783. Wit. Elizabeth Brough, Ann Brough, Robert Brough. Codicil: Whereas my friend William Ballard has died, Exs. wife Mary, friend Robert Brough and son Francis Tarrant. D. October 15, 1784. R. October 28, 1784. Wit. Elizabeth Brough, Ann Brough, Sally Wilson. Original Will.

TARRANT, Elizabeth. Leg.- niece Jane Seaton, daughter of my sister Ann Seaton; niece Priscilla Mitchell, daughter of Mary Carlton; sister Jane Talbott; sister Catherine Tarrant; brother Francis Tarrant; to my relation Mary the daughter of Nicholas Powell. D. January 13, 1778. R. Wit. Moss Armistead, William Ballard, Jr. Original Will.

TARRANT, Mary. Leg.- sister Frances Bayley; nephew William Bayley, a bond due me from James Latimer; nephew Charles Bayley, a bond due me from Miles King, Esq.; nephew Thomas Bayley; if a claim due me from the United States Government be recovered to be divided between my nephews Servant and John Ballard and niece Rebecca Baker. Exs. George Wray and John Ashton Wray. D. ------- 1790. R. April 22, 1796. Wit. Pascow Herbert, William King, Samuel Healy. Book 1787-1800, p. 297. Original Will.

TAYLOR, Robert. Of Hampton. Leg.- nephew Daniel Taylor; nephew Cathern Taylor; nephew Sarah Taylor; daughter Martha Taylor a house and lot in Hampton, now in the occupation of Samuel Sweny; wife Martha; son Robert Taylor. Exs wife and son Robert Taylor. D. July 18, 1719. R. January 20, 1719. Wit. Joshua Curle, Samuel Sweny, Jo. Wragg. Book 1715-21, p. 235. Estate appraised by F. Ballard, Joshua Curle, Joseph Banister, Jo. Wragg. March 3, 1719. Book 1715-21, p. 246.

TAYLOR, Thomas. Leg.- son William in England; daughter Katherine; daughter Elizabeth; daughter Jane; to my sister Mary; to Major William Wilson; to Captain Anthony Armistead; the money for my children is to be remitted to Mr. John Hall Minister of Finchly in ye County of Middlesex; to Mr. James Wallace; the money in the hands of Mr. Corbans in England and of Mr. Bullits in the Barbadoes to my wife Frances. Exs. Capt. Anthony Armistead and Major William Wilson. D. January 7, 1692/93. R. March 21, 1692/93. Wit. James Wallace, Minister, Roger Massenburg, Nathaniel Whitaker, Edward Powell. Book 1689-1699, p. 32 & 104. Probation granted to Frances Taylor. April 29, 1693. Book 1689-1699, p. 118.

TAYLOR, Thomas. Administration of his estate granted to Mary Taylor his relict. Appraisers, William Smelt and William Hudson. February 19, 1699/1700. Order Book 1689-1699, p. 170.

TAYLOR, Pol (?). In case of my death my land transferred from Waff and wife to me to Robert Whitfield, son of Mary Ann Whitfield, with reversion to the said Mary Ann Whitfield. No date. Wit. George Wray, Jr., George Wray, Sr. Book 1763-71, p. 45.

TEWILL, Mathew. Estate appraised by Anthony Tucker, James Smith and Joseph Jegitts. June 6, 1749. Book 1737-49, p. 336.

ap THOMAS, William. (Original in the Library of Congress. Complete text is given, because it is not available in the Clerk's Office of Elizabeth County or in any printed source.) In the name of God Amen: I, William ap Thomas of Elizabeth City County, being weak of body, but of good and perfect mind and memory praised be God for it, do make and ordain this my last will and testament in manner and form following: That is to say first and principally I commend my soul into the hands of Almighty God hoping through the merits of Death and Passion of my Savior Jesus Christ to have pardon and forgiveness of all my sins and to have everlasting life and my body I commit to the Earth to be decently buried as my Executrix hereafter named shall think fitting and as touching of all such temporal estate as it hath pleased God to bestow upon me I give and bequeath as followeth: Item: I give and bequeath unto my son-in-law John Stone one mare of two years old, two cows and two breeding sows. Item, 2nd.: I give and bequeath unto my daughter-in-law Mary Cumberland one weanable mare colt. Item, 3rd.: I give unto my wife Elizabeth ap Thomas her thirds of all my estate, the plantation and orchard where I now live on only excepted. Item 4th.: I give and bequeath unto my daughter Anne ap Thomas all the rest of my whole estate, moveables and immoveables to her and her heirs forever. Item 5th.: My will is further that my wife Elizabeth ap Thomas shall have one third of the plantation and orchard where I now live and to enjoy my whole estate during the time of her widowhood not wasting or destroying anything. My will is further that no lease shall be let of any part or parcel of land or estate for above seven years and that the Court shall have nothing to do with my estate only proving the will. My will is further that if in case my daughter Anne shall die without issue my whole estate to fall to the nearest of my own relations and their heirs forever. Item: It is my desire that my daughter Anne ap Thomas shall be my full and whole Executrix of all only to be guided and directed by the Overseer hereafter mentioned, not to act anything without the advice of her said Overseer and I do appoint my trusty and well beloved friend, Mr. John Robertson of the Parish of new Poquoson in the County of York as Overseer to see my last will and testament performed in every point. And I do hereby revoke, disannul and make void all former wills and testaments by me heretofore made and do own this to be my last will and testament as witness my hand and seal this thirteenth day January One thousand six hundred and seventy eight. Signed, William ap Thomas. Signed, sealed and delivered in the presence of us, John Moore, Antho. Robinson and Edward Hawkins. Proved in the Court of Elizabeth City County the eighteenth day of June One thousand six hundred and seventy nine by the oaths of John Moore and Anthony Robinson. Recorded the twenty first day of June 1679. George Walker, Clk. Cur. Papers in a suit give the following information:- that the daughter Anne ap Thomas married John Parsons. That John Parsons and Anne his wife conveyed land to Thomas Curle, March 18, 1689. John Parsons was then of New Poquoson Parish, York County. The property conveyed was known as Beaver Dams (but formerly called Otter Dams) and was bounded by William Hampton's patent assigned unto William ap Thomas. The assignment was dated December 11, 1640. John Parsons the elder died in 1717.

By deed May 20, 1720, Anne Parsons assigned land to her son William Parsons, the said Anne then being of Charles Parish, York County, being all the land on which Joseph Hull formerly lived and whereon Daniel Marro lately lived, lying on the Back River of Elizabeth City County, adjoining the land of George Rogers. Anne ap Thomas Parsons died in 1742 and John Parsons, Jr. died in 1753 leaving issue John Parsons, III, his eldest son. It is stated that William ap Thomas died seized of 1280 acres of land. Of this his daughter Anne and John Parsons, her husband, deeded 550 acres to Thomas Curle, cordwainer and about 400 to William Parsons their second son. This 400 acres is the property in question. John Parsons III brings this suit of ejectment against his uncle William Parsons. The jury before whom the case was heard were Edward Booker, Robert Miller, William McKoy, Archibald Ritchie, Charles Hamlin, Francis Anderson, George Watkins, James Dillard, Richard Selden, William Dowsing, Lewis Hansford and John Cary. Judgment was granted for the defendant on April 10, 1763. Library of Congress, Washington, D.C.

THOMAS, George. Leg.- son Cornelius; wife Mary; daughter Ann Massenburg. Extx. wife Mary Thomas. D. May 7, 1767. Wit. Arch'd. Wager, John Cardy Fox, Allen Wood, Ann Massenburg. Original Will.

THOMAS, Richard. Account estate. Indexed. Book 1689-1699.

Thomson and Thompson

THOMSON, Andrew. Appraisal of estate taken at the house of Mrs. Ann Wallace by Simon Hollier, John Lowry and Edward Lattimore. Signed, Ann Wallace and Thomas Wythe. Book 1715-21, p. 263.

THOMPSON, John. Frances Thompson, relict of John Thompson deed of gift to son John Thompson. January 9, 1688. Acknowledged by George Giggles her husband to be recorded by his consent. Book 1689-1699, p. 75.

THOMPSON, William. Of Naury in the County of Aunagh, Merchant. Leg.- to brother Acheson Thompson, brother Andrew Thompson. Ex. brother Andrew Thompson. D. April 10, 1783. P. February Court 1808. Wit. Francis McKenny, John Maxwell, Alexander Falls. Proved by the oath of Oswald Lawson, August 26, 1824. Original Will.

THURMER, Samuel. Mariner, of his Majesty's Ship, Lizard, Captain James Doake, Commander. Leg.- wife Martha. Extx. wife Martha Thurmer. D. August 21, 1761. R. Wit. James Doake, Captain, Alex'r Allen, Master, William Scott, Boatswain. Original Will.

Tilly and Tylley

TILLY, John. Inventory. Indexed. Book 1689-1699.

TYLLEY, John. Account current of estate, signed by William Browne. September 18, 1693. Book 1689-1699, p. 185.

TODD, Isaac. Estate appraised by Carter Tarrant, Henry Batts and Charles Cooper. November 28, 1761. Book 1763-71, p. 120. Account of sales. April 5, 1761. Signed, John Riddlehurst. Audited by H. King, John Jones and Roe Cooper. August 27, 1768. Book 1763-71, p. 244 & 247.

TOMPKINS, James. Leg.- to Mrs. Rebecca Goodwin, daughter of

Captain John Goodwin; to honoured father, Samuel Tompkins, the land which was the inheritance of my mother; to sister Martha Tompkins; to my daughter Mary Tompkins at twenty-one or marriage, reversion of the bequest to my five sisters, Mary, Martha, Sarah, Anne and Elizabeth Tompkins. Tuition of my daughter Mary to Mrs. Martha Kerby and Thomas Kerby of Elizabeth City, if they should die to my father Samuel Tompkins. Ex. father Samuel Tompkins. D. January 17, 1755. R. Wit. Thomas Roberts, Abraham Allen and Abraham Bailif (?). Original Will.

TOMPKINS, James. Appraisal of estate ordered November 9, 1796. Appraised by Augustine Moore, William Armistead, Augustine Moore, Jr. January 26, 1797. Book 1787-1800, p. 338. Account estate, signed by Miles King. Audited by Augustine Moore, Sr., Augustine Moore, Jr. and Henry Tabb. February Court 1798. Book 1787-1800, p. 391.

TOMPKINS, Mary. Administration refused by Samuel Tompkins. Edward Armistead and William Read, qualified. Starky Robinson and William Tompkins, securities. Appr. Edward Lattimer, Robert Sandefur and William Tuell. May 6, 1760. Order Book 1755-60, p. 286. Estate appraised by John Presson, Edward Latimer and William Tuell. July 1, 1760. Book 1758-64, p. 162.

TOMPKINS, William. Administration granted to William Reade, security George Ware. Appraisers, Robert Sandefur, Edward Lattimer, John Presson and William Tuell. August 5, 1760. Order Book 1755-60, p. 300. Book 1758-64, p. 224.

Traverse and Travis

TRAVERSE, William. Administration granted to William Smelt and wife Elizabeth, relict of William Traverse. May 18, 1699. Order Book 1689-1699, p. 147.

TRAVIS, William. Estate appraised by William Armistead, Robert Taylor, Richard Street and John Theddam. Signed, Elizabeth Smelt. August 18, 1699. Book 1689-1699, p. 271.

TREADWAY, Francis. Administration of estate granted to John Bordland. August --, 1718. Book 1715-21, p. 9.

TUCKER, Anthony. Leg.- wife Rosea; son Curle; daughter Sarah Dixon; daughter Mary Armistead; to my two aforesaid daughters my plantation on Salford's Creek; grandson Anthony Tucker Dixon; grandson Anthony Armistead. Extx. wife Rosea Tucker. D. September 15, 1758. R. January 2, 1759. Codicil: Jane Block to have the liberty to live on my land during her life. Daughter Mary Armistead the land bought of Charles Jenings and Hannah his wife, decd., with reversion to grandson Anthony Armistead. Rosea Tucker qualified, security, Charles Jenings and Anthony Armistead. Wit. Ann Armistead, Rt. Armistead, Jane White. Book 1758-64, p. 24. Original Will. Appraisers of the estate, John Moore, Robert Armistead, Jr., John Herbert and John Creek. February 6, 1759. Order Book 1755-60, p. 201 & 208. Book 1758-64, p. 60.

TUCKER, Elizabeth. Leg.- refers to deceased husband Thomas Tucker; son Thomas; daughter Mary (both under sixteen); to Charles Cooper and John Moore the debts which they owe me. John Moore to keep my son Thomas Tucker and Charles Cooper to keep my daughter Mary Tucker. Exs. John Moore and Charles Cooper. Overseer, my brother-in-law Charles Tucker. D. January 16, 1718. R. July 15, 1719. Wit. Charles Jenings,

Will Westwood. Book 1715-21, p. 203.

TUCKER, Robert. Administration granted to Mathew Small and Barbara his wife, relict of Robert Tucker. May 18, 1698. Thomas Tucker the son of Robert Tucker brings suit against Mathew Small and wife Barbara. Order Book 1689-1699, p. 132, 157 and 167.

TUCKER, Robert. Leg.- loving wife, reversion to son Robert Tucker Casey at twenty-one; reversion to cousin Thomas Kibble. Ex. friend Cary Selden. D. June 29, 1763. R. November 1, 1763. Wit. Thomas Dixon, William Weymouth, Rebecca Weymouth, Thomas Davis. Cary Selden qualified, security, William Smith. Book 1758-64, p. 515. Original Will.

TUCKER, Rosea. Leg.- granddaughter Elizabeth Armistead, with reversion of the bequest to my four grandsons, Anthony, Robert, Westwood and Alexander Carver Armistead, sons of my daughter Mary by her husband Anthony Armistead; rest of my estate between my three daughters, Mary King, Judith Herbert and Mary Armistead and Sarah Dixon if she lives until after my death. Friend William Armistead to be guardian to my granddaughter Elizabeth Armistead. Ex. William Armistead. D. September 8, 1766. R. January 6, 1767. Wit. John Riddlehurst, James Sebie (?). Book 1763-71, p. 108.

TUCKER, Thomas. Sr. Leg.- granddaughter Elizabeth Cooper, daughter of Charles Cooper, with reversion of the bequest to her sister; son Thomas; daughter Mary. Extx. wife Elizabeth. D. March 17, 1718/18. R. July 15, 1719. Codicil:- to daughter Elizabeth Moore and daughter Barbery Cooper. Wit. Robert Bright, John Batte, Charles Jenings. Administration granted to Charles Cooper and John Moore. Estate appraised by James Naylor, William Copland and James Baker. February 19, 1718. Order Book 1704-30, p. 316. Book 1715-21, p. 166 & 255.

TUCKER, Thomas. Nuncupative Will. Wife Elizabeth; son William, among the rest of my five children. D. April 7, 1718. R. July 18, 1722. Wit. William Spicer, Elizabeth Reidge (?). Book 1721-23, p. 58. Elizabeth Tucker qualified, security, William Tucker and John Massenburg. Book 1721-23, p. 64. Appraisers of estate, William Spicer and Thomas Hawkins, who also appraised the estate of Elizabeth Tucker, decd., which was ordered recorded. July 18, 1722. R. December 19, 1722. Book 1721-23, p. 69.

TUCKER, Thomas. Administration granted to Mary Tucker. Appraisers of the estate, James Baker, George Latimer, Leonard Whiting and Charles Jenings. June 16, 1736. Order Book 1731-47, p. 116. Account of the settlement of estate to the widow's third; to Elizabeth Tucker one-third; to Mary Tucker one-third. Divided by R. Brough, John Dunn and Rt. Armistead. September 15, 1742. Book 1737-49, p. 143.

TUCKER, William, Jr. Leg.- brother Robert Tucker; rest of my estate to my wife Usley Tucker. Extx. wife Usley Tucker. D. March 14, 1721/22. R. June 20, 1722. Wit. Thomas Jones, John Corlee (?). Usley Tucker qualified, security, Mathew Small and Thomas Jones. Book 1721-23, p. 50. Inventory, p. 59.

TUCKER, William. Leg.- son Robert one-half of my land in Hampton and my plantation on Saltsford Creek; son William the other half of my land in Hampton and my plantation on Salford's Creek purchased of Jeremiah Knight; daughter Barbara Boyce; daughter Mary Loyal; daughter Elizabeth Corprew; daughter Sarah Bruce; granddaughter Jane Butts; wife Susannah Tucker. Exs. wife Susanna and son Robert Tucker. D. August 7, 1758. R. March 2, 1763. Wit. Alexander Rhonnalds, David Wilson Curle, J. Westwood. Codicil: changing bequests, witnessed by George Wray, David Wilson Curle and James Westwood. Book 1758-64, p. 458.

TYLLEY, John. (See under Tilley). Ordered William Browne to produce an account of his estate. September 11, 1693. William Browne and Susanna the relict of John Tylley returned the estate of the orphan. John Harron of Nansemond County appointed guardian to Elizabeth Tylley, orphan of John Tylley. Order Book 1689-1699, p. 49, 70 and 72.

VAN BURKELLO, (Burkelo) Catherine. Leg.- granddaughter Margaret Davis; son William Van Burkelo; daughter Margaret Davis. Ex. son-in-law Capt. William Davis. D. September 27, 1762. R. November 2, 1762. Wit. James Wallace, Henry Batts, William Mallory. Book 1758-64, p. 369. Original Will. Estate appraised by Charles Pasteur, Carter Tarrant and Wil. Mitchell. May 3, 1763. Book 1758-64, p. 438.

WAFFE, George. Leg.- son-in-law William Winterton and my daughter Jane Winterton; grandson George, son of my son George Waffe. Exs. William Winterton and my daughter Jane Winterton. D. July 19, 1718. R. January 22, 1718. Wit. Henry Jenkins, John Mitchell, Bridgett Jenkins. Book 1715-21, p. 159.

WAFFE, George. Estate appraised by Samuel Hawkins, James Robertson and John Henry Rombough. February 16, 1736. R. May 18, 1737. Book 1737-49, p. 3. Estate settled by Charles Jenings, Jr. and Rt. Armistead. November 18, 1742. Book 1737-49, p. 155.

WAGER, William. Leg.- wife Bethia; provision for an unborn child. Extx. wife Bethia Wager. D. October 20, 1765. R. October 28, 1784. Wit. George Johnson, William Davis, Solomon Allmand. George Booker qualified as Executor, when Bethia Wager refused. Original Will.

WALKE, Thomas. Catherine Walke and Anthony Walke qualified as Executors. November 18, 1725. Order Book 1723-29, p. 139.

WALKER, George. Appraisal ordered recorded, July 19, 1732. Order Book 1731-47, p. 29.

WALKER, Jacob. Administration granted to George Walker, Jr. November 18, 1697. Order Book 1689-1699, p. 217. Estate appraised by George Wauffe, John Smith, Walter Bayley and Thomas Tucker. October 25, 1697. Signed, George Walker, Jr. Book 1689-1699, p. 275.

WALKER, Rebecca. Widow of Jacob Walker. Leg.- sister Mary Servant; brother James Servant; sister Frances George; rest of estate to be divided into six parts to go to my sister Jane Long's five children, viz.- Peter, John, Bertram, Thomas Proby Long and Rebecca Long. Ex. honorable father, Bertrand Servant. D. September 20, 1697. R. November 18, 1697. Wit. Joseph Arrosmith, Peter Heyman. Book 1689-1699, p. 228.

WALKER, Samuel. Settlement of estate, among items, to Charles Cooper's wife her one-third part and the balance due the orphans. Dated 1752. R. June 4, 1765. Audited by George Wray, H. King and John Riddlehurst. Book 1763-71, p. 48. Charles Cooper in account with Thomas Walker, orphan of Samuel Walker. Paid for rent of pew in Williamsburg Church; one-third of profits of estate in right of his wife; one-third due Susanna Walker; balance due the said orphan (Thomas ?). October 7, 1766. Book 1763-71, p. 97.

WALKER, William. Estate appraised by William Moore, William Parsons and Thomas Tabb. D. February 21, 1727. R. May 15, 1728. Book 1704-30, p. 122.

WALLACE, Ann. Leg.- granddaughter Mary Westwood; grandson James Westwood; the children of my daughter Ann Armistead; grandson Mathew Ballard; grandson George Wythe; granddaughter Mary Wallace; daughter-in-law Martha Wallace; son James Wallace. Ex. son James Wallace. D. March 14, 1739. R. February 18, 1740. Wit. John Selden, Lucy Ballard. Book 1737-49, 99. Original Will.

WALLACE, James. Leg.- son Robert, with reversion to son James at twenty-one; reversion to son William Westwood Wallace; to sister Ann Wray; nephews, James and Wilson Wallace, sons of deceased brother Robert Wallace; sister Mary Ball with reversion of bequest to nephew James Ball; to my children, Mary, Martha, Euphan, Elizabeth, James and William Westwood Wallace; to Anne Fenn for her service during my illness; to friend William Selden. Exs. wife Elizabeth, mother Martha Wallace, Captain Henry King and Captain John Tabb. D. 31st day of March 1775. R. Wit. Martha Wallace, Samuel Allyne, William Selden. Original Will. (bad condition)

WALLACE, (Wallis) John, Sr. Estate appraised by Joseph Banister, Nicholas Parker, John Bordland, John Meredith. February 1, 1724/25. Administration granted to Susannah Wallis the Widow. November 18, 1724. Book 1704-30, p. 22. Order Book 1723-29, p. 59 & 72.

WALLACE, John. Estate appraised by Robert Brough, Nicholas Parker and John Henry Rombough. January 30, 1726. R. June 21, 1727. Book 1704-30, p. 92.

WALLACE, Martha. Leg.- son James; grandson James, son of Robert Wallace, deceased the plantation bought of Thomas Wilson; reversion to grandson Wilson Wallace the younger son of Robert Wallace, decd.; reversion to the children of my daughters Martha Tabb and Elizabeth Selden; the plantation bought of Thomas Davis to be sold and the money arising to be divided between my daughters, Mary Ball, Martha Tabb, Euphan Curle, Ann Wray, Elizabeth Selden and my two grandsons James and Wilson Wallace; to daughter Elizabeth the wife of John Selden. Exs. Thomas Tabb, George Wray, William Roscow Wilson Curle and James Wallace. D. December 10, 1768. R. December 26, 1776. Wit. James Selden, James Wallace, Will Selden. William Roscow Wilson Curle and Thomas Tabb qualified, security John Cary and Merritt Westwood. Original Will.

WALLACE, Robert. Suit brought by Mary Wallace and Wilson Wallace infant, versus William Roscow Curle, administrator of Robert Wallace decd. and James Wallace, Jr. an infant and heir-at-law of said Robert Wallace. The widow was allotted her dower, part paid to Capt. James Wallace for James Wallace, Jr., son of Robert Wallace; part paid to Wilson Wallace, youngest son of Robert Wallace. Divided by George Wray and Jacob Wray. January 25, 1771. Book 1763-71, p. 411. Further appraisal by John Selden, H. King and W. Wager. January 25, 1771. Book 1763-71, p. 412.

WALLACE, Robert. Leg.- wife Elizabeth; son James Westwood Wallace, with reversion to unborn child and my brother James Wallace; to my said brother one half of my land in lieu of bequest my father left him, if he should die before he comes of age to return to my heirs; the negroes which my wife possesses either as a legacy or dower after her death to my son James Westwood; to my mother Elizabeth Mason. Exs. Mother Elizabeth Mason, uncle Worlich Westwood, George Latimer and Joseph Cooper. D. October 24, 1788. R. January 23, 1789. Wit. Joseph Cooper, George Latimer, William Westwood, Worlich Westwood. Worlich Westwood qualified, security, Robert Armistead and David Brodie. Original Will. Estate appraised by George Latimer, Joseph Cooper, William Latimer. December 4, 1788. Book 1787-1800, p. 473 & 474. Audited by M.E. Chisman, John S. Westwood and Charles Jenings. February 27, 1800. Book 1787-1800, p. 528.

WARD, Edward. Leg.- daughter Martha my whole estate. Extx. daughter Martha Ward. D. December 16, 1739. R. November 19, 1741. Wit. Francis Mallory, John Young, Johnson Mallory. (John Young died before the probation of the will.) Book 1737-49, p. 109.

WARE, George. Leg.- wife Elizabeth; son George when he is twenty-one; reversion to William Young. Ex. Francis Jones. D. January 31, 1752. R. Wit. Abraham Bailif (?), Gerrard Young, Nehemiah Nicholls. Original Will. Estate audited by Anthony Tucker, Charles Jenings, Cary Selden and William Wager. June 1, 1756. Order Book 1755-60, p. 52.

WATERS, Andrew. John Marshall administrator is sued by Andrew Giles for counter security. March 15, 1732. Order Book 1731-47, p. 20.

WATKINS, William. Account of the sale of estate by Robert Armistead, Sheriff. (The widow bought many items.) February 5, 1798. Book 1787-1800, p. 392.

WATERSON, -------. Account of estate. Indexed. Book 1689-1699.

WATTS, Jane. Leg.- grandson John Cooper; granddaughter Susanna Cooper; grandson William Cooper; granddaughter Euphan Naylor Russell; granddaughter Betsey Buxton; granddaughter Sally Buxton. D. September 22, 1794. R. September 22, 1794. Wit. Joseph Cooper, James N. Cooper, Joseph Cooper, Jr. Book 1787-1800, p. 176.

WATTS, Jean. Leg.- my husband Samuel Watts; granddaughter Euphan Russell; daughter Sarah Lunsford; granddaughter Elizabeth Buxton; granddaughter Sarah N. Buxton. Ex. grandson John Cooper. D. April 26, 1797. R. January Court 1798. Wit. Samuel Watts, Jr., Ann Sheppard. Book 1787-1800, p. 376. Original Will. (Williamsburg Wills lists Sarah Lunsford as Sarah Sandefur, a study of the original plainly shows that Lunsford is correct.)

WATTS, Mathew. Leg.- son Samuel; daughter Ann when she is sixteen;

brother Samuel. Exs. wife and Charles Tucker. D. R. August 15, 1716. Wit. Thomas Jones, William Creeke, Cassander Spicer. Probation granted to Hannah Armistead, Extx. Book 1715-21, p. 41. Estate appraised by Charles Jenings, John Howard and Robert Johnson. June 15, 1717. Book 1715-21, p. 85. Account of estate examined by Samuel Sweny and Joseph Banister. Among items, we find that Richard Hawkins and wife Hannah are indebted to the said estate. May 21, 1724. Book 1704-30, p. 21.

WATTS, Samuel. Leg.- son Mathew the tract bought of Andrew Laws; son Thomas; wife Elizabeth; daughter Judith. Exs. wife and father-in-law William Brasie (Bressie). D. March 19, 1726/27. R. June 21, 1727. Wit. Rt. Armistead, John King, William Tucker. Book 1704-30, p. 72. Estate appraised by Hugh Ross, Thomas Batts, Abraham Parish. July 19, 1727. Book 1704-30, p. 86.

WATTS, Samuel, Jr. Leg.- Pilot Boat "Favorite" to be sold. Wife Susanna; daughter Mary Wilson Watts at sixteen or marriage; to my lov'd relation Charles Jenings, son of Charles Jenings of Hampton; friend William Hunt; to George Lattimer, son of Thomas Lattimer; to relations, Thomas Minson Watts, Euphan Lattimer Watts, Mary Walker Watts and Jean Sinclear Jenings and Charles Jenings, son of Charles Jenings. Exs. wife Susanna and Charles Jenings. D. January 2, 1787. Wit. John Sheppard, William Short, Ann Hunt, Joseph Cooper. Susanna Watts qualified, security, William Hunt and Thomas Lattimer, Jr. Original Will.

WATTS, Samuel, Sr. Leg.- son Thomas land bought of Daniel Routten; son Samuel land bought of George Walker and William Williams; daughter Mary Bright; daughter Susannah Haynes; daughter Ann Jenings; daughter Sarah Williams; daughter Elizabeth King; to Mr. Charles Jenings. Exs. sons Thomas and Samuel Watts. D. December 26, 1797. R. July 28, 1798. Wit. James N. Cooper, Thomas Latimer, Thomas Lowry, John Bean. Book 1787-1800, p. 409. Original Will.

WATTS, Thomas. Leg.- son Samuel land adjoining Richard Routon, Joseph Selden and John Armistead, when he is sixteen; to mother-in-law Jane Bloudworth; wife Mary with reversion of bequest to the children of my brother Samuel Watts; provision for an unborn child. Wife, Extx. D. September 30, 1726. R. September 21, 1727. Wit. Baldwin Sheppard, Francis Massenburg, Thomas Jones. Book 1704-30, p. 104. Estate appraised by Edward Lattimer, Charles Jenings and James Naylor. August 21, 1728. Book 1704-30, p. 147.

WATTS, Thomas. Account of estate, returned by Baldwin Sheppard. Paid his wife's part of the personal estate. Audited by Thomas Latimer, Rt. Brough and Charles Jenings. March 21, 1738. Book 1736-53, p. 62.

WATTS, Thomas. Ordered that Robert Armistead settle the estate and that Mary Berry be paid a sum out of the estate. November 4, 1760. Order Book 1755-60, p. 310.

WATTS, Thomas. October 5, 1762. Estate appraised by Banister Minson, James Naylor, John Minson. February 1, 1763. Book 1758-64, p. 388.

WATTS, Thomas. Leg.- wife Ann; sister Mary Watts; provision for an unborn child. Wife, Extx. D. October 18, 1778. Wit.

John Sheppard, John Cooper Sheppard. Original Will.

WATTS, Thomas, Sr. Leg.- wife Ann to educate my child or children. D. March 1, 1782. R. July 22, 1784. Wit. Thomas Watts, Jr., Thomas Minson. Original Will.

WEBB, William. Administration granted to James Parsons, security, William Westwood. Appraisers appointed, George Johnson, John Allmand, Joseph Slee and Nicholas Morris. October 5, 1756. Order Book 1755-60, p. 80. Estate audited by Jacob Wray, George Wray and H. King. January 2, 1759. Book 1758-64, p. 26.

WEBSTER, Thomas. Leg.- daughter Mary Bullock, with reversion of the bequest to grandson Thomas Webster Bullock; granddaughter Elizabeth Haley, with the bequest to be left in the care of her aunt Mary Bullock until she is twenty-one; granddaughter Martha Skinner; great granddaughter Ann Webster Skinner; God-son William Baley; to Ann Haley. Exs. John Skinner, Jr. and Mary Bullock. D. October 26, 1787. R. January 28, 1790. Wit. Samuel Burkit, John Skinner, Mary Bullock, Elizabeth Coke. Book 1787-1800, p.

WELLINGS, Robert. Estate appraised by Nathaniel Bell, John Wood and John Allen. August 25, 1785. Book 1787-1800, p. 9. Account of estate returned by Robert Wellings, Ex. To sundries sold Mrs. Wellings when a widow. Audited by John Allen and W. Seymour. April 28, 1791. Book 1787-1800, p. 23.

WESTEBY, Samuel. Stephen Howard brings suit as marrying the widow of Samuel Westeby. November 20, 1693. Order Book 1689-1699, p. 23.

WESTWOOD, James. Leg.- wife Elizabeth, with reversion to son Merrit Westwood; daughter Sarah a lot in Blandford in the County of Prince George, bought of Col. William Poythress as by deed from Col. Samuel Gordon; daughter Ann. D. November 3, 1768. R. February 23, 1769. Wife, Extx. Wit. Mary King, Rt. Armistead, H. King. Elizabeth Westwood qualified, security John Tabb and Henry King. Book 1763-71, p. 279. Fragment of original preserved.

WESTWOOD, Merrit. Leg.- wife Elizabeth; daughter Sarah; provision of an unborn child; reversion to William and John Stith Westwood, sons of William Westwood, with reversion to Worlich Westwood, son of Worlich Westwood. Exs. wife, Capt. Miles King and Capt. Worlich Westwood. D. March 25, 1777. Wit. H. King, Francis Mallory, Samuel Jones. Original Will.

WESTWOOD, Thomas. Estate appraised by William Smelt, J. Meredith and Thomas Howard. Exs. James Servant and Henry Turner. June 16, 1715. Book 1715-21, p. 9 & 12.

WESTWOOD, William. Leg.- grandson Merrit Westwood; my daughter-in-law Elizabeth, widow of my son James Westwood; son William land bought of Joshua Curle, William Allen and wife Bethia and Henry Jenkins; grandson Merrit Westwood the tract bought of Thomas Mingham; son Worlich land bought of John Nixon, William King, Mathew Williams, John Noblin and Thomas Manning; grandson John Stith Westwood land bought of Thomas Williams and Edward Latimer; daughter Mary Armistead, lot bought of Francis Ballard, formerly belonging to Henry Irwin, decd. which he bought of Abraham Mitchel, Jr.; daughter Mary the wife of Robert Armistead; to daughter Elizabeth, wife of James Wallace a lot bought of John Meredith; daughter Martha a lot bought of Thomas Ryland and one bought of John Nelson on which George Johnson now lives; daughter Rachel, the wife of Henry King the tract I hold under a mortgate from William Henry late of Nansemond, land in Nansemond, a lot in Hampton adjoining Henry Sinclair and land bought of Richard Street and Thomas Trotter in Charles Parish, York County; to granddaughter Sarah, daughter of James Westwood. Exs. Capt. James Wallace and Henry King. D. May 7, 1770. R. June 28, 1770. Wit. Rt. Armistead, Joseph Selden, William Selden. Security for Exs. Robert Armistead and William Armistead. Book 1763-71, p. 349. Original Will.

WESTWOOD, William. Leg.- son William, land adjoining the land of Merrit Westwood and John Stith Westwood; to son John Stith Westwood land bought of Edward Parish, which adjoins the land given him by his grandfather; wife Ann and my daughter; provision for an unborn child. Exs. wife Ann, John Tabb, Worlich Westwood and Stith Hardiman. D. December 24, 1780. R. January 24, 1782. Wit. James Bray Armistead, John Brodie, Frances Armistead. Ann Westwood qualified, security Worlich Westwood and Miles King. Original Will.

WETHERSBY, Thomas. Estate appraised by Richard Joanes and Charles Jenings. February 21, 1693/94. Signed by Bridgett Wethersby. Book 1689-1699, p. 184 & 187.

Weymouth and Waymouth

WAYMOUTH, John. Leg.- eldest son Robert; son John; son William; son James Waymouth. Ex. son Robert Waymouth. D. December 9, 1743. R. February 15, 1743. Wit. Baldwin Shepard, John Shepard, James Manson. Book 1737-49, p. 180. Estate appraised by William Tucker, Thomas Massenburg and John Rombough. July 18, 1744. Book 1737-49, p. 186. Account of estate audited by Charles King and Dunn Armistead, May 3, 1748. Book 1737-49, p. 287.

WEYMOUTH, John. Leg.- wife Sarah; daughter Elizabeth; daughter Rebecca; provision for an unborn child. Exs. James Burk and brother-in-law William Allen. D. December 10, 1789. Wit. Thomas Humphlet, James Burk, Mary Wilson Brown. Original Will. Estate appraised by William Gooch, Thomas Minson and Thomas Humphlet. January 27, 1791. Book 1787-1900, p. 5. Estate audited by Charles Jenings, William Smith and Worlich Westwood. James Burk, Ex. October 25, 1798. Book 1787-1800, p. 442.

WEYMOUTH, John. Leg.- wife Ann and her heirs forever. Exs. wife Ann and John Wilson, Jr. D. January 4, 1793. R. September 26, 1793. Wit. John Drewry, William Allen, William Drewry. Ann qualified, security William Allen. Book 1787-1800, p. 134. Original Will.

WEYMOUTH, Rebecca. Leg.- son John; granddaughter Rebecca Yeargain, money which is due me from her father William Yeargain; son William; daughter Rebecca; daughter Hannah; daughter Sarah Weymouth. D. May 4, 1776. Wit. William Bean, Mary Dixon. Original Will.

WEYMOUTH, Robert. Inventory. Indexed. Book 1689-1699.

WEYMOUTH, William. Leg.- wife Rebecca; eldest son John; son James; son William; reversion of the bequest to my wife to my four daughters. Exs. wife and Samuel Rowland. D. December 26,

1766. R. July 23, 1767. Wit. Edward Hurst, King Humphlet, Thomas Davis. Book 1763-71, p. 168. Original Will. Estate appraised by King Humphlet, J. Casey and John Smith. Book 1763-71, p. 285.

WHEELER, Robert. Leg.- wife Jannett and son -----Wheeler. Wife, Extx. D. December 30, 1747. R. June 8, 1748. Wit. W. Wager, Thomas Smith, Mary Bordland. Jannett Wheeler qualified, security, John Proby and William Wager. Book 1737-49, p. 288. Estate appraised by William Tucker, John Nelson and John Jones. August 2, 1748. Book 1737-49, p. 303. Audited by George Wray, Cary Selden, George Walker and William Wager. August 6, 1755. Order Book 1755-60, p. 8.

WHITAKER, Nathaniel, formely of Cana in the State of Massachusetts. Leg.- wife Saralie; son Jonathan; son William Smith Whitaker, my papers in a green large pocket book which I traveled with in England, also all debts due to us in connection of our partnership as physicians in Elizabeth City County; son Nathaniel; daughter Sarah Whitaker. Wife Saralie Whitaker, Extx. D. January 20, 1795. R. September 24, 1795. Wit. Benjamin Bryen, George Hope, Minson T. Proby, John Jenings. Codicil: Mr. George Hope and Mr. Benjamin Bryan to send a copy of my will to my wife in Canan in Massachusetts. My wife to divide estate in her hands at her discretion between Mrs. Sarah Trowbridge, widow and son Nathaniel. Book 1787-1800, p. 251. Original Will.

WHITE, Isaac. Late of the County of Gloucester. Leg.- to wife; son William White. D. September 29, 1767. R. March 22, 1770. Wit. Benjamin Bryan, W. Wager. Joanna White, qualified, security William Wager. Original Will. Book 1763-71, p. 339. Estate appraised by William Latimer, Banister Minson, John Sheppard, Jr. June 28, 1770. Book 1763-71, p. 361. Account estate audited by James Naylor, Banister Minson and Samuel Watts. August 23, 1770. Book 1763-71, p. 379.

WHITE, John. Leg.- wife Jane, with reversion to son David White; daughter Ann White. Wife, Extx. D. December 1, 1750. R. Wit. Richard Taylor, William Hilsman (?), Sarah Jones. Original Will.

WHITEFIELD, Elizabeth. Of the Town of Hampton. Leg.- son Abraham; son William; son Joseph; daughter Mary Anne Whitfield. Mary Geirr is to live in my house until my son Abraham is eighteen. Ex., friend Charles Jenings. D. February 2, 1727. R. May 16, 1728. Wit. Richard Kerkin, Susannah Kerkin, Richard Nusum. Book 1704-30, p. 123. Estate appraised by John Servant, George Waffe, William Loyall. August 21, 1728. Signed Charles Jenings. Book 1704-30, p. 148 & 167. Estate audited by Joseph Banister and Merrit Sweny. July 18, 1739. Book 1737-49, p. 70.

WHITFIELD, John. Estate appraised by Leonard Whiting, James Naylor and Thomas Jones. June 21, 1727. Book 1704-30, p. 85.

WHITFIELD, Thomas. Administration of his estate granted to Ann Whitfield his reliet. 16 of 9ber 1695. Book 1689-1699, p. 156. Leg.- wife Ann one-half of my land from George Bells; other one-half to my son John at sixteen; son Thomas; daughter Mary; daughter Elizabeth. Wife, Extx. D. July 26, 1694. R. November 26, 1694. Wit. Thomas Tyler, Peter Manson, Thomas Poole. Book 1689-1699, p. 194. Estate appraised by Thomas House, John Bushell, Thomas Bailey and Christopher Copeland. November 18, 1695. Book 1689-1699, p. 224.

WHITING, Easter. Leg.- grandson Henry, son of William Minson, decd., land called "Whiting's Landing" adjoining the land of Latimer and Baker; granddaughter Easter Minson, sister of the aforesaid Henry; to granddaughter Easter Whiting Minson, daughter of Thomas Minson; to grandson Banister Minson the land called Purvis land; to my overseer Samuel White; my servants Joseph Wally and Alice Walley their freedom. Ex., son Thomas Minson. D. January 22, 1736/37. R. February --, 1736. Wit. Ed Carrington, Joseph Walley. Original Will.

WHITING, Leonard. Nuncupative will proven by Joseph Banister and Alice Wooly. Thomas Minson qualified as Executor. January 19, 1736. Order Book 1731-47, p. 127. Appraisers of the estate were H. Irwin, John White, Angus McKey. May 18, 1737. Book 1737-49, p. 5. Account of the estate, among items money paid by the Government for the house at the Fort; by the sale of William Minson's estate. Audited by Alexander Hamilton, Robert Armistead, Charles Jenings, Jr. and Thomas Everard. August 17, 1743. Book 1737-49, p. 174.

WHITTICARS, William. Indexed. Book 1689-1699.

WILCOCKS, Captain John, late of Plymouth, now of Accomac intending to go on service against the Indians, made his will in Elizabeth City, Virginia, 10th of September 1622. Proved the last of June 1628. Leg.- wife Temperance; daughter-in-law Grace Burges the legitimate daughter of his said wife; sister Katherine Wilcocks; sister Susanna Wilcocks Water's Gleanings, p. 3.

WILLIAMS, James. Leg.- wife Christiania; son Richard; son James; daughter Sarah Hall; daughter Ann Williams. Exs. wife, Mark Hall, and son Richard Williams. D. February 12, 1790. R. June 24, 1790. Wit. Susanna Kelley, Elizabeth ------, Benjamin Stores. Original Will. Estate appraised by Thomas Fenn, John Sheppard, William Pierce. February 24, 1796. Book 1787-1800, p. 290.

WILLIAMS, John. Leg.- son Robert; daughter Ann the cattle in the hands of John Parson, Sr. and John Parson, Jr.; to daughter Mary when she is seventeen. Exs., William Browne and John Harron. D. April 9, 1692. R. May 18, 1692. Wit. Robert Crooke, John Allen. Book 1689-1699, p. 116 & 117. Estate appraised by John Cotten and John Allen. June 5, 1692. Book 1689-1699, p. 129.

WILLIAMS, John. Will proved by Thomas Cook and Thomas Read. Anne Read, Extx., qualified. February 21, 1732. Order Book 1731-47, p. 47.

WILLIAMS, John. Leg.- wife Nancy; daughter Mary; my lot next to Mr. George Massenburg to be sold to pay my debts. Exs., wife and Captain Edward Ballard. D. August 30, 1797. R. October 25, 1798. Wit. Richard W. Hurst, John Britain, Sarah Barron. Book 1787-1800, p. 441. Original Will.

WILLIAMS, Mary. Widow. Leg.- cousin John Beane; nephew Joel Dunn. Ex., Joel Dunn. D. October 14, 1741. R. November 19, 1741. Wit. William Westwood, Thomas Jones, John Nelson. Book 1737-49, p. 109.

WILLIAMS, Mathew. Leg.- wife Mary. Wife Extx. D. June 10, 1736. R. June 18, 1739. Wit. John Tabb, David Davidson, Mary Rimes (?). Book 1737-49, p. 69. Original Will.

WILLIAMS, William. Inventory, signed by Francis Mallory, Sub Sheriff. May 23, 1720. Estate appraised by Brian Penne, Richard Nusum and Thomas Batts. June 19, 1720. Mary Bridge's bond as guardian to Ann, orphan of William Williams. Security Brian Penne and Richard Nusum. June 16, 1720. Book 1715-21, p. 265, 282 & 286.

WILLS, Mary,- wife of Mathew Wills, Gent. of Warwick County. Leg.- son John Tabb, Jr.; son Thomas Tabb; daughter Elizabeth King; daughter Rachel Fiveash; daughter Martha Lattimer; grandson Thomas Tabb Wills; to Sarah and Elizabeth Smelt, daughters of my late sister Elizabeth Smelt, decd. Exs., son John Tabb, daughter Elizabeth King and Mr. William Lattimer. D. February 9, 1758. R. June 3, 1766. Wit. Thomas Tabb, Francis Parker, H. King. James Westwood qualified as having married Elizabeth King, security, William Westwood, Sr., William Latimer. Book 1763-71, p. 78.

WILSON, Ann. Leg.- granddaughter Elizabeth Bean; granddaughter Martha Bean; grandson John Bean; grandson James Bean. Ex. John Skinner. D. March 13, 1786. R. April 28, 1791. Wit. James Bullock, Mary Bullock, John Skinner. John Bean qualified. Book 1787-1800, p. 20. Original Will. Estate appraised by Thomas Minson, John Skinner, Jr., Thomas Humphlett. July 26, 1792. Book 1787-1800, p. 87.

WILSON, Dorothy. Estate appraised by Peter Manson, John Yergin and John Massenburg. July 20, 1738. Book 1737-49, p. 54.

WILSON, John, Jr. EState appraised by John Banes, John Wilson and John Allen. 1795. R. February 24, 1796. Book 1787-18--, p. 291.

WILSON, Mary. Leg.- daughter Ann Wooten; granddaughter Ann Wooten; daughter Mary Watts; grandson Thomas Watts; grandson Samuel Watts, reversion to either son or daughter Mary Watts may have; grandson Thomas Wooten; grandson John Wooten; son Thomas Wilson; grandson Thomas Wilson Exs. Thomas Wooten and Thomas Watts. D. January 31, 1755. Wit. --------- Baylis, -------- Bushell. Original Will. Will proved by Thomas Baylis and Thomas Baylis, Jr. Thomas Wooten qualified, security William Wager and James Wallace. D. February 7, 1758. Order Book 1755-60, p. 164.

WILSON, Thomas. Leg.- son Thomas; to wife, reversion to two daughters. Exs. wife and son Thomas Wilson. D. May 15, 1740. R. July 15, 1741. Wit. Thomas Davis, Mary Dun, Thomas Wilson. Probation granted Mary Wilson. Book 1737-49, p. 105. Estate appraised by John Dunn, Thomas Minson, John Webb. November 19, 1741. Book 1737-49, p. 107.

WILSON, Colonel William. Died testate August 20, 1713. Book 1736-70, Ejectments, p. 19.

WILSON, (Willson) William, Sr. Leg.- son William; son John; daughter Frances Skinner; daughter Martha; daughter Jane; son Edward. Ex. son Edward Wilson. D. April 11, 1720. R. May 17, 1721. Wit. Jacob Face, George Pain, Mary Pain. Book 1715-21, p. 287. Edward Wilson qualified, security John King and Emanuel Alkin. January 18, 1721. Book 1721-23, p. 39 & 48.

WINN, Thomas. Administration of estate granted to Sarah Winn. Security, William Hatchell and Henry ------. June 21, 1727. Order Book 1723-29, p.   Estate appraised by Thomas Allen and Philip Williams. Book 1704-30, p. 103.

WINTERTON, John. Leg.- son William; reversion to son John; daughter Elizabeth; daughter Rebecca. Wife Extx. D. July 5, 1694. R. July 26, 1694. Wit. Sidwell Minson, Charles Jones, John Minson. Book 1689-1699, p. 193. Probation granted to Joseph Harris in right of Elinor his wife. Book 1689-1699, p. 156.

WOOD, John. Leg.- wife Hannah; son Bennett; daughter Martha; son Robert; son James; son William; son John Wood. Exs. sons John and Bennett Wood. D. January 30, 1799. R. September 26, 1799. Wit. John Drewry, Sally Wilson. Book 1787-1800, p. 487. Original Will.

WOOD, Mary. Leg.- granddaughter Mary Wilson Brown; granddaughter Elizabeth Brown; grandson John Allen; grandson Wilson Saunders; son-in-law John Allen; daughter Judith Saunders; son William Wood. Ex. son-in-law John Allen. D. September 24, 1784. R. January 27, 1785. Wit. Mary Armistead, Ann Armistead, William Armistead. Original Will.

WOOD, William. Ordered Booth Armistead, Thomas Watts, Josiah Massenburg and Thomas Smith to audit the estate. September 4, 1759. Order Book 1755-60, p. 243. Book 1758-64, p. 92.

WOODWORTH, Isaac. Account of estate, examined by Cary Selden and William Wager. Thomas Dixon, Administrator. March 3, 1767. Book 1763-71, p. 118.

Wootten and Wooten

WOOTTEN, Thomas. Leg.- son Thomas; son William; daughter Ann Trigg; son Benjamin land bought of Mr. William Latimer; wife Ann, reversion of bequest to my youngest son John. Exs. wife and Commodore James Barron. D. September 24, 1784. R. October 28, 1790. Wit. John Perry, John Skinner, William King. October 27, 1791. Benjamin Wootten relinquished his right of administration. Miles King qualified, security Johnson Tabb. Original Will. Book 1787-1800, p. 48.

WRAY, George. Leg.- wife Hellen; son Jacob; houses in England in Poplar Nove, London, also lots adjoining Mr. Charles Jenings; son George lots bought of Mr. Charles Sweny, adjoining Mr. Archer Bolling; daughter Ann Stith; son James land in Appomatox bought of Captain Taylor; son Keith. Exs. wife, son Jacob, son George and daughter Ann Stith. D. May 1, 1750. R. May 2, 1758. Wit. Will Tucker, Morris Jones, Benjamin McDowell. Original Will. Administration granted to Jacob and George Wray, security William Young and John Jones. Estate appraised by James Glasford, James Westwood, Abram Maer, Yavid Curle, Henry King, Alexander Rhonnald. May 2, 1758. Order Book 1755-60, p. 178.

WRAY, Jacob. Leg.- son George Wray; son John Ashton Wray; to Mrs. Charles Stuart; granddaughter Elizabeth Stuart; granddaughter Helen Wray Stuart; grandson Jacob Wray Stuart; granddaughter Nancy Stuart; to John A. Stuart; granddaughter Mary Ann Wray. D. February 2, 1797. R. November 29, 1798. Wit. George Booker, Thomas Jones, John L. Westwood. Codicil states that son John S. Wray has died. Ex. son George Wray. Book 1787-1800, p. 519. Original Will.

WYTHE, Thomas, Sr. Leg.- grandson Thomas Wythe land which I bought of Mr. Sweny; son John Tomer; granddaughter Ann Wythe;

on Thomas Wythe; to Elizabeth Russell and Elizabeth Savory, if they serve out their time; to Mr. Crook; to Ga---- Rouse; to my loving wife. Exs. son Thomas and grandson Thomas Wythe. Overseers, Mr. Armiger Wade and John Tomer. D. December 14, 1693. March 19, 1693/94. Wit. John Bean, Jr., John Cheryton, Francis Kuibreton (?). Book 1689-1699, p. 165.

WYTHE, Thomas. Leg.- son Thomas at sixteen; loving brother John Tomer; daughter Ann; wife Ann after the decease of my Mother; Godson Francis Mallory; Godson John Tomer; Godson William Wilson. Wife Ann, Extx. Overseers, Mr. Armiger Wade and Mr. John Tomer. D. March 10, 1693/94. R. September 18, 1694. Wit. Robert Crooke, Hugh Rosse, John Allen. Book 1689-1699, p. 163. Appraisers for the widow, Captain Anthony Armistead and William Armistead, for the orphans, Mathew Watts and Robert Crooke. Order Book 1689-1699, p. 45. Probation granted Ann Wythe on the estate of Thomas Wythe, Jr. Security, Captain Anthony Armistead and Captain William Armistead. September 18, 1694. Book 1689-1699, p. 155.

WYTHE, Thomas. Leg.- wife Margaret my slaves except those which are hired to Robert Ballard of York County; son Thomas; son George; daughter Ann; (all children under 18); my nephew Mathew Ballard; brother James Wallace; mother Ann Wallace; debts due Cole Digges and Major Lightfoot to be paid. D. November 3, 1728. R. October 15, 1729. Wit. John Tabb, Sarah Walker, Abraham George. Book 1704-30, p. 188.

WYTHE, Thomas. Leg.- the land I bought of George Picket and Frances to my brother George to repay the debt I owe him; slaves to be divided between my wife and Fanny Sweny, my wife to have the use of Uphan Sweny's part during her natural life. D. May 2, 1754. R. January 7, 1755. George Wythe, Esq., brother and heir-at-law to said Thomas Wythe, qualified, security Jacob Walker. Original Will.

YANCEY, Archelaus. Leg.- wife Mary. Exs. Thomas Fenn and William Pierce. D. February 2, 1795. R. June 25, 1795. Wit. William Pierce, John McHollon, John B. Saubot. Book 1787-1800, p. 225. Original Will. Estate appraised by William Latimer, Sr., William Latimer, Jr., John Shepherd. September 24, 1795. Book 1787-1800, p. 260 & 496. Account estate, audited by John Nicholson, John Shepard, William King. October 24, 1799. Book 1787-1800, p. 507.

YANCEY, Nathan. Leg.- nephew Nathan, son of John Yancey and his wife Elizabeth, reversion to Joel, son of my brother Joel Yancey; reversion of the aforesaid bequests in case my nephews die without heirs to the inhabitants of the southside of Back River the plantations Greenland and Fox Hill for benefit and education of poor children, no children of Baptist parents to be allowed and none but those of the Protestant Episcopal Church; to Martha Elliott the money due from Elizabeth Mingham decd. Exs. Colonel John Cary and Joseph Cooper, who are also to be guardians to nephew Nathan Yancey. D. November 19, 1789. Wit. Thomas Watts, William Hunt. Codicil: I desire my brother John Yancey and his wife come to live on my plantation during their lives. March 15, 1790. R. April 27, 1790. Wit. Arthur Henderson, Joseph Cooper. John Yancey qualified, security Archelus Young. Original Will.

Yeargain and Yergin

YEARGAIN, John. Leg.- wife Katherine; daughter Mary; daughter Judith; son William. Wife, Extx. D. November 1, 1770. R.

R. March 28, 1771. Wit. William Armistead, Penuel Russell, Penuel Sands. Katherine Yeargain qualified, security William Armistead. Book 1763-71, p. 426. Original Will.

YERGIN, John. Estate appraised by William Merritt, Alexander Carver, Armistead King. Signed, Mary Yergin. September 17, 1745. Book 1737-49, p. 208.

YEO, George. Leg.- cousin George Arnold of the Kingdom of England and Merchant in London all my estate in England; cousin John Selden; cousin Elizabeth Selden; to Joseph the son of cousin John Selden; to Elizabeth the daughter of cousin John Selden; to Robert Brough, son of William Brough, decd.; if cousin Arnold thinks proper to divide my wife's clothes between her children and grandchildren; to my wife's granddaughter Agnes Howard; to her granddaughter Mary Douglas; remainder of wife's clothes to her daughter Grace Selden. Exs. cousin George Arnold of England and cousin John Selden of Virginia. D. March 15, 1742. R. April 20, 1743. Wit. Charles Jenings, John Webb, George Cooper. Book 1737-49, p. 182.

YEO, Leonard. Of Back River. Leg.- wife Mary whole estate. Wife Extx. D. July 8, 1690. R. November 18, 1690. Wit. George Cooper, William Malory, Richard Parker. Book 1689-1699, p. 113.

YOUNG, Gerard. Leg.- son William; to George Ware the land on which he now lives; daughter Margaret; after debts are paid my estate to be divided between my son William, son Gerard, daughter Mary Jegits, Martha Ware, Ann Morgan and Margaret Young. Exs. son William and Guardian Jegits. D. April 17, 1765. R. July 2, 1765. Wit. William Mallory, George Jarvis, Simon Stuckey. Book 1763-71, p. 53. Estate appraised by Robert Sandefur, Edward Armistead, Lockey Collier. September 3, 1764. Book 1763-71, p. 65. Account of estate audited by C. Clausel, Locky Collier and W. Reade. January 29, 1768. Book 1763-71, p. 185.

YOUNG, John. Estate appraised by William Smelt, Francis Mallory and Samuel Tompkins. June 17, 1741. Dower allotted the widow Ann Young. Audited by John Lowry, William Parsons and William Allen. July 17, 1745. Book 1737-49, p. 104 & 207.

———— o ————

Elizabeth City County Suits.

(William and Mary College Quarterly, Vol. 20. Second Series, pages 547-553.)

Armistead vs. Sweny and wife Ex'rs of N. Curle.

Curle, Nicholas, of Elizabeth City County, died with a will. Seized of considerable estate including slaves, goods, chattels, ready money and outstanding debts. Survived by children (who are not named) and by his widow Jane who married James Rickets who wasted the estate and thirdly a Mr. Sweney, of whom Samuel Sweny purchased slaves. Nicholas Curle's Executors were George Walker, John Curle and Harry Jenkins. Their securities were George Walker, Edmund Keary (?), Joshua Curle and John Smith.

Doe Lessee of Myhill against Myhill.

Myhill, Edward died with a will. (See will which refers to wife leaving him and that he is not the father of the child, which she now has.) Stated that after the death of testator she married Mallory. Suit in reference to land devised daughter Elizabeth who died without issue, with reversion to Edward the son of Lockey Myhill and to Joshua Myhill and his own right heirs.

Denn, (Dunn ?) vs. Smith.

Powell, -------- of Elizabeth City County, died with a will. Devised land to Mary, died in 1680, wife of Ephraim Thomas, died in 1690. They conveyed the same in deed dated 0 April 1675 to Owen Davis in fee. Ephraim Thomas and his wife Mary had issue two daughters:

1. Elizabeth, who was two years old when her mother died, married at the age of 18, Giles Dewberry. Both died on the same day in December 1716, leaving issue, two sons:
   1. Giles Dewberry, died without issue in 1719, age 21.
   2. Thomas Dewberry, surviving son and heir, being about 22 years of age.
2. Mary, six months of age when her mother died, married at the age of 17, Anthony Simons, who died two years afterwards. She married secondly in 1703, John Roberts, who died in 1710. She died in 1719 leaving issue, son
   1. John Roberts.

Sweny vs. Dandridge.

Roscow, Wilson died with a will dated 26 August 1713. Possessed of considerable estate. Survived by his widow, now the wife of Dandridge. Testator provided a legacy for his Godson Pasco Curle when he should arrive at the age of 21 years. Curle died under age.

Dunn and Als against Wythe.

Simmonds, Samuel, died with a will. Survived by his widow, who did not remarry, and is deceased. Legacies to the children of Daniel Dunn and children of Matthew Noblin. The question in this suit was whether Simmond's estate should go to Dunn's and Noblin's children by force of the devisee, or as next of kin, or to the wife's Executor. Oct. Court, 1738.

Tucker etc. vs. Tucker's Executors.

Tucker, ----- died with a will. "Devised estate to his nephews: Robert Tucker, John Tucker, John Cooke, Robert Cooke and to Mr. Jacob Walker's four children, whose mother, the testator's niece is now deceased." April Court 1740.

Will of William Tucker, Member of the House of Burgesses from Elizabeth City County, 1619-1625.

TUCKER, William of the City of London (endorsed St. Dunstans in the East) Esq. now bound for the Kingdom of Ireland. Oct. 12, 1642. Proved Feb. 17, 1643/44. To wife Frances. Remainder of my estate in these parts to my three children, viz.-sonne William; sonne Thomas and daughter Mary Tucker. If daughter deceased before she is twenty-one or married reversion to my sonnes William and Thomas Tucker. If all of my children die to the children of brother Thomas Tucker then living. If wife die before my return from Ireland, then whole estate to my three children. Overseers: brother Edmund Smythe, Esq.; brother Maurice Thompson, Merchant; brother Elias Roberts, Merchant and cousin Mr. Thomas Dawney, Citizen and Merchant of London. For my land in Virginia, I bequeath unto my son William Tucker to enjoy to him and his heirs forever, which is for my adventure of Fiftie pounds as per letters of Adventure may appear. I have transported divers servants thither which for every servant I am to have fifty acres of land, for my first dividend, which will amount unto 3000 acres, 3000 acres for the second dividend and 3000 acres for the third, which land may prove beneficial in time to my heire. The record bookes in Virginia will produce the number of men I have transported thither. Wit. John Bodington, Letitia Atkinson. Seal, a griffin sejent. Proved by oath of the relict. Virginia Historical Magazine, Volume 22, page 267.

GENEALOGICAL AND HISTORICAL ITEMS

Hotten's Original Lists of Persons of Quality. . . Who Went From Great Britain to the American Plantations, 1600-1700.

A List of Names of the Living in Virginia. Febr. 16, 1623.

At Elizabeth Cittye. Living.

Cap. Isacke Whittakers
Mary Whittakers
Charles Atkinson
Charles Calthrop
John Lankfeild
Bridg's Freeman
Nicholas Wese-l
Edward Loyd
Thomas North
Anthony Middleton
Richard Popely
Thomas Harding
William Joy
Raph Osborne
Edward Barnes
Thomas Thorngood
Ann Attkinson
Lankfield
Medclalfe
George Nuce
Elizabeth Whittakers
George Roads
Edward Johnson
William Fouller
Reinold Goodwyn
James Larmount
John Jackson
vid's Johnson
vid's Fowler
2 french men
George Medcalfe
Walter Ely
Thomas Lane
Barthelmew Hopkins
John Jefferson
Robert Thresher
John Rowes
Mr. Yates
Robert Goodman
ux Ely
infans Ely
Cap Rawleigh Crashaw
Robert Wright
James Sleight
John Welchman
John More
Henry Potter
Mr. Roswell
William Gawntlett
Osborne Smith
ux More
ux Wright
ux Wright
filia Wright
Thomas Dowse
Samwell Bennett
William Browne
William Allen
Lewis Welchman
Robert More
Mrs. Dowse
ux Bennett
pue (Bennett
(Bennett

At Bucke Row

Thomas Flint
John Hampton
Richard Peirsby
William Rookins
Rowland Williams
Steven Dixon
Thomas Risby
Henry Wheeler
James Brooks
Samwell Kennell
John Carning
Thomas Neares
Robert Salvadge
William Barry
Joseph Hatfield
Edward Marshall
Ambrose Griffith
Petter Arrundell
Anthony Bonall) french
La Gaurd) men
James Bonall
John Arrundell
John Hanie (or Haine)
Nich: Row
Richard Althrop
John Loyd
ux Hame
ux Hampton
Elizabeth Arrundell
Margreat Arrundell

Sheppard

John Powell
John Wooley
Cathren Powell
John Bradston
Franc's Pitts
Gilbert Whitfield

Peter Hereford
Thomas Faulkner
Esaw De La Ware
William Cornie
Thomas Curtise
Robert Brittaine
Roger Walker
Henry Kersley
Edward Morgaine
Anthony Ebsworth
Elinor Harris
Thomas Addison
William Longe
William Smith
William Pinsen
Agnes Ebsworth

Cap Wm. Tucker
Cap Nich: Marteaw
Leftennt Ed: Barkly
Daniell Tanner
John Morris
Georg Thomson
Paule Thomson
William Thomson
Pasta Champin
Stephen Shere
Jeffery Hall
Rich: Jones
William Hutchinson
Richard Apleton
Thomas Evans
Weston Browne
Robert Mounday
Steven Cvlloe
Raph Adams
Thomas Phillips
Francis Barrett
Mary Tucker
Jane Brakley
Elizabeth Higgins
Mary Mounday
Choupouke an Indian
Leftennt Lupo
Phillip Lupo
Bartholmew Wethersby
Henry Draper
Joseph Haman
Elizabeth Lupo
Albiano Wethersly
Henry Draper
Joseph Haman
Elizabeth Lupo
Albiano Wethersly
John Laydon
Ann Laydon
Virginia Laydon
Alice Laydon
Katherne Laydon
William Evans
William Julian
William Kemp
Richard With'e (Withere)
John Jornall

Walter Mason
Sara Julian
Sara Gouldocke
John Salter
William Coale
Jereny Dickenson
Lawrence Peele
John Evans
Marke Evans
George Evans
John Downeman
Elizabeth Downeman
William Baldwin
John Sibsey
William Clarke
Rice Griffine
Joseph Mosley
Anthony) negres
Issabella)
Robert Smith
John Cheesman
Thomas Cheesman
Edward Cheesman
Petter Dickson
John Baynan
Robert Sweet
John Parrett
William Fouks
John Glackson
John Hill
William Morten
William Clarke
Edward Stockdell
Elizabeth Baynam
George Davies
Elizabeth Davies
Ann Harrison
John Curtise
John Walton
Edward Aston
Toby Hurt
Cornelius May
Elizabeth May
Henry May, child
Thomas Willowbey
Oliuer Jenkinson
John Chandeler
Nicholas Davies
Jone Jenkins
Mary Jenkins
Henry Gouldwell
Henry Prichard
Henry Barber
Ann Barber
John Hutton
Elizabeth Hutton
Thomas Baldwin
John Billiard
Reynold Booth
Mary
Elizabeth Booth, child
Cap. Tho. Davies
John Davies
Thomas Huges
William Kildridge

Alexander Mountney
Edward Bryan
Persivall Ibotson
John Penrice
Robert Locke
Elizabeth Ibotson
Ann Ibotson
Edward Hill
Thomas Best
Hanna Hill
Elizabeth Hill
Robert Salford
John Salford
Philip Chapman
Thomas Parter
Mary Salford
Francis Chamberlin
William Hill
William Harris
William Worlidge
John Forth
Thomas Spilman
Rebecca Chamberlin
Alice Harris
Pharow Phlinton
Arthur Smith
Hugh Hall
Robert Sabin
John Cooker
Hugh Dicken
William Gayne
Richard Mintren Junior
Joan Flinton
Elizabeth Flinton
Rebecca Coubber
Richard Mintren Senior
John Frye
William Brooks
Sibile Brooks
William Brooks
Thomas Crispe
Richard Packe
Miles Prichett
Thomas Bodby
Margery Prichett
Jone Goody
Jone Grindry
John Juiman
Mary Grindy, child
John Waine
Ann Waine
Mary Ackland
George Ackland
John Harlow
William Capp's
Edward Watters
Paule Harwood
Nich. Browne
Adam Throughood
Richard East
Stephen Read
Grace Watters
William Watters
William Ganey
Henry Ganey
John Robinson
Robert Browne
Thomas Parrish
Edmond Spalden
Roger Farbracke
Theoder Jones
William Baldwin
Luke Aden
Anna Gany
Anna Gany fillia
Elizabeth Pope
Rebecca Hatch
Thomasin Loxmore
Thomas Garnett
Elizabeth Garnett
Sussan Garnett
Frances Michell
Jonas Stockton
Thimothee Stockton
William Cooke
Richard Boulten
Frances Hill
John Jackson
Richard Davies
Ann Cooke
Dictras Chrismus
Thomas Hill
Arthur Davies
William Newcome
Elizabeth Chrismus
Joane Davies
Thomas Hethersall
William Douglas
Thomas Douthorn
Elizabeth Douthorn
Samwell Douthorn a bo(y)
Thomas an Indian
John Hazard
Joane Hazard
Henry
Frances Mason
Michaell Wilcocks
Mr. Keth, mister
John Bush
John Coop (Cooper)
Jonadab Illett
John Barnaby
John Seawar
Robert Newman
William Parker
Thomas Snapp
Clement Evans
Thomas Spilman
Thomas Parrish

A list of the names of the dead in Virginia since April last. Feb. 16, 1623.

At Elizabeth Cittie

Charle Marshall
William Hopkicke
Dorithie Parkinson

William Robertts
John Farrar
Martin Cuffe
Thomas Hall
Thomas Smith
Christoph' Robertts
Thomas Browne
Henry Fearne
Thomas Parkins
Mr. Hussy
James Collis
Raph Rockly
William Geales
George Jones
Andrew Allinson
William Downes
Richard Gillett
Goodwife Nonn (or Noun)
Hugo Smale
Thomas Wintersall
John Wright
James Fenton
Cisely, a maid
John Gavett
James)
John) Irishmen

Jocky Armestronge
Wolston Pelsant
Sampson Pelsant
Cathrin Capps
William Elbridg
John Sanderson
John Benbricke
John Baker, kild
William Lupo
Timothy Burley
Margery Frisle
Henry West
Jasper Tayler
Brigett Searle
Anthony Andrew
Edmond Cartter
Thomas
William Gauntlett
Gilbert ______ kild
Christo. Welchman
John Hilliard
Gregory Hilliard
John Hilliard

William Richards
Elizabeth, a maid
Cap. Hitchcocke
Thomas Keninston
Cap. Lincolne
Chad. Gulstons
ux Gulstons
infans Gulstons
George Cooke
Richard Goodchild
Chrismus his child
Elizabeth Mason
Symon With
Whitney Guy
Thomas Brodbanke
William Burnhouse
John Sparks
Robert Morgaine
John Locke
William Thompson
Thomas Fulham
Cutberd Brooks
Innocent Poore
Edward Dupper
Elizabeth Davies
Thomas Buwen
Ann Barber
William Lucott
Nicholas ------ kild
Henry Bridges
Henry Payton
Richard Griffin
Raphe Harrison
Samwell Harvie
John Box
Benianino Box
Thomas, a servant
Frances Chamberline
Bridgett Dameron
Isarell Knowles
Edward Bendige
William Davies
John Phillips
Daniell Sauewell

William Jones
Robert Balls wife
Robert Leauer
Huch Nichcott
John Knight

Muster
of the
Inhabitants in Virginia
1624/5

Elizabeth Cittie
Capt. William Tucker his Muster

Capt. William Tucker, aged 36, in the Mary and James 1610
Mrs. Mary Tucker aged 26, in the George 1623
Elizabeth Tucker borne in Virginia in August

George Tomson aged 17)
Paule Tomson aged 14)- in the George 1623
William Thomson aged 11)
Pascoe Champion aged 23)
Strenght Sheere aged 23)- in the Elloner 1621
Thomas Evand's aged 23)
Stephen Collowe aged 23)- in the George 1623
Robart Munday aged 18)
Mathewe Robinsonn aged 24 in the Greate Hopewll 1623
Richard Appleton aged 19 in the James 1622
John Morris aged 24 in the Bona Nova 1619
Mary Morris aged 22 in the George 1623
William Hutchinson aged 21 in the Diana 1618
Peeter Porter aged 20 in the Tyger 1621
William Crawshaw an Indean Baptised
Antoney, Negro: Isabell, Negro: and William their child

John Downeman his Muster

John Downeman aged 33 in the John and Francis 1611
Elzabeth Downeman aged 22 in the Warwicke 1621
Moyses Stones aged 16 in the Bone Bes 1623

John Laydon his Muster

John Laydon aged 44 in the Susan 1606
Anne Laydon aged 30 in the Mary Marett 1608
Virginia Laydon)
Alce Laydon)
Katherin Laydon) borne in Virginia
Margerett Laydon)

William Cole his Muster

William Cole aged 26 in the Neptune 1618
Francis Cole aged 27 in the Susan 1616
Roger Farbrase aged 26 in the Elzabeth 1621

Miles Prickett and Francis Mitchell their Musters

Miles Prickett aged 36 in the Starr 1610
Francis Mitchall aged 38 in the Neptune 1618
Maudlin Mitchell aged 21 in the Bona Nova 1620
John Mitchell borne in Virginia 1624

Richard Yonge his Muster

Richard Yonge aged 31 in the George 1616
Joane Yonge aged 26 in the Guifte 1618
Joane Yonge aged 2 borne in Virginia
Susan aged 12 in the Swan 1624

Leiueten. Albiano Lupo his Muster

Albiano Lupo aged 40 in the Swan 1610
Wlizabeth Lupo aged 28 in the George 1616
Temperance Lupo aged 4 borne in Virginia
Servants

Henrie Draper aged 14 in the George 1621
Joseph Ham aged 16 in the Warwicke 1621

John Powell his Muster

John Powell aged 29 in the Swallowe 1609
Kathren Powell aged 22 in the Flying Hart 1622
John Powell borne in Virginia
Servant's
Thomas Prater aged 20 in the Marie Providene 1622

Larence Peale his Muster

Larence Peale aged 23 in the Margett and John 1620
William Smith aged 30 in the Jacob 1624

Robert Brittin his Muster

Robert Brittin aged 30 in the Edwin 1618

Mihell Wilcockes and John Slater their Muster

Mihell Wilcockes aged 31 in the Prosporouse 1610
Elzabeth Willcockes aged 23 in the Concord 1621
John Slater aged 22 in the George 1617
Anne Slater aged 17 in the Guyft 1622
Servant's
James Feild aged 20 in the Swan 1624
John Jornall aged 20 in the Ann 1623
Theodore Joones aged 16 in the Margett and John 1620

Joseph Cobb his Muster

Joseph Cobb aged 25 in the Treasoror 1613
Elizabeth Cobb aged 25 in the Bone Bes 1623
John Snowood aged 25

Cornelius May his Muster

Cornelius May aged 25 in the Providence 1616

William Morgan als Broockes his Muster

William Morgan aged 30 in the Starr 1610
William Morgan aged 2 borne in Virginia

Mr. William Julian his Muster

William Julian aged 43 in the Hercules 1609
Sara Julian aged 25 in the Neptune 1618
William Kemp aged 33 in the William and Thomas 1618
Thomas Sully aged 36 in the Sara 1611
Maudlyn Sully aged 30 in the London Marchant 1620
Servant's
Thomas Flower aged 22 in the George 1623
Wyatt Masonn aged 16 in the Ann 1623

Leiuten, Thomas Purfray his Muster

Thomas Purfry aged 43 in the George 1621
Cjristopher Colethorpe aged 18 in the Furtherance 1622
Danniell Tanner aged 40 in the Sampson 1618
Servant's
Henries Feeldes aged 26 in the Jacob 1624
William Bauldwin

John Barnabe his Muster

John Barnabie aged 21 in the London Marchant 1620

John Hazard his Muster

John Hazard aged 40 in the William and Thomas 1618
Servant's
Abraham Pelteare aged 14 in the Swan 1624

Jeremiah Dickinson his Muster

Jeremiah Dickinson aged 26 in the Margett and John 1620
Elizabeth Dickinson aged 38 in the Margett and John 1623

Phillip Lupo his Muster

Phillip Lupo aged 42 in the George 1621

Ensigne Thomas Willoby his Muster

Thomas Willoby aged 23 in the Prosporouse 1610
Servant's
John Chaundler aged 24 in the Hercules 1609
Thomas aged 20 in the Greate Hopewell 1623
Robert Bennett aged 24 in the Jacob 1624
Niccolas Davis aged 13 in the Mariegould 1618

John Hatton his Muster

John Hatton aged 26 in the Trsorer 1613
Oliue Hatton aged 32 in the Abigall 1620

Mr. Cisse Minister his Muster

Mr. George Keth aged 40)
James Whitinge aged 16) - in the George 1617
John Keth aged 11)

Susan Bush her Muster

Susan Bush aged 20 in the George 1617
Sara Spence aged 4 borne in Virginia
Servant's
Clemant Evand's aged 30 in the Edwin 1616
William Parker aged 20 in the Charles 1616
John Seward aged 30 in the Geife 1622

Gilbert Marburie aged 32 in the Southampton 1622
Thomas Killson aged 21 in the Truelove 1623

Capt. Niccolas Martue his Muster
Niccolas Martue aged 33 in the Francis Bonaventure
Peter Eccallowe aged 30 in the Southampton
William Stafford aged 17 in the Futherance

Mr. John Banum and Robert Sweete theire Muster

John Banum aged 54 in the Susan 1616
Elizabeth Banum aged 43 in the Bona Nova 1620
Robart Sweete aged 42 in the Neptune 1618
Servant's
Niccolas Thredder aged 30 in the Katherin 1623
Richard Robinsonn aged 22 in the Bona Nova 1620
John Hill aged 26 in the Bona Nova 1620
William Morton aged 20 in the Margett and John 1620
James Pascell aged 20 in the Warwicke 1621
Robert Draper aged 16 in the Jacob 1624
Sara Gouldinge aged 20 in the Ann 1623

Richard Mintrene his Muster

Richard Mintrene aged 40 in the Margett and John 1620
William Beane aged 25 in the Diana 1618
Edward Mintrone aged 12 in the Margett and John 1620
John Inman aged 26 in the Falcon 1619
William Browne aged 14 in the Southampton 1622

Anthoney Burroos his Muster

John Waine aged 30 in the Neptune 1618
Amyte Waine aged 30 in the Swan 1610
George Ackland aged 7)
Mary Ackland aged 4) borne in Virginia
John Harlow aged 28 in the Sampson 1619
Robart Sabyn aged 30 in the Marget and John 1622
Phillip Chapman aged 23 in the Flying Hart 1621

Mr. Robart Salford his Muster and John Salford

Mr. Robert Salford aged 56 in the John and Francis 1611
John Slaford aged 24 in the George 1616
Mary Salford aged 24 in the Bona Nova 1620
Servant's
William Ellison aged 44 in the Swan 1624
Thomas Faulkner aged 28 in the Mary Providense 1622

Bartholemew Wethersbie and Richard Boulton their Musters

Batholemew Wethersbie aged 30 in the Providence 1616
Dorythie Wethersbie aged 30 in the London Marchant 1620
Richard Boulton aged 28 in the Mary and James 1610
Richard aged 15 in the Swan 1624

John Gundrie his Muster

John Gundrie aged 33 in the Starr 1610

Marie Gundrie aged 20 in the George 1618
John Gundrie aged 2 borne in Virginia

Francis Mason his Muster

Francis Mason aged 40 in the John and Francis 1613
Alice Mason aged 26 in the Margett and John 1622
Francis Mason borne in Virginia
Servant's
William Querke aged 30 in the Marmaduke 1621
Thomas Worthall aged 14 in the Marmaducke 1621
William Stafford aged 16 in the Futherance 1622
Henrie Gany aged 21 in the Dutie 1619
John Robinson aged 21 in the Margett and John 1622

Farrar Flinton his Muster

Farrar Flinton aged 36 in the Elzabeth 1612
Joane Flinton aged 38 in the Elzabeth 1612
William Bentlie aged 36 in the Jacob 1624
Servant's
Arthur Smyth aged 25)
Hugh Hall aged 13)- in the Margett and John 1622
Mathew Hardcastle aged 20 in the Jacob 1624
Henrie Nasfield aged 19 in the Swan 1624

James Sleight and Francis Huff their Muster

Francis Huff aged 20 in the Swan 1624
James Sleight aged 42 in the Tryall 1610

Leiutrn. John Chisman his Muster

John Chisman aged 27 in the Flying Hart 1621
Edward Chisman aged 22 in the Providence 1623

Mr. Thomas Spilman his Muster

Thomas Spilman aged 24 in the George 1616
Hanna Spilman aged 23 in the Bona Nova 1620
Elizabeth Hill borne in Virginia
Servant's
Robart Browne aged 25 in the Mary Gould 1618
Rebecca Browne aged 24 in the Southampton 1623
Thomas Parrish aged 26 in the Charity 1622
John Harris aged 21 in the Jacob 1624

Oliver Jinkins his Muster

Oliver Jinkins aged 30 in the Mary James 1610
Joane Jinkins aged 26 in the George 1617
Allexnad' Jinkins borne in Virginia

Williame Gayne and Robart Newman theire Muster

Robart Newman aged 25 in the Neptune 1618

William Gayne aged 36 in the Bona Nova 1620
John Taylor aged 34 in the Swan 1610
Rebecca Taylor aged 22 in the Margett and John 1623
John Coker aged 20
Richard Packe aged 23 in the Warwicke 1621
Abraham Avelin aged 23)
Arthur Avelin aged 26)-in the Elizabeth 1620

Thomas Godby his Muster

Thomas Godby aged 38 in the Deli'ance 1608
Joane Godby aged 42 in the Flyinge Hart 1621
John Curtis aged 22 in the Flyinge Hart 1621
Christopher Smith aged 23 in the Returne 1624

Mr. Edward Waters his Muster

Edward Waters aged 40 in the Patience 1608
Grace Waters aged 21 in the Diana 1618
William Waters)
Margerett Waters)-borne in Virginia
William Hampton aged 40 in the Bona Nova 1620
Joane Hampton aged 25 in the Abigall 1621
Thomas Lane aged 30 in the Treasorer 1613
Alice Lane aged 24 in the Bona Nova 1620
Thomas Thornebury aged 20 in the George 1616
Servant's
Adam Thorogood aged 18)
Niccolas Browne aged 18)-in the Charles 1621
Paule Harwood aged 20 in the Bona Nova 1622
Stephen Reede aged 17 in the George 1618
Mathias Francisco aged 18 in the Jacob 1624
Robart Penrise aged 12 in the Bona Nova 1620

Capt. Thomas Davis his Muster

Capt Thomas Davis aged 40 in the John and Francis 1623
Thomas Hewes aged 40 in the John and Francis 1623

Mr. Francis Chamberlin his Muster

Francis Chamberlin aged 45 in the Marmaducke 1621
Rebecca Chamberlin aged 37 in the Bona Nova 1622
Francis Chamberlin aged 3 borne in Virginia
Servant's
John Forth aged 16)-in the Bona Nova 1622
William Worlidge aged 18)
Sionell Rowlston aged 30 in the God's Guifte 1623
Richard Burton aged 28 in the Swan 1624

Percivall Ibottson his Muster
Percivall Ibottson aged 24 in the Neptune 1618
Elizabeth Ibottson aged 23 in the Flyinge Hart 1621
John Davis aged 24 in the John and Francis 1623
Servant's
William Greene aged 28 in the Hopewell 1623
Robart Locke aged 18 in the Warwicke 1621

Mr. Daniell Cookins his Muster (Gookins ?)

William Wadsworth aged 26
William Foulke aged 24
Thomas Curtis aged 24
Peeter Sherewood aged 21

Thomas Bouldinge his Muster

Thomas Bouldinge aged 40 in the Swan 1610
William Bouldinge borne in Virginia
William Coxe aged 26 in the Godspeede 1610
Richard Edwards aged 23)
Niccolas Dale aged 20)-in the Jacob 1624

Reynold Booth aged 32 in the Hercules 1609
Elizabeth Booth aged 24 in the Ann 1623
Servant's
George Levett aged 29 in the Bona Nova 1619
Thomas Seywell aged 20 in the Tyger 1623

Thomas Garnett his Muster

Thomas Garnett aged 40 in the Swan 1610
Elizabeth Garnett aged 26 in the Neptune 1618
Susan Garnett aged 3 borne in Virginia
Ambrose Gyffith aged 33 in the Bona Nova 1619
Joyse Gyffith aged 20 in the Jacob 1624

Thomas Dunthorne his Muster

Thomas Dunthorne aged 27 in the Margett and John 1620
Elizabeth Dunthorne aged 38 in the Tryall 1610
Srvant's
William Tomson aged 22)
George Turner aged 27)-in the Swan 1624
George Banckes aged 15)
Thomas an Indian Boaye
Elizabeth Joones aged 30 in the Patience 1609
Sara Joones aged 5 borne in Virginia

Thomas Stepney his Muster

Thomas Stepney aged 35 in the Swan 1610

Mr. Stockton his Muster

Jonas Stockton aged 40 in the Bona Nova 1620
Richard Popeley aged 26)
Richard Davis aged 22)
Walter Barrett aged 26)-in the Bona Nova 1620
Timothey Stockton aged 14)
Servant's
William Duglas aged 16 in the Margett and John 1621
John Watson aged 24 in the Swan 1624

Tobias Hurst his Muster

Tobias Hurst aged 22 in the Treasurer 1618

Mr. William Gany his Muster

William Gany aged 33 in the George 1616
Anna Gany aged 24 in the Bona Nova 1620
Servant's
Anna Gany borne in Virginia
Thomasin Eester aged 26 in the Falcon 1617
Elizabeth Pope aged 8 in the Abbigall 1621
John Wright aged 20)
William Clarke aged 20)
Hather Tomson aged 18)-in the Ambrose 1623
Thomas Savadge aged 18)

Alexander Mountney his Muster

Allexand. Mountney aged 33 in the Mary James 1610
Lenord Mountney aged 21 in the Bona Nova 1620
John Walton aged 28 in the Elzabeth 1621
Bryan Rogers aged 18 in the Elzabeth 1621
John Washborne aged 25 in the Jonathan 1619

A list of the Burialles in Elizabeth Citty 1624

Weston Browne Aprill 20
Richard Wiffe Aprill 26
John Mileman Aprill 28
John Jackson Maye 12
Edward Hill Maye 15
Peeter Maye 16
James More June 24
Mr. Tomson
Phillip Coocke July 8
Thomas Ebes July 12
Mr. Chamberlin's Man July 17
Sibill Morgon July 18
Wethersby August 8
James Chamberlin August 11
Mr. Fenton Minister Sept. 5
William White Septemb. 12
James Chamberlin Septemb. 22
Mary Downeman a child Novemb. 23
John Stamford Septemb. 30
Thomas Davis
Peeter Dickenson
Richard Easte
Thomas Hunter
John Simnell
Henrie Middleton
Sammuell Lambert
John Bush

A Muster of the Inhabitente of Elizabeth Cittie beyond Hampton River. Beinge the Companyes land.

Capt. Francis West his Muster

Capt. Francis West Counseler aged 36 in the Mary Ann Margett 1610
Mrs. Francis West Widdowe in the Supply 1620
Nathaniel West borne in Virginia
Servant's
Joane Fairechild aged 20 in the George 1618
Benjamin Owin aged 18 in the Swan 1623
William Parnell aged 18 in the Southampton 1622
Walter Couper aged 22 in the Neptune 1618
Reinould Godwin aged 30 in the Abigall 1620
John Pedro a Neger aged 30 in the Swan 1623

Capt. John Martin his Muster
Capt John Martin)
Sackford Wetherell aged 21)
John Smith aged 31)- in the Swan 1624
John Howard aged 24)
John Anthonie aged 23)

George Medcalfe his Muster

George Medcalfe aged 46
Sara Medcalfe aged 30 in the Hopewell 1624
Joane a child

Edward Johnson his Muster

Edward Johnson aged 26 in the Abigall 1621
in the Bona Nova 1621
A child borne in Virginia

John Lauckfild his Muster

John Lauckfild aged 24 in the Bona Nova 1621
Alice Lauckfild aged 24 in the Abbigall 1621
Sammuell Kennell aged 30 in the Abigall 1621

William Fowler his Muster

William Fowler aged 30 in the Abigall 1621
Margrett Fowler aged 30 in the Abigall 1621

Walter Ely his Muster

Walter Ely
Elizabeth Ely aged 30 in the Warwicke 1622
Ann Ely borne in Virginia

William Tiler his Muster

William Tiler in the Francis Bonaventure 1620
Elizabeth Tiler in the Francis Bonaventure 1620
Servant's
Robart More aged 50 in the Providence 1622
William Browne aged 26 in the Providence 1622
Robart Todd aged 20 in the Hopewell 1622
Anthonie Burt aged 18 in the Hopewell 1622
Samiell Bennett aged 40 in the Providence 1622
Joane Bennett in the Providence 1622

Thomas Flynt his Muster

Thomas Flynt in the Diana 1618
Thomas Morres aged 21 in the Francis Bona Venture 1620
Henrie Wheeler aged 20 in the Tryall 1620
John Brocke aged 19 in the Bona Nova 1619
James Brookes aged 19 in the Jonathan 1619
Robert Savadge aged 18 in the Elzabeth 1621

John Ward his Muster

John Ward in the Elzabeth 1621
Adam Rimwell aged 24 in the Bona Nova 1619
Christopher Wynwill aged 26 in the Bona Nova 1619
Oliuer Jenkins aged 40
Joane Jenkins, a little child
Henrie Potter aged 50

Ann Potter in the London Marchant
Robart Goodman aged 24 in the Bona Nova 1619

Gregorie Dorie his Muster

Gregorie Dorie aged 36 in the Bona Nova 1620
his wife and a littell child borne in Virginia

John More his Muster

John More aged 36 in the Bona Nova in 1620
Elizabeth More in the Abigall 1622

Sargent William Barry his Muster

William Barry in the Bona Nova 1619
Servant's
Richard Frisbie aged 34 in the Jonathan 1619
William Rookines aged 26 in the Bona Nova 1619
Joseph Hattfild aged 24 in the Bona Nova 1619
Cutbert Seirson aged 22 in the Bona Nova 1619
John Gibbes aged 24 in the Abigall 1621
Francis Hill aged 22 in the Bona Nova 1619
John Vaghan aged 23 in the Bona Nova 1619
Edward Marshall aged 26 in the Abigall 1621
William Joyce aged 26 in the Abigall 1621
William Evand's aged 23 in the Bona Nova 1619
Ralph Osborne aged 22 in the Bona Nova 1619
Morris Stanley aged 26 in the Hopewell 1624
Niccolas Weasoll aged 28 in the Abigall 1621
Stephen Dickson aged 25 in the Bona Nova 1619
Thomas Calder aged 24 in the Bona Nova 1619

William Hampter his Muster

William Hampton age 34 in the Bona Nova 1621
Joane Hampton
John Arndell age 22 in the Abigall 1621

Anthonie Bonall his Muster

Anthonie Bonall age 42)
Elias Legardo age 38)-in the Abigall 1621
Robart Wright age 45 in the Swan 1608
Joane Wright and two children borne in Virginia
William Binsley age 18 in the Jacob 1624
Robart Godwin age 19 in the Swan 1624
Virbritt)
Oble Hero) two Frenchmen in the Abigall 1622

Robart Thrasher his Muster

Robart Thrasher age 22 in the Bona Nova 1620
Roland Williames age 20 in the Jonathan 1623
Servant
John Sacker age 20 in the Marget and John 1623

John Haney age 27 in the Margett and John 1621
Elizabeth Hanie in the Abigall 1622
Nicholas Rowe in the Elzabeth 1621
Mary Rowe in the London Marchant 1620
Servant's
Thomas Moreland)
Ralph Hoode) age 19 in the Abigall 1621

A list of Dead beyond Hampton River

of Mr. Bonales Servant -----1
Mr. Dowse his men ----------2
Mr. Peeter Arndell

The Corporacon of Elizabeth Cittie 1626

Newports Newes ------------	1300	Acres	planted)
The Gleab Land ------------	100		planted)
Mr. Keyth -----------------	100		planted)
Thomas Taylor -------------	50		planted)by pattent
John Powell ---------------	150		planted)
Capt. Wm. Tucker ----------	150		.......)
Richard Boulton -----------	50		claimed & planted
John Salford --------------	50		planted)
Robert Salford ------------	100		planted)
Robert Salford ------------	100		)
Miles Prickett ------------	150		planted)
John Bush -----------------	300	Acres	planted)
William Julian ------------	150		planted)
Leift. Lupo ---------------	350		planted)
Elizabeth Lupo ------------	50		)
Thomas Spilman ------------	50		planted)by pattent
Edward Hill ---------------	100		planted)
Alexander Mountney --------	100		planted)
William Cole --------------	50		planted)
William Brooks ------------	100		planted)
The Gleab Land ------------	100		planted
Eliza Donthrne ------------	100		planted)
William Gany --------------	200		planted)by pattent
William Capps divident planted			
William Landsdell ---------	100		planted)
Mr. Wm. Claybourne --------	150		planted)
John Gunnery --------------	150		planted)
Mary Bouldin --------------	100		planted)
Thomas Bouldin ------------	200		planted)
Mr. Petter Arundell -------	200		)
Bartholmew Hoskins --------	100		)
Capt Raughly Croshaw) between Fox Hill and) Pemonkey ----------)	500		)))
Tho. Willowsaby about 2) miles within the mouth) of Pemonkey River	200	Acres	by order of Court

On the Easterly side of Southampton River, their are 3000 Acres, belonging to the Company at Elizabeth Cittie, planted and 1500 Acres Comon Land.

On ye South Side of the maine River against Elizabeth Cittie

Thomas Willoughbye -----	100 Acres	)
Thomas Chapman ---------	100	)
Thomas Brewood ---------	200	)
John Downman -----------	100	)by pattent
Capt. William Tucker ---	650	)
John Sipsey ------------	250	)
Leift. Jo. Cheesman ----	200	)

ELIZABETH CITY COUNTY PATENTS

Issued During the Royal Government

(Copied from the Index of Patents to be found in the State Land Office, Richmond, Virginia.)

John Taylor- Sept. 20, 1624. 50 Acres. (This patent was renewed in Court the 28th of November 1633, see Memo. at foot of the record). Corporation of Elizabeth City abutting Eastward upon the land of John Powell and Westward upon a swamp etc. from the land of Francis Michaell. Land Book 1, p. 26.

John Powell. Sept. 20, 1624. 150 Acres within the Corp. of Elizabeth City, abutting Eastward upon a green swamp, which parteth it from the land of Capt. William Tucker. Land Book 1, p. 27.

Capt. William Tucker. Sept. 20, 1624. 150 Acres within the Corp. of Elizabeth City abutting Eastward upon the land of Richard Boulton. Land Book 1, p. 29.

John Bush. Dec. 1, 1624. 300 Acres, in the Corp. of Elizabeth City, 100 Acres of same, abutting Eastward upon the land of Lt. Albina Lupo and Westward upon the land of William Julian. Land Book 1, p. 31.

William Julian. Sept. 20, 1624. 150 Acres within the Corp. of Elizabeth City, Eastward upon the land of John Bush and Westward upon another parcell of the said John Bush. Land Book 1, p. 32.

Lt. Albiana Lupo. Sept. 1, 1624. 350 Acres in the Corp of Elizabeth City, abutting Eastward upon the mouth of the creek by the old pines. Land Book 1, p. 33.

Elizabeth Lupo, the wife of Albiano Lupo in the Corp of Elizabeth City. Sept. 20, 1624. 50 Acres abutting Southward upon the Broad Creek, by the old pines. Land Book 1, p. 34.

Thomas Spilman. Dec. 1, 1624. 50 Acres in the Corp. of Elizabeth City upon the Broad Creek by the old pines which parteth it from the land of Lt. Albiana Lupo. Land Book 1, p. 35.

Alexander Mountney. Sept. 20, 1624. 100 Acres in the Corp. of Elizabeth City, butting Westward on the land of Edward Hill, Eastward upon the dividend of William Cole, now in the tenure and possession of Capt. Thomas Davis. Land Book 1, p. 37.

Elizabeth Dunthorne. Dec. 20, 1624. 100 Acres, Northward upon a creek, which divideth the same from the land of William Gainye, Southward etc. upon a Sandy Point lying out of the mouth of Southampton River in the Corp. of Elizabeth City. Land Book 1, p. 38.

William Gainye. Jan. 12, 1624. 200 Acres Eastward on the harbour of Southampton River, Westward upon the main land unto the head of Church Creek in the Corp. of Elizabeth City. Land Book 1, p. 39.

William Lansden. June 3, 1624. 100 Acres on the West side of Southampton River, within the Corp. of Elizabeth City thence and Northward upon a small creek, which divideth it from the land of William Clayborne. Land Book 1, p. 40.

William Clayborne of James City. June 3, 1624. 150 Acres on the West side of Southampton River within the Corp. of Elizabeth City, 50 Acres of the same abutting Northward on the land of John Gunnery and Southward etc. until a small creek, which parteth it from the land of William Lansden, the other 100 Acres adjoining on the other side of the said William Lansden's land. Land Book 1, p. 41.

Mary Bouldin. Jan. 12, 1624. 100 Acres about a mile and a half up Southampton River, within the Corp. of Elizabeth City. Land Book 1, p. 42.

Peter Arundell of Buck Roe. Nov. 8, 1624. 200 Acres, in the Corp. of Elizabeth City upon the Back River and abutting Northward upon the main land, tending toward the head of Southampton River. Land Book 1, p. 44.

Bartholomew Hoskins. Nov. 3, 1624. 100 Acres on Back River in the Corp. of Elizabeth City, Northward upon a creek that divideth the same from the land of Peter Arundell. Land Book 1, p. 45.

Ensign Thomas Willoughby. Nov. 17, 1624. 50 Acres in Corp. of Elizabeth City, abutting Westerly upon the creek called Salford's Creek. Land Book 1, p. 61.

Mary Flint. March 14, 1628. 100 Acres within the Corp. of Elizabeth City and commonly called Foxhill. Land Book 1, p. 73.

Thomas Flint (Lease). Feb. 20, 1626. 50 Acres at Elizabeth City commonly called the Indian House. Land Book 1, p. 77.

Edward Johnson (Lease). Nov. 20, 1627. 50 Acres in the precincts of James City, being part of the Strawberry Bancks, Westerly upon a creek commonly called Thomas his Creek. Land Book 1, p. 77.

Dictoris Christmas. Aug. 20, 1627. 50 Acres, being part of the Strawberry Bancks, abutting and bounding Westerly on the land of Edward Waters. Land Book 1, p. 78.

Jonas Stockde, Minister (Lease). Sept. 8, 1627. 50 Acres, lying on the Easterly side of Southampton River- within the precincts of the Companies land at Elizabet City- beginning on land of Thomas Flint's, commonly called the Indian House thickett. Land Book 1, p. 79.

David Poole (Lease). Dec. 11, 1627. 60 Acres, lying at Buck Roe within the precincts of Elizabeth City. Land Book 1, p. 80.

John Arundell (Lease). Dec. 12, 1627. 12 Acres, within the precincts of Elizabeth City at Buck Roe. Land Book 1, p. 81.

James Benall (Lease). Dec. 12, 1627. 50 Acres, lying at Buck Roe within the precincts of Elizabeth City. Land Book 1, p. 82.

John Henry (Lease). Now granted to Henry Coleman. Dec. 12, 1627. 150 Acres, lying at Buck Roe within the precincts of Elizabeth City. Land Book 1, p. 83.

John Sipsey, Yeoman of Kiccoughtan. Sept. 2, 1624. 250 Acres on the South side of the river over against Kiccoughtan, abutting upon the land of Capt. William Tucker and Lt. John Cheesman. Land Book 1, p. 46. (omitted from Index).

John Cheesman, Gent. of Kiccoughtan. Sept. 2, 1624. 200 Acres on the South side of the river over against Kiccoughtan, abutting upon the land of John Sipsey. Land Book 1, p. 47. (omitted from Index).

William Hampton, Planter (Lease). Dec. 10, 1627. 50 Acres, lying at Buckroe within the precints of Elizabeth City, abutting upon James Bonall, Frenchman and the land of John Henry. Land Book 1, p. 84.

Richard Ball, Planter. Dec. 10, 1627. (Lease). 6 Acres, lying at Buckroe within the precincts of Elizabeth City, abutting upon the land of David Poole, Frenchman. Land Book 1, p. 84.

Lt. Thomas Purfury. Sept. 20, 1628. 100 Acres, within the precincts of Elizabeth City, abutting upon the fields called Fort Henry. Land Book 1, p. 88.

William Cox (Lease). Sept. 20, 1628. 100 Acres, within the precincts of Elizabeth City, bounding Easterly on the ground formerly in like manner granted to Dictoris Cdristmas. Land Book 1, p. 89.

Christopher Windmell (Lease). Sept. 20, 1628. 60 Acres within the precincts of Elizabeth City, Southerly upon the plantation commonly called the Indian House thickett.

Walter Heyley (Lease). Sept. 20, 1628. 60 Acres within the precincts of Elizabeth City, Southerly on the ground formerly granted unto Jonas Stockton, Minister. Land Book 1, p. 91.

Edward Waters (Lease). Oct. 20, 1628. 100 Acres, within the precincts of Elizabeth City being part of the Strawberry Bancks. Land Book 1, p. 93.

Christopher Windmell (Lease). Nov. 30, 1628. 50 Acres lying within the precincts of Elizabeth City, Southerly on a creek which lyeth towards the land of Walter Heley. Land Book 1, p. 93.

Nicholas Roe (Lease). Dec. 2, 1628. 40 Acres, within the precincts of Elizabeth City, Westerly on the long creek, parting the same from the land of Giles Jones. Land Book 1, p. 96.

Elias la Guard, Vignerone. March 14, 1628. 100 Acres, lying upon the Westerly side of the creek called Harris his creek, within the precincts of Elizabeth City. Land Book 1, p. 99.

Nicholas Browne (Lease). June 6, 1630. 50 Acres within the precincts of Elizabeth City, abutting on the land formerly granted to Walter Huley. Land Book 1, p. 101.

John Arundell, Gent. Aug. 1, 1632. 100 Acres within the Corp. of Elizabeth City, upon the Back River, Westerly upon the land granted by patent unto Bartolomew Hoskins. Land Book 1, p. 109.

John Arundell, of the Back River within the Corp. of Elizabeth City, sonn and heir apparent of Peter Arundell Gent., decd. Sept. 7, 1632. 100 Acres, abutting upon the land granted by patent to Bartholomew Hoskins, toward the land of Capt. Richard Stephens, now in the tenure of John Chandler, Planter. Land Book 1, p. 116.

Elizabeth Jones, wife of Giles Jones, Gent. 100 Acres within the Island of Point Comfort. Oct. 16, 1628. Her first personal devident, being an Ancient Planter. Land Book 1, p. 60. (omitted from Index).

Bartholomew Hoskins. Sept. 7, 1632. 100 Acres, lying at the Back River within the Corp. of Elizabeth City, Westerly upon a small creek, that divides the same from the land granted by patent unto Peter Arundell. Land Book 1, p. 117.

John Robins, the Younger. Sept. 7, 1632. 300 Acres, being on the Back River, within the Corp. of Elizabeth City, Easterly upon the land granted by patent unto Peter Arundell, decd. Land Book 1, p. 119.

Capt. William Tucker. June 1, 1632. 100 Acres, being at the Back River within the precincts of Elizabeth City. Land Book 1, p. 122.

James Knott (Lease). March 12, 1632. 50 Acres at the mouth of Hampton River within the precincts of Elizabeth City. Land Book 1, p. 133.

Dictoris Christmas, Planter of Elizabeth City to Lyonell Roulston, Gent., assignment of title of least, 50 Acres, upon the Strawberry Banckes. Sept. 29, 1628.

Lyonell Roulston, Gent. of Koskyake to loving friend John Neale. Jan. 14, 1630.

John Neale, Merchant (Lease). Feb. 12, 1632. 50 Acres upon the Strawberry Banckes witin the precinct of Elizabeth City, Easterly upon the land granted Lt. Edward Waters. Land Book p. 134 & 135.

William Hampton (Lease). March 12, 1632. 50 Acres, lying at Buck Roe within the precincts of Elizabeth City. Land Book 1, p. 136.

James Bonall (Lease). May 8, 1633. 50 Acres, at Buck Roe, within the precincts of Elizabeth City, abutting upon the land of Elias la Guard. Land Book 1, p. 139.

Elias la Guard, Vignerone. Assigned. April 12, 1633. 12 Acres, lying at Buck Roe, within the precincts of Elizabeth City. Land Book 1, p. 141.

Lancelott Barnes (Lease). April 12, 1633. 100 Acres, within the precincts of Elizabeth City, commonly known by the name of the Indian Thickett. Land Book 1, p. 142.

Joseph Hatfield of Elizabeth City. Oct. 31, 1633. 50 Acres, lying and being with the precinct of Elizabeth City, abutting upon the land of Walter Heyley. Land Book 1, p. 145.

Henry Coleman (Lease from Francis Hough). May 30, 1634. 60 Acres within the precincts of Elizabeth City, upon the plantation commonly called the Indian House Thickett. Land Book 1, p. 147.

Thomas Watts (Lease). May 30, 1634. 50 Acres, being at the Back River, within the Corp of Elizabeth City, upon a creek called the Broad Creek. Land Book 1, p. 149.

William Conner (Lease). Aug. 13, 1634. 60 Acres in the Corp of Elizabeth City, about two miles within the narrow of said Back River, on the side of a Dam called the Otterdam. Land Book 1, p. 152.

William Hampton (Lease). Aug. 13, 1634. 100 Acres on the Easterly side of Harris Creek. Land Book 1, p. 153.

William Ramshaw. July 1, 1635. 200 Acres, North up the mouth of the Elizabeth River. Land Book 1, p. 193.

Thomas Vicount. July 13, 1635. 100 Acres, adjoining the land of John Moore and John Garnett, etc. Land Book 1, p. 226.

Capt. Christopher Calthorpe. April 26, 1631. 500 Acres, in the New Poquoson, in the County of Elizabeth City, upon a creek called Calthorpe Creek. Land Book 1, p. 227.

Thomas Ranshaw. July 8, 1635. 250 Acres at the New Pocoson, abutting upon the land of Christopher Stoakes. Land Book 1, p. 264.

Christopher Stoakes. July 8, 1635. 300 Acres at the New Pocoson, abutting upon the land of John Watson. Land Book 1, p. 265.

Robert Glascocke. October 7, 1635. 300 Acres, upon the Great Creek and Lt. Cheesman's land. Land Book 1, p. 290.

William Woolritch. June 17, 1635. 400 Acres, upon the land belonging to Capt. Christopher Calthorpe. Land Book 1, p. 309.

William Clarke. Nov. 18, 1635. 100 Acres, upon the land of George White, Minister. Land Book 1, p. 310.

Captain Thomas Willowby. November 15, 1635. 300 Acres up the Hither Creek, between Francis Mason and his own land. Land Book 1, p. 312.

Thomas Keeling. November 18, 1635. 100 Acres, north upon the land of Henry Southwell. Land Book 1, p. 313.

Dictoris Christmas. November 21, 1635. 300 Acres on the north side of the Poquoson River, called the Poquoson, joining upon the East the land of Gilbert Perkin. Land Book 1, p. 317.

Thomas Purifye. November 28, 1635. 100 Acres on the Northwest upon a Creek, the Fort Field and John Neale's land. Land Book 1, p. 323.

Thomas Normanton. -----------. 50 Acres adjoining the land of Robert Huett. Land Book 1, p. 334.

James Knott. March 23, 1635. 1200 Acres, Northeast facing upon the Nansemond River. Land Book 1, p. 334.

John Yates. May 4, 1636. 150 Acres, being a neck of land upon the Eastwide of the Elizabeth River, the Southern Branch of the river. Land Book 1, p. 340.

John Yates. May 4, 1636. 200 Acres, being a neck of land upon the west side of the southward Branch of the Elizabeth River. Land Book 1, p. 340.

Christopher Burroughes. May 4, 1636. 200 Acres, northwardly upon the land of Captain Adam Thorroughgood. Land Book 1, p. 341.

Robert West. May 4, 1636. 100 Acres, adjoining the land of John Graves, Adam Thoroughgood and the said Robert West. Land Book 1, p. 342.

Thomas Watts. May 5, 1636. 50 Acres, upon the Back River and Broad Creek, adjoining the land of Captain Thomas Purifye. Land Book 1, p. 342.

John Place. March 1636. 150 Acres, at the head of Hampton River, adjoining the land of William Wells. Land Book 1, p. 356.

William Wells. March 1636. 50 Acres, near the head of Hampton River, adjoining the land of William Stafford. Land Book 1, p. 356.

Joseph Moore. June 2, 1636. 200 Acres, on the Old Poquoson River and a creek called Football Quarter. Land Book 1, p. 357.

William Coleman. March 10, 1635. 100 Acres, at the Old Poquoson called by the name of the Football Quarter. Land Book 1, p. 360.

John Chandler. June 6, 1636. 1000 Acres on the west side of a creek called Harris Creek. Land Book 1, p. 368.

William Armistead. July 7, 1636. 450 Acres, upon the land of Mr. Southell. Land Book 1, p. 370.

Thomas Allen. September 14, 1636. 550 Acres, on the first branch of the Long Creek, on the east side of the Chisopeacke, toward the Great Indian Field. Land Book 1, p. 381.

Thomas Beast. September 15, 1636. 200 Acres, beginning on the branch of a creek adjoining the land of Michaell Peasley. Land Book 1, p. 382.

William Rainshaw. September 14, 1636. 150 Acres being a neck of land, lying some three miles up the Elizabeth River. Land Book 1, p. 382.

William Rainshaw. September 14, 1636. 100 Acres, being a neck of land lying some two miles up Elizabeth River. Land Book 1, p. 383.

John Roberts. September 16, 1636. 100 Acres, being a neck of land on the south branch of Elizabeth River. Land Book 1, p. 383.

Thomas Burbage. September 16, 1636. 300 Acres adjoining the land of John Sipsey on the Elizabeth River. Land Book 1, p. 385.

Samuel Stephens. September 20, 1636. 2000 Acres, being a neck of land stretching eastward upon the main bay of Chisopeian. Land Book 1, p. 387.

William Julian. July 4, 1636. 600 Acres, part of the land being three necks of land, upon the entrance into Elizabeth River, the remainder adjoining the land of Francis Mason. Land Book 1, p. 388.

John Gates. September 21, 1636. 300 Acres being a neck of the eastern branch of the Elizabeth River. Land Book 1, p. 389.

John Gates. September 21, 1636. Patent renewed of 300 Acres on Elizabeth River. Land Book 1, p. 389.

John Gater (Gates). September 21, 1636. 200 Acres, being on the southern branch of Elizabeth River. Land Book 1, p. 389.

Cornelius Loyd. June 2, 1635. 800 Acres, on the south side of the western branch of the Elizabeth River. Land Book 1, p. 394.

Thomas Bensteed. September 28, 1636. 50 Acres commonly called Pascall's Neck. Land Book 1, p. 395.

James Vanerit. October 19, 1636. 1000 Acres, from Sandy Bay, along Point Creek. Land Book 1, p. 396.

George Saphier. November 26, 1636. 300 Acres upon the Old Pequoson River, upon the land of John Layden. Land Book 1, p. 401.

Thomas Andrews. Lease. November 28, 1636. 50 Acres upon the school land, formerly called Benjamin Syms' land. Land Book 1, p. 403.

William Morgan als Brookes. 100 Acres, upon the narrows of Back River. Land Book 1, p. 426.

John Graves. August 9, 1637. 600 Acres, near unto the upper end of the Back River. Land Book 1, p. 443.

Leonard Yeo. August 9, 1637. 850 Acres upon the head of a branch of the Old Poquoson Creek. Land Book 1, p. 444.

Captain Francis Hooke. August 9, 1637. 100 Acres upon the Strawberry Brancke and a creek near the Fort Field. Land Book 1, p. 445.

Captain Francis Hooke. August 10, 1637. 50 Acres commonly called Pascall's Neck. Land Book 1, p. 446.

Captain Francis Hooke. (Also to his successors, who shall be Captain of the Fort.) August 28, 1637. A tract called by the name of Fort Field, situated upon the Strawberry Banckes. Land Book 1, p. 473.

John Gundry. December 6, 1720. 150 Acres, within the territories of Elizabeth City, upon the Southampton River and the land now in the occupation of William Capp. Land Book 1, p. 476.

John Gundry's bill of sale to Captain Thorogood. December 6, 1626. 150 Acres on the Southampton River. Land Book 1, p. 477.

William Landsden. June 3, 1624. 100 Acres in the Corporation of Elizabeth City on the west side of the Southampton River, adjoining the land of William Clayborne. Land Book 1, p. 479.

Captain Adam Thorogood. September 20, 1637. 200 Acres, upon the land lately belonging to John Gundry. Land Book 1, p. 481.

George Slaughier. November 23, 1637. 200 Acres, adjoining the land of Robert Gould. Land Book 1, p. 501.

Robert Partin. Lease. November 24, 1637. 40 Acres on the land which the widow Tompson possesseth and south on the Fort Field. Land Book 1, p. 503.

Humphry Tabb. November 25, 1637. 50 Acres on Harris' Creek. Land Book 1, p. 505.

Nicholas Hill. November 25, 1637. 100 Acres, upon the Broad Creek. Land Book 1, p. 506.

Captain Adam Thorogood. February 10, 1637. 200 Acres upon Hampton River, commonly called by the name of Capp's Point. Land Book 1, p. 516.

Captain Adam Thorogood. March 12, 1634. 200 Acres, upon the Back River and the land of John Robinson. Land Book 1, p. 518.

Thomas Eaton. June 5, 1638. 650 Acres, upon the Beaver Dams and the head of the Back River. Land Book 1, p. 542.

John Graves. May 15, 1638. 200 Acres, near the Back River and adjoining the land formerly granted to the said Graves. Land Book 1, p. 556.

Peter Stafferton. May 13, 1638. 200 Acres, abutting upon the head of the little Poquoson Creek. Land Book 1, p. 557.

John Powell. May 2, 1638. 50 Acres upon the narrows of Back River. Land Book 1, p. 564.

William Armistead. May 16, 1638. 300 Acres upon the mouth of Broad Creek. Land Book 1, p. 564.

Humphry Tabb. May 6, 1638. 300 Acres upon a branch of Harris' Creek. Land Book 1, p. 567.

Joseph Moore. August 28, 1638. 200 Acres at the old Poquoson River and bounded upon the west with a creek called Football Quarter Creek. Land Book 1, p. 594.

John Gibbs. September 27, 1638. 300 Acres, adjoining the land of Thomas Purifye and Thomas Sewall's patented land. Land Book 1, p. 601.

Thomas Boulding. September 27, 1638. 200 Acres, adjoining the land of Thomas Sewall, now in the possession of Henry Batt. Land Book 1, p. 620.

John Laydon. October 3, 1638. 500 Acres, at the old Poquoson, lying by a neck called Burrowes Neck. Land Book 1, p. 620.

Aron Corsestam and Derrick Corsestam. March 23, 1638. 860 Acres abutting upon the main river and paralell to the land of Bartholomew Wethersbye. Land Book 1, p. 629.

John Robins. April 1, 1639. 200 Acres on the Back River, adjoining the land of the said Robins. Land Book 1, p. 638.

George Hull. June 12, 1639. 50 Acres, abutting upon the old Poquoson and Broad Creek. Land Book 1, p. 654.

John Graves. May 20, 1639. 150 Acres, at the head of the Back River. Land Book 1, p. 655.

Christopher Dawcey. August 13, 1639. 50 Acres upon Harris' Creek, adjoining the land of Humphry Moore. Land Book 1, p. 663.

William Parry. October 10, 1639. 350 Acres abutting upon the Hampton River and a creek that divides this land from the land called Indian Thickett. Land Book 1, p. 679.

John Smith and Christopher Bea. Last day of October 1639. 100 Acres at the head of Old Poquoson River, upon the great Otterdams. Land Book 1, p. 679.

Marke Johnson. Last day of October 1639. 50 Acres on the Back River, in two parcells of 25 Acres, abutting upon the land formerly taken up by Captain William Tucker. Land Book 1, p. 680.

Thomas Boulding. Last day of October 1639. 400 Acres upon the Middle Ridge, lying upon the P----simon Ponds. Land Book 1, p. 680.

Dictoris Christmas. October 24, 1639. 300 Acres on the old Pocquoson River and adjoining the land of Gilbert Perkins. Land Book 1, p. 688.

Thomas Oldis. Lease. March 22, 1639. 50 Acres at the Strawberry Banckes, whereon he now liveth. Land Book 1, p. 737.

William Armistead's bill of sale to John Bowles. June 11, 1641. 20 Acres on the north side of the land of the said Bowles and 50 Acres that he holdeth by deed of gift from Mrs. Elizabeth Southwell. Land Book 1, p. 737.

William Hampton. December 11, 1640. 550 Acres on the edge of the Otterdams. Land Book 1, p. 752.

Thomas Oldis. January 27, 1641. 50 Acres upon the river. Land Book 1, p. 760.

Richard Gregson. December 8, 1642. 400 Acres beginning on a path that leadeth from Nutmeg Corner unto the poquoson. Land Book 1, p. 776.

William Morgan als Brooke. August 1642. 50 Acres upon his first divident at the Oyster Bancks. Land Book 1, p. 795.

Humphry Tabb. June 19, 1642. 100 Acres upon Harris' Creek and a branch of the said creek. Land Book 1, p. 824.

Humphry Tabb. January 6, 1642. 150 Acres on Long Branch and adjoining the land of Dr. Calvert. Land Book 1, p. 825.

Henry Poole. October 18, 1642. 116 Acres adjoining the Hampton River and the Gleav land. Land Book 1, p. 834.

Henry Coleman. October 17, 1642. 104 Acres on the Hampton River and adjoining the land of Henry Pool. Land Book 1, p. 836.

Adam Thorrogood. February 10, 1637. 200 Acres upon the Hampton River and commonly called Capps. Land Book 1, p. 890.

William Wilkinson. Minister. August 28, 1644. 100 Acres in or near Buckerowe. Land Book 2, p. 9.

William Cock. June 5, 1645. 100 Acres, late in the tenure of John Roberts decd., abutting upon the late in the possession of Captain Albiano Lupo and now in the possession of John Chandler. Land Book 2, p. 23.

John Baker. June 5, 1645. 175 Acres. 50 Acres former leased land granted Nicholas Brown and by him assigned to said Baker and adjoining the land formerly granted unto Walter Hely. Land Book 2, p. 24.

Marke Johnson. July 31, 1645. 198 Acres, beginning on a branch that divides his land from Thomas Watts. Land Book 2, p. 27.

Thomas Watts. August 2, 1645. 423 Acres on the branch of the Broad Creek, which divides the land from that of Mr. Johnson. Land Book 2, p. 35.

John Ingrame. March 2, 1642. 150 Acres upon the Point Comfort Creek, beginning at the Indian Spring. Land Book 2, p. 42.

Ralph Barlow. March 18, 1642. 150 Acres, adjoining the land of Richard Bolton. Land Book 2, p. 45.

Richard Grigson. April 10, 1646. 400 Acres beginning at a path that leadeth from Nutmeg Quarter unto the Poquoson. Land Book 2, p. 64.

Elizabeth Ambrose, widow. August 6, 1646. 100 Acres on the main river, adjoining the land of George Keth. Land Book 2, p. 73.

Elizabeth Claiborne, the wife of Captain William Claiborne. October 29, 1647. 700 Acres in the Corporation of Elizabeth City, partly on the land commonly called the Strawberry land. Land Book 2, p. 81.

Thomas Hopkins. January 6, 1647. 300 Acres, 200 Acres of which begins at the bridge at the narrow of the Back River, the other on Stones Dams. Land Book 2, p. 114.

Thomas Todd. March 6, 1647. 50 Acres at the head of the Ould Poquoson River. Land Book 2, p. 114.

Major Richard Morrison. June 1648. 110 Acres commonly called the Fort Field. Land Book 2, p. 128.

John Howitt, carpenter. June 1, 1648. 204 Acres on the Ould Poquoson River, adjoining the land of George Hull. Land Book 2, p. 138.

Ralph Hunt. November 28, 1645. 300 Acres near the head of Salford's Creek. Land Book 2, p. 138.

John Houlder. October 25, 1647. 50 Acres upon a swamp near the head of Salford's Creek. Land Book 2, p. 138.

William ap Thomas. June 2, 1648. 335 Acres, upon the Broad Creek and adjoining the land of Thomas Watts. Land Book 2, p. 139.

John Ingram. November 23, 1647. 300 Acres upon the Point Comfort Creek and the land of Humphry Tabb. Land Book 2, p. 140.

Edward Parish. Last day of May 1648. 200 Acres on the head of the Back River. Land Book 2, p. 140.

William Parry. June 6, 1648. 90 Acres adjoining the dividend of Florentine Payne. Land Book 2, p. 142.

Lieutenant William Worleich. October 14, 1649. 150 Acres upon a creek called Carson's Creek in Hampton River. Land Book 2, p. 188.

Thom Preston. December 19, 1650. 100 Acres, upon the Patch Tree Dam and the Long Pond. Land Book 2, p. 274.

Samuel Thorowgood. March 10, 1650. 50 Acres upon the head of the Long Ponds and the Swanes Dams. Land Book 2, p. 288.

Captain Leonard Yeo. 1644. 35 Acres at the head of the Southampton River, abutting on a creek, parting the same from the land of Captain Thorowgood, decd., and now in the possession of Thomas Oxley. Land Book 2, p. 363.

Thomas Coniers. July 30, 1649. 40 Acres beginning by Basnet's house to the creek which parts this land from the Fort Field. Land Book 2, p. 201.

Symon Thorogood. April 18, 1653. 200 Acres upon the head of the Long Pond and the land granted by patent to Toby Smith. Land Book 3, p. 25.

Richard Allen. March 10, 1652. 285 Acres at the head of Scoones Dam, adjoining the land of William Houlder. Land Book 3, p. 188.

Richard Hull. October 15, 1655. 116 Acres on the Hampton River and the Gleab land. Land Book 3, p. 393.

William Parry. May 6, 1656. 100 Acres lately belonging unto William Cock, decd, adjoining the land now in the possession of Henry Withers. Land Book 4, p. 52.

Humphry Tabb. (This patent was renewed in Thomas Tabb's name, son and heir of the said Humphry Tabb. March 18, 1662.) September 20, 1656. 900 Acres between Harris Creek and Point

Comfort Creek, beginning at a branch called Old Wills Canoe. Land Book 4, p. 59.

Robert Gray. October 7, 1658. 50 Acres from the head of Otterdam, near the Back River, to a swamp called by the name of Dixell's Woodyard. Land Book 4, p. 325.

William ap Thomas. March 18, 1663. 300 Acres in the Poquoson adjoining the land of Thomas Purifoy. Land Book 5, p.

Richard Jones. February 5, 1663. 100 Acres adjoining the land the said Jones lately purchased of Thomas Ceely and the land of Richard Allen. Land Book 5, p. 280.

Thomas Spery. August 13, 1664. 100 Acres upon the head of the Long Pond, formerly granted to Symon Thorowgood. Land Book 5, p. 382.

Richard Pinner. March 18, 1662. 500 Acres, a part of which lies between the two main branches of the Church Creek and the other part lies on the Western Branch of the Elizabeth River. Land Book 5, p. 389.

Richard Todd. October 9, 1665. 600 Acres adjoining the land of Edward Pace. Land Book 5, p. 474.

Major Theophilus Hone. September 21, 1663. 1000 Acres being escheat land formerly granted to James Vauerick. Land Book 5, p. 453.

Major Theophilus Hone. September 21, 1663. 50 Acres being escheat land formerly granted to Henry Withers. Land Book 5, p. 544.

Captain Charles Morryson. July 24, 1669. 350 Acres, being escheat land formerly granted to Richard Hull, decd. Land Book 6, p. 250.

Ann Wilson, relict of John Wilson. July 24, 1669. 75 Acres being escheat land, formerly granted to John Gundrey, decd. Land Book 6, p. 251.

William Morris. July 24, 1669. One Acre, formerly granted to Hen. Hawley, decd. Land Book 6, p. 251.

Augustine Moore. October 28, 1672. Escheat land, formerly granted Thomas Shirley. 225 Acres. Land Book 6, p. 408.

Thomas Tabb. October 28, 1672. 300 Acres, escheat land formerly granted John Gibbs. Land Book 6, p. 408.

Richard Jones. May 30, 1675. 240 Acres, adjoining the land of Richard Allen and Richard Thomas. Land Book 6, p. 462.

Captain Anthony Armistead. June 1, 1676. 928 Acres on the Back River and adjoining the land of Marke Morgan's orphans. Land Book 6, p. 611.

Augustine Moore. June 19, 1676. 235 Acres at the head of little Poquoson Creek. Land Book 6, p. 614.

Henry Presson. April 23, 1681. Land upon the Patch Tree Dam, toward the Long Pond. Land Book 7, p. 82.

Richard Hurstly. September 28, 1681. 94 Acres upon Hampton River, at the mouth of Baldwyn's Creek. Land Book 7, p. 102.

Anthony Armistead. April 20, 1682. 50 Acres of escheat land, part of 150 Acres, which John Powell died seized of. Land Book 7, p. 129.

John Tilley. April 20, 1682. 50 Acres of escheat land part of 150 Acres, which John Powell died seized of. Land Book 7, p. 129.

John Symone. April 20, 1682. 50 Acres of escheat land part of 150 Acres, which John Powell died seized of. Land Book 7, p. 129.

Thomas Allamby. December 22, 1682. 184 Acres on the bank of the James River, adjoining the land now in the possession of Robert Combes. Land Book 7, p. 217.

Baldwin Sheppard. November 22, 1682. 360 Acres, near the head of Harris' Creek. Land Book 7, p. 229.

Quintillian Gothrick. April 26, 1684. 200 Acres on the Hampton River and now in the possession of John Spinkes. Land Book 7, p. 396.

Pasco Dunn. April 20, 1685. 146 Acres at a place called the Ridge of Land. Land Book 7, p. 435.

Coleman Brough. April 11, 1689. 50 Acres of escheat land formerly bequeathed by William Bradfield, Sr., the will bears date, September 26, 1664. Land Book 7, p. 712.

Richard Shewell. October 20, 1689. 115 Acres, adjoining the dividend of Pasco Dunn. Land Book 8, p. 15.

Richard Shewell. April 21, 1690. 115 Acres recorded again. Land Book 8, p. 33.

John Lear and Rebecca his wife. October 20, 1691. 180 Acres between Hampton River and Back River and on ye side of ye Deep Creek issueing into Hampton River. Land Book 8, p. 214.

Christopher Copeland. April 29, 1692. 220 Acres on Harris Creek and adjoining Needham's old line. Land Book 8, p. 228.

Jacob Walker and George Walker the Younger. April 29, 1692. 125 Acres on the Mill Creek and on the branch of John's alias Hook's Creek. Land Book 8, p. 229.

Henry Copeland. April 29, 1692. 220 Acres on the west side Harris Creek, adjoining the land of Henry Dunn. Land Book 8, p. 229.

Captain Anthony Armistead. April 21, 1695. 150 Acres, adjoining his own land at the mill and the land of John Archer and Captain Henry Jenkins. Land Book 8, p. 404.

Walter Bayley. April 21, 1696. 106 Acres on the Back River and adjoining the land of Eaton's Free School. Land Book 8, p. 406.

John Archer. April 21, 1695. 375 Acres, adjoining the land of Pascho Curle, Captain Henry Jenkins and Captain Henry Armistead. Land Book 8, p. 406.

Captain William Armistead. October 29, 1696. 130 Acres adjoining his father's and John Parson's land. Land Book 9, p. 52.

Philip Johnson. October 29, 1696. 400 Acres on a branch of Broad Creek. Land Book 9, p. 63.

John Heron. October 28, 1696. 124 Acres, adjoining the land of Captain Anthony Armistead, Mark Parrish and Thomas Curle. Land Book 9, p. 102.

Robert Holmes. October 28, 1697. 195 Acres near Scoans Dam, adjoining the land of the heirs of George Kemp, decd. Land Book 9, p. 113.

Henry Royall. October 28, 1697. 586 Acres adjoining the land of John Pignall, Samuel Dewborne and the bridge Scons Dams. Land Book 9, p. 121.

Mark Parrish. October 28, 1697. 35 Acres, adjoining his own land, Captain Anthony Armistead at the mill and John Heron, etc. Land Book 9, p. 122.

Robert Beverley. October 15, 1698. 570 Acres. 110 Acres commonly called Fort Field, 160 Acres called Downs Field and 300 Acres called Buckrow, late in the possession of Colonel Charles Morrison, decd., being escheat land. Land Book 9, p. 158.

Robert Hollins. October 15, 1698. 195 Acres, near Scones Dam, adjoining the land of George Kemp, decd., Captain Henry Jenkins, etc. Land Book 9, p. 173.

Pascho Dunn. June 6, 1699. 443 Acres, on the Oaken Swamp which parts this county from Warwick County. Land Book 9, p. 192.

Charles Jenings. June 6, 1699. 443 Acres, adjoining the land now in the possession of Thomas Batts. Land Book 9, p. 202.

Richard Crussell. June 6, 1699. 70 Acres, adjoining the land of Samuel Groves. Land Book 9, p. 213.

Henry Robinson. June 6, 1699. 188 Acres, adjoining the land of George Cooper, Charles Jenings and Thomas Needham. Land Book 9, p. 215.

Thomas Roberts, Jr. October 26, 1699. 249 Acres, adjoining the land of Captain Anthony Armistead and Edward Millas, etc. Land Book 9, p. 229.

Robert Beverley. April 24, 1700. 813 Acres on the land of George Walker, Jr., and the head of the Long Creek. Land Book 9, p. 243.

William Armistead. April 24, 1700. 125 Acres, being land formerly granted to Captain Anthony Armistead and is added to a patent of 928 Acres, dated, June 1, 1676. Land Book 9, p. 257.

James Baker. April 25, 1702. 225 Acres, adjoining the land of Nicholas Curle, Mr. Shepheard and Edward Lattimore. Land Book 9, p. 453.

George Walker, Jr. October 23, 1703. 25 Acres on the main branch of John's Creek, adjoining the land of Edward Roe. Land Book 9, p. 565.

Thomas Poole. April 26, 1704. 474 Acres, escheat land, late in the possession of Jane Poole, decd. Land Book 9, p. 610.

George Walker. October 20, 1704. 115 Acres, adjoining his own land, that lies next to Buck Roe. Land Book 9, p. 615.

Mathew Watts. May 2, 1705. 50 Acres, escheat land, late in the possession of Anne Symonds, decd. Land Book 9, p. 650.

Walter Bayley. May 2, 1705. 150 Acres, escheat land, late in the possession of John Powell, decd. Land Book 9, p. 650.

Colonel William Wilson. May 2, 1705. 200 Acres, adjoining the land of Woolridge Westwood, decd., Robert Taylor, William Smelt, Richard Street, decd. and John Chanlers. Land Book 9, p. 652.

Robert Beverley. May 2, 1705. 120 Acres, being all that neck or part of land, sand and marsh on the south west end of Point Comfort. Land Book 9, p. 717.

William Mallory. May 2, 1706. 274 Acres on a branch which falls into the Old Poquoson River. Land Book 9, p. 723.

Robert Taylor. May 2, 1706. 3 half Acres, escheat land, late in the possession of William Hudson, decd. Land Book 9, p. 727.

George Walker. --------. 126 Acres, adjoining the land of William Knight, the school land, Thomas Tucker and Colonel William Wilson. Land Book 10, p.

Nicholas Curle. ----------. 200 Acres, escheat land late in the possession of William Guterick. Land Book 10, p. 3.

James Wallace. December 19, 1711. 583 Acres on the land of Henry Robinson. Land Book 10, p. 45.

William Hachell. December 10, 1711. 74 Acres, adjoining the land of John Young, heirs of Richard Sewall, decd., and the heirs of Pasco Dunn, decd. Land Book 10, p. 54.

Joshua Curle. May 2, 1713. 134 Acres adjoining the school land. Land Book 10, p. 69.

William Armistead. November 13, 1713. 200 Acres adjoining the land of the heirs of Thomas Curle, Merchant, decd. Land Book 10, p. 95.

John Parsons, Jr. November 13, 1713. 300 Acres, adjoining the land of Anthony Armistead and Major William Armistead. Land Book 10, p. 85.

Charles Cellis. November 13, 1713. 124 Acres, beginning upon a branch which parts this land from that of Thomas Tucker and of William Knight. Land Book 10, p. 86.

Mark Johnson. June 16, 1714. 150 Acres, adjoining the land of Thomas Roberts, Major William Armistead and John Parsons. Land Book 10, p. 139.

Thomas Allen. June 16, 1714. 328 Acres, adjoining the land of James Hollins, Captain Henry Royall and the heirs of John Archer, decd. Land Book 10, p. 192.

John Hayward. November 4, 1714. 58 Acres, adjoining the land of John Jeggett and Samuel Dewberry. Land Book 10, p. 197.

James Burtell. February 23, 1714. One-half Acres on the west side of King's Street and on the south side of Hampton Town. Land Book lo, p. 235.

Thomas Wilcoks. April 1, 1717. 214 Acres adjoining the land of Mark Johnson, Thomas Roberts and Benjamin Smith. Land Book 10, p. 316.

Joshua Curle. July 12, 1718. 452 Acres, near the head of a cove on George Walker's lott. Land Book 10, p. 374.

George Walker. July 12, 1718. 1000 square feet, adjoining the town of Hampton at the end of King's Street. Land Book 10, p. 375.

John Ballie. January 2, 1718. 69 Acres, adjoining the land of George Walker, Thomas Redd and Ealton's school land. Land Book 10, p. 416.

William Dandridge and Thomas Wythe. July 11, 1719. 32 poles adjoining to Hampton Town on the east side of King's Street. Land Book 10, p. 450.

Henry Irwin. August 20, 1719. 19 poles, adjoining to the town of Hampton, on Joshua Curle's land. Land Book 10, p. 450.

William Armistead. August 17, 1720. 9 Acres. Land Book 11, p. 24.

John Dandridge. April 21, 1722. 32 poles, adjoining Hampton Town, on the east side of King's Street. Land Book 11, p. 84.

Anthony Armistead. June 22, 1722. 93 Acres, adjoining the land of Richard Harvey and Thomas Roberts. Land Book 11, p. 142.

William Hatchell. June 22, 1722. 83 Acres adjoining the land of William Bracie, John King, etc. Land Book 11, p. 143.

William Allen. June 5, 1723. 150 Acres, adjoining the land of Anthony Armistead and William Armistead. Land Book 11, p. 235.

Miles Cary. May 10, 1729. 200 Acres, adjoining the land of Thomas Curle, Merchant, decd., Captain Henry Irwin and the heirs of John Archer, decd. Land Book 13, p.

John Casey. August 1, 1734. 62 Acres, beginning on the head of Slippery Pine Branch and the land of Edward Andres. Land Book 15, p.

Edward Andros. August 20, 1634. 50 Acres, begging on a branch called the Slippery Pine, falling into Salford's Creek and adjoining the land of Joseph Jeggits. Land Book 15, p. 286.

William King and Mary his wife and Judith Curle. September 22, 1739. 637 Acres, beginning on a ridge commonly called the Great Ridge, near the main road and adjoining the land of Isaac Vollins and the heirs of Mark Johnson. Land Book 18, p. 18.

Thomas Smith. June 16, 1738. 225 Acres on the Back River and the mouth of the Otterdams. Land Book , p. 12.

John Massenburgh. August 20, 1747. 75 Acres on the Scones Dams, adjoining his own and the land of Alexander Carver. Land Book 28, p. 154.

Thomas Townshend Mingham. November 3, 1750. 90 Acres on Back River, adjoining the land of the heirs of Captain Wilson Curle. Land Book 29, p. 361.

Benjamin Lester. Assignee. May 23, 1763. 214 Acres, adjoining the land of Mark Johnson, Thomas Roberts, the heirs of Thomas Curle, Merchant, decd. Land Book 35, p. 111.

George Wythe. August 30, 1763. 40 Acres at the north end of Old Point Comfort. Land Book 35, p. 327.

William Morehead. August 15, 1764. 57 Acres, escheat land on the north side of the James River at a place known by the name of Newport News. Land Book 36, p. 583.

James Wallace Bayley. October 31, 1765. 10 1/2 Acres, adjoining the land of William Westwood, Judith Robinson and John Nelson. Land Book 36, p. 916.

Anne and John Smith. July 5, 1774. 94 Acres in the counties of Warwick and Elizabeth City, being escheat land from Rebecca and Mary Newberry (Dewberry ?). Land Book 42, p. 745.

Commonwealth Grants or Patents

George Hope. April 20, 1785. One Acre, escheat land, beginning on the corner of the said Hope's warehouse. Land Book 0, p. 320.

Robert Walker. April 20, 1685. One Acre, escheat land beginning at the corner where the road from Hampton and Back River meet. Land Book 0, p. 322.

Worlich Westwood. June 25, 1788. 27 Acres, escheat land being part of the tract commonly known as Little England. Land Book 17, p. 222.

Miles Cary. June 24, 1788. Two lotts, number 4 and 5, each on the water side of escheat land. Land Book 17, p. 223.

Miles Cary. June 24, 1788. Two lotts, number 6 and 7 on escheat land. Land Book 17, p. 224.

Miles Cary. June 23, 1788. Three lotts, number 1, 2, and 3 on escheat land. Land Book 17, p. 225.

Miles Cary. June 23, 1788. 10 Acres, escheat land called Hanover and lot number 15, being part of the land known as Little England. Land Book 17, p. 227.

QUIT RENT ROLL --1704

Total 29560 Acres

Henry Royall, Sheriff.

Name	Acres
Allin, Thomas	227
Armistead, Col. Anthony	2140
Armistead, Maj. William	460
Babb, Thomas-per Selden	300
Baines, Thomas	50
Baker, James	225
Ballard, Francis-per Selden	460
Ballis, Widdo.	350
Bayley, John	415
Bell, George	80
Beverley, Robert	777
Booker, Mr. Rvend. (pro Rev. James Bowker)	526
Boswell, William	220
Bowles, John	360
Breltnen, Michael	100
Bright, Robert, Sr.	100
Bushnell, John, Jr.	150
Chandler, John	150
Charwell, Robert per John Young	440
Cooley, Charles	200
Cooper, Charles	100
Cooper, George, Sr.	100
Copeland, Christopher	340
Cotton, John	50
Croashell, Widdo.	100
Curle, Nicholas	950
Curle, Pasquo	300
Davill, Paltey	100
Davill, Samuel	100
Davis, Christopher	25
Davis, Moses	150
Davis, William	42
Diggs, Col. Dudley	216
Dunn, Henry	50
Dunn, William	100
Dupra, Giles	150
Faulkner, Thomas	50
Fingall, Samuel	333
Francis, John	25
Gibbs, Thomas	630
Griggs, Anthony	50
Harris, Joseph	50
Haslyitt, William	100
Hawkins, Thomas	270
Hollier, Simon	200
Horsley, Richard	90
House, John	157
James, Henry	100
Jenings, Charles	225
Jenings, Mary	250
Jenkins, Mrs. Bridgett	100
Jenkins, Capt. Henry	300
Johnson, Mark	400
Lais, Henry	50
Latham, William	90
Lattimore, Edward	190
Lowry, John per Selden	110
Lowry, William	526
Mallory, William	200
Masnibrod, Roger	50
Moory, Mr. or Mrs. Dunn	500
Mihill, Edward	600
More, Capt. Augustino	285
More, John	250
Morgan, Rebecka	50
Nagleer (Naylor) Sarah	230
Naylor, Thomas	100
Needham, Thomas	100
Nichols, Jane	50
Nobling, Thomas per Archer	212
Parish, Abraham	100
Parish, John	50
Parish, Mark	200
Passones (Parsons) John	780
Pearce, Peter	50
Pearce, Samuel	100
Penny, Bryan	50
Poole, Thomas	1200
Powell, Mark	184
Powers, Charles	400
Preeday, Daniel	50
Priest, James	50
Roatton, Richard	50
Roberts, Thomas	250
Robinson, Henry	200
Robinson, William	50
Roe, Edward	100
Rogers, Francis	200
Royall, Capt. Henry	750
Savoy, Francis	50
Servant, Bertram	418
Shepherd, John	210
Simmons, Mary	200
Skinner, John	50
Smelt, Mathew	100
Smelt, William	150
Smith, Benjamin	650
Spicer, William	60
Taylor, Robert	50
Theodam, John	100
Tucker, Charles	240
Tucker, Thomas	60
Turner, John	50
Umplese (Umphlet), William	25
Walker, George	325

Wallace, James	1300	Williams, William per ye school	600
Watts, Mathew	454	Williams, William	260
Wethersby, Bartho.	300	Wilson, Col. William	1024
Wheatland, John	66	Winsor, William	150
White, Joseph	200	Winter, William	70

0 0

A POLL FOR THE ELECTION OF BURGESSES for County of Elizabeth City July 11, 1758

Colonel John Tabb and Captain William Wager were elected. Other names on the ticket were, Captain Roscow Sweny, George Wythe, Robert Brough, Captain Cary Selden, Mr. James Wallace, Mr. William Westwood, and Mr. William Armistead.

Allen, James
Allen, Henry
Armistead, Booth
Armistead, John
Armistead, Robert
Armistead, Westwood
Armistead, William
Baker, William
Ballard, Francis
Ballard, William
Banister, Joseph
Batts, Henry
Bayley, James Wallace
Bayley, John
Bayley, Nicholas
Baylis, Thomas, Jr.
Baylis, Thomas
Baylis, William
Bickardick, Richard
Brough, Robert
Brown, James
Buck, John
Butt, Thomas
Casey, John
Cooper, Charles
Cooper, Philip
Creek, John
Cross, William
Curle, Joshua
Curle, Samuel
Dailie, Owen
Davis, David
Davis, Thomas
Dixon, Thomas
Duberry, Samuel
Dunn, William
Face, William
Fenn, Thomas
Ham, Benjamin
Hawkins, Anthony
Hatton, Thomas
Hawkins, Thomas
Herbert, John
Hicks, John
Hundley, Robert
Jegitts, Joseph
Jones, John
Jones, Morris
Kerby, John
Kerby, Thomas
King, Henry
Latimer, Edward
Latimer, James
Latimer, Thomas
Latimer, William
Lester, Benjamin
Lowry, John
Loyell, John
Loyell, William
Mallory, Johnson
Massenburg, Josiah
Matthews, John
Meredith, Joseph
Michell, Cary
Minson, Banister
Minson, John
Moore, Augustine
Moore, John
Moore, Meritt
Morehead, William
Naylor, James
Naylor, William
Nelson, John
Parish, Signey
Parsons, John
Pasteur, Charles
Pierce, Christopher
Pierce, Peter
Pool, John
Proby, Minson
Puryear, Peter
Read, William

Robinson, Henry
Robinson, Starkey
Roland, Samuel
Ross, Mallory
Routon, Daniel
Selden, Cary
Selden, Joseph
Servant, Bertram
Shepard, John, Jr.
Shepard, John
Skinner, Thomas, Jr.
Skinner, Thomas
Smelt, William
Smith, John
Smith, Thomas
Stores, Frasey
Stores, John
Sweny, Roscow
Tabb, John, Jr.
Tabb, John
Tarrant, Carter
Thomas, George
Tompkins, Samuel
Tucker, Curle
Tucker, Robert
Umphlet, King
Waff, George
Wager, William
Walker, George
Wallace, James
Wallace, Richard
Ward, Edward
Watts, Thomas, Jr.
Watts, Thomas
Williams, William
Wilson, Richard
Wooten, Thomas
Wray, George

———— 0 0 ————

A POLL FOR THE ELECTION OF BURGESSES
for
County of Elizabeth City
August 23, 1765

George Wythe, Esq. and Colonel Wilson M. Cary were elected. Captain James Wallace was the other candidate.

Allen, Henry
Allen, John, Jr.
Allen, John, Sr.
Armistead, Anthony
Armistead, Booth
Armistead, John
Armistead, Moseley
Armistead, Robert, Sr.
Armistead, William
Bains, Samuel
Baker, James
Ballard, Francis
Banes, Samuel
Batts, Henry
Bayley, James Wallace
Bayley, John
Bayley, Wilson Roscow
Baylis, Thomas, Jr.
Bean, William
Bell, Nathaniel
Bennett, John
Boutwell, Samuel
Bright, Robert
Brodie, John
Brough, Robert
Brown, Robert
Brown, William
Bullock, James
Butt, Thomas
Cary, Wilson M.
Collier, Lockey
Cooper, Charles
Cooper, Joseph
Cowper, Edward
Cross, William
Cunningham, James
Curle, David Wilson
Curle, Samuel
Davis, David
Davis, William
Dewbre, Samuel, Sr.
Dixon, Thomas
Dunn, William
Face, William
Fenn, Thomas
Gill, James
Ham, Benjamin
House, Thomas
Humphlett, King
Jegitts, Joseph
Johnson, George
Jones, Cooper
Jones, John
Kerby, John
King, Henry
Langley, John
Latimer, Edward
Latimer, George
Latimer, George, Sr.
Latimer, Thomas, Sr.
Latimer, William
Lewis, John
Lowry, John, Sr.
Loyall, Paul

Loyall, Ann
Mallory, Francis
Mallory, William
Massenburg, Josiah
Massenburg, Robert
Meredith, Joseph
Minson, Banister
Minson, John
Minson, William
Moore, Augustine
Morehead, William
Moreland, Young
Naylor, James
Naylor, William
Nelson, John
Parish, Mark
Pasteur, Charlès, Sr.
Poole, Robert
Poole, William
Riddlehurst, Francis
Riddlehurst, John
Roberts, Samuel
Roscow, James
Ross, Mallory
Rowland, Samuel
Sandefer, Robert
Scott, Richard
Scott, Willis
Selden, Cary
Selden, John
Selden, Joseph
Sheppard, John, Jr.
Sheppard, John, Sr.
Sinnclair, Henry
Skinner, Thomas
Skinner, Thomas, Sr.
Skinner, William
Skinner, William, Sr.
Smelt, William
Smith, John
Smith, Thomas
Smith, William
Spearing, John
Stores, Frazey
Stores, John
Sweny, Roscow
Tabb, John
Tarrant, Carter
Thomas, George, Jr.
Thomas, George, Sr.
Tucker, Curle
Tuell, William
Van Burkello, William
Wager, William
Walker, George, Jr.
Walker, George, Sr.
Wallace, James
Wallace, Robert
Ward, Edward
Warrington, Rev. Thomas
Watts, Samuel
Weir, George
Westwood, James
Westwood, William, Sr.
Weymouth, William
Williams, William
Wilson, Richard
Wootten, Thomas
Wray, Jacob
Wythe, George
Yeargain, Edward

0 0

TITHABLES

A list of tithables in the County of Elizabeth City for the year 1782, taken agreeable to an act for ascertaining taxes and duties and for establishing a permanent revenue. Free male persons above the age of 21 and slaves above the age of 16 years. (The numbers listed below refer to aforesaid classifications, persons listed without numbers hold other taxable property.)

	F.	M.	N.
Allen, Edward		6	
Allen, John		2	
Allen, Thomas		2	6
Allen, William		1	
Almand, John		1	
Almand, William		2	2
Armistead, Ann			
Armistead, Baker		4	
Armistead, Frances		17	15
paid for Vicanious Nettles			
Armistead, James Bray		3	
Armistead, John		5	3
Armistead, Moses		3	9

	F.	M.	N.
Armistead, Robert			
paid for by Wm. Armistead			
Armistead, Samuel		3	3
Armistead, Westwood		7	7
Armistead, William		21	24
paid for Wm. Armistead			
Avera, Hannah		1	
Bains, Henry		1	
Bains, John		1	
Ballard, Edward		2	1
Ballard, Francis		5	2
Ballard, William			
paid for by Charles Baylis			
Banks, John		1	

	F.	M.	N.
Barron, James		2	2
Barron, Richard		5	4
Bayley, Hannah		6	7
Bayley, James Wallace			
Bayley, William A.		3	3
Baylis, Charles		5	
paid for Wm. Ballard			
Baylis, Thomas		5	5
Bell, John			
paid for by Woolich Westwood			
Bell, Nathaniel		1	
Bennett, William		1	1
Berry, Edward		1	
Biscow, James		1	
Booker, George		10	17
Boutwell, Ann		1	
Boutwell, Edward		2	1
Bowry, Elioner		2	1
Bright, Robert		6	15
Brodie, John		6	3
Brough, William		11	4
Brown, Robt. Kipling		1	
Brown, William		3	
Brown, William		3	1
Bryan, Benjamin		4	2
Bryan, Richard		2	
Bullock, James		2	5
Bully, Andrew		1	
Bully, John		1	
Burnham, John			
paid for by John Seymore			
Burges, William		2	1
Burt, Richard		3	6
Bushell, John, Jr.		1	
Bushell, John, Sr.		1	
Campbell, Priscilla		1	
Carter, John		1	2
Carter, William		1	
Cary, John		12	9
Ceely, William		1	1
Clarke, Benjamin		1	
Clarke, John		1	
Cooper, Joseph		5	3
Counsel, Michael		2	
Cowper, Edward		7	5
Cowper, Roe		10	3
Crandol, Thomas		1	1
Crook, Pennuel		2	2
Cunningham, James		2	1
Cunningham, Samuel B.		8	3
paid for by Ruben Mitchell			
Cunningham, William		1	
Cunningham, William		2	2
Curle, Mary		3	7
Curle, Mary		8	14
Dames, John		2	
Davis, James		1	
Davis, William		2	
Dewbry, Rebecca		2	2
Dewbry, Samuel		5	
Dixon, James		10	9
Dixon, Sarah		5	5
Dunn, Anthony		1	
Dunn, Martha			1

	F.	M.	N.
Dunn, William		2	2
Face, Edward		2	1
Fenn, Thomas		2	
Fields, Bartlet		5	3
Field, John		12	18
paid for by Thomas Stevens			
Frazier, Ann			
Frazier, John		1	1
Gibson, James		1	
Gill, James		1	
Gooch, William		3	2
Goodwin, James		5	6
Grey, George		2	
Haley, Samuel		1	
Hatton, Samuel		1	
Hatton, Thomas		2	
Hatton, William		1	1
Hawkins, James		5	4
Hawkins, William		3	
Henry, James			
paid for by Charles Jenings			
Herbert, Pascow		6	5
Hicks, John		1	
Hicks, William		1	
Hollier, Simon		11	10
Hope, George		11	3
House, Mary			
Humphlett, King		2	
Hunter, John		5	1
Hurst, Edward		1	
Huson, Elizabeth			
Huson, William		1	
Huson, William			
paid for by Wm. Moore			
Jarvis, George		2	1
Jenkins, Henry		5	5
Jenkins, Richard		1	
Jenings, Charles		5	4
paid for Henry Sinclair			
James Henry			
Jenings, Thomas		3	4
Jenings, William		3	1
Jenkins, James		1	
Jones, John		10	2
Jones, Samuel		4	
King, Michael		6	3
King, Miles		10	3
King, William		2	4
Kirby, Thomas		12	13
Lane, Zachariah		1	
Langley, Elizabeth		1	
Langley, William		1	
Langley, Wilson		2	
Latimer, George		7	8
Latimer, Rosea		5	2
Latimer, Thomas		1	
Latimer, William		10	10
Lee, Richard E.		4	2
Lewellin, Frances		1	1
Lewellings, Alexander		1	
Lewis, John, Jr.		1	
Lewis, Mathew		1	
Lewis, Thomas		1	
Lewis, William		2	

	F.	M.	N.
Lowry, John		20	14
McCaa, Sarah		1	1
McClurg, Walter		4	5
McHolland, William		2	
McLachlen, Mary		3	2
Mallory, Edward		9	8
Mallory, Mary		13	17
Mallory, William		11	10
Massenburg, Robert		3	1
Minson, Euphan		5	10
Mitchell, Edward		2	
Mitchell, Ross		2	
Mitchell, Ruben			
paid for by Sam. B. Cunningham			
Moore, Augustine		11	6
paid for Merrit Moore			
Moore, William		8	10
paid for William Huson			
Morris, Baldwin Sheppard		1	2
Morris, Christopher		1	
Morris, William		3	5
Moss, Shelden		6	7
Mossom, David		2	
Naylor, Jane		9	10
Needham, Joseph		4	8
Nettles, John		3	
Nettles, Vicanious			
paid for Frances Armistead			
Newton, Thomas		1	
Noble, Cornelius		2	
Nicholas, Joseph		2	3
Palmer, Lydia			
Parish, Jane		1	4
Parish, John		1	
Parish, John		1	1
Parish, Mary		1	1
Parish, Natheniel		1	
Parish, Sarah		1	2
Parsons, John		7	4
paid for William Aplomas Parsons			
Parsons, Thomas		6	
Parsons, William Aplomas			
paid for by John Parsons			
Pasteur, Blovet		1	
Pasteur, Elizabeth		1	
Paul, John		3	
Payne, Thomas		4	
Perry, John		1	
Phillips, John		2	
Picket, Abram		1	
Peirce, Thomas		2	
Peirce, William		1	1
Poole, Francis		2	
Pool, John		2	
Poole, Robert		5	
Randolph, William		1	
Riddlehurst, Francis		5	3
Robinson, John		10	3
Rogers, John		2	4
Roland, Phebe		3	1
Ross, Francis		3	2
Ross, J. M.			
paid for by Mallory Ross			

	F.	M.	N.
Ross, Mallory, Jr.		2	
Ross, Mallory		3	4
paid for Thomas Ross			
Ross, Thomas			
paid for by Mallory Ross			
Routon, Richard		1	
Rudd, Edward		4	5
Russel, James		4	5
Sanders, Judeth			
Sandifur, Samuel		1	
Sandifur, Samuel, Jr.		1	
Sandifur, William		1	1
Saunders, David		1	
Selden, Ann		1	3
Selden, Cary		25	14
Selden, John		1	
Selden, Joseph		1	1
Selden, Revd. William		7	11
Seymore, John			
paid for John Burnham			
Seymour, William		1	1
Shepard, Ann		4	8
Sheppard, John		2	
Sinclair, Henry			
paid for by Charles Jenings			
Skinner, Ellyson		5	2
Skinner, Howard		1	
Skinner, John		3	1
Skinner, John, Jr.		3	
Skinner, Willis		1	
Smelt, David		2	2
Smelt, John		3	2
Smelt, Joseph		1	
Smith, Elizabeth		1	1
Spruce, David		1	
Stevens, Thomas			
paid for by John Fields			
Stores, Charles		1	
Stores, Frazier, Jr.		2	
Stores, Frazier, Sr.		4	
Stores, John		1	
Stores, Savage		1	
Tabb, John		16	14
paid for Thomas Tabb			
paid for Johnson Tabb			
Tabb, Thomas			
paid for by John Tabb			
Tabb, Johnson			
paid for by John Tabb			
Tarrant, Carter		7	3
Turnbull, Stephen		5	9
Wager, William		4	2
Walker, Robert		3	3
Wallace, Robert		11	1
Watkins, George			
paid for by William Watkins			
Watkins, William		3	
paid for George Watkins			
Watts, Littleton		1	
Watts, Samuel, Jr.		3	6
Watts, Samuel		16	6
paid for Thomas Watts, Jr.			
Watts, Thomas, Jr.			
paid for by Samuel Watts			

	F.	M.	N.
Watts, Thomas, Sr.		3	4
Webb, Armiger		2	
Webb, John		1	
Webster, Thomas		3	3
Westwood, Woolich		10	6
paid for John Bell			
Whitaker, Thomas		2	
White, William			
Widdows, Robert		2	
Williams, James		5	4
Wilson, Ann		1	
Wilson, John		1	
Wilson, John		1	1
Wilson, William		1	
Wise, William		2	
Wood, John		1	
Wood, Mary		2	4
Wootten, Thomas, Sr.		8	2
Wray, George		4	1
Wray, Jacob		7	7
Wythe, George		11	16
Yancy, Nathan		6	13
Yeargin, William		1	

A copy. W. W. Wager, Deputy, Clerk. A list of Ordinary Licenses granted in the Court of Elizabeth City County, February 1782, vizt., Bryan, Richard; Crook, Pennuel; Mitchell, Edward; Pasteur, Elizabeth; Paul, John; Riddlehurst. April 25, 1782.

White and black tithes	904
Young blacks	648
Total	1552

Memo-Recapitulation for 1783, 252 whites, 1051 (799) blacks. Deduct 252 whites charged above as the 1051 tithables included both white and blacks.

List of those persons who have not paid the specific tax in Elizabeth City County. September 1, 1782.

Allen, Samuel	1
Armistead, Martha	3
Carter, William	1
Gill, James	1
Hayley, Samuel	1
Jervis, George	2
Lewis, Thomas	1
McCaa, Sarah	1
Manson, Robert	2
Nettles, John	3
Parish, Edward	1
Parish, Nathenial	1
Ross, Francis	3
Ross, Thomas	1
Smelt, David	2
Smith, John (unknown)	
Russell, Elizabeth	1
Webb, Armager	2
Willson, John	1
Wilson, Ann	1

0 0

A PARTIAL LIST of the Civil Officers of the County

Members of the Governor's Council:

Thomas Purefey of "Drayton", Elizabeth City County. 1631. Born in England and died in Virginia.

Francis Hooke of Elizabeth City County. 1637. Born in England, died in Virginia in 1637.

Richard Morrison of Elizabeth City County. 1641. Born in England, died before 1656.

Anthony Elliott of Elizabeth City, Lancaster and Middlesex Counties. 1657. Born in England, died about 1666 in Virginia.

0 0

MEMBERS of the HOUSE of BURGESSES

1619 Kiccowtan- William Tucker, William Capp.
1623/24 Incorporation of Elizabeth City- William Tucker, Nicholas Martian.
Beyond the Hampton River- Rev. Jabez Whitaker, Raleigh (Rawley) Crashaw.
1625 William Tucker, Abrah Peirsey.
1626
1627
1628
1629 George Thompson, William English, Adam Thoroughgood, Lionel Rowlton, John Browning, John Dowman.
1629/30 Upper part of Elizabeth City County- Thomas Willoughby, William Kempe, Thomas Hayrick.
Lower part of Elizabeth City County- Thomas Purifoy, Adam Thoroughgood, Lancelot Barnes.
1631/32 Upper part of Elizabeth City County and Water's Creek- Thomas Willoughby.
Lower part of Elizabeth City County- George Downes.
1632 Upper part of Elizabeth City County- Thomas Willoughby, Henry Seawell, John Sipsey.
Lower part of Elizabeth City County- Adam Thoroughgood, William English, George Downes.
1632/33 Upper part of Elizabeth City County- Thomas Sheppard, John Sipsey.
Lower part of Elizabeth City County- William English, John Arundel.
1634
1635
1636
1637
1638
1639/40 Thomas Oldis, Mr. Stafferton.
1641/42 John Branch, John Hoddin.
1642/43 John Branch, John Hoddin.
1643/44 Willm. Woolridg, John Holden.
1644 William Worbrigh (Wooldridge) John Hodin.
1644/45 Leonard Yeo, X'pher Caulthropp, Arthur Price.
1645/46 Leonard Yeo, John Chandler.
1646 John Robbins, Hen. Ball.
1647/48 Anth. Elliot, John Chandler, Hen. Poole.
1648
1649 William Worlich, Jo. Robbins.
1650
1651
1652 April, May. Peter Ransom, John Sheppard.
November. Peter Ransome, Theo. Hone.
1653 John Sheppard, Thomas Thornbury.
1654/55 William (Wooldridge) Worlich, John Sheppard.
1655/56 Peter Ashton.
1657/58 William (Wooldridge), John Powell.
1658/59 William Batte, Florentine Paine.
1659/60 William Worleich, John Powell.
1661
1662
1663 John Powel, Leonard Yeo.
1664
1665
1666 John Powell, Leonard Yeo.
1667
1668

1669	
1670	
1671	
1672	
1673	
1674	
1675	
1676	
1677	
1678	
1679	
1680	Thomas Jarvis, Edward Mihill.
1681	
1682	Thomas Jarvis, Edward Mihill.
1683	Captain Anthony Armistead, Baldwin Shepherd.
1684	William Wilson, Thomas Allomby (Allainby).
1685/86	Henry Jenkins, William Wilson.
1687	
1688	William Wilson, Thomas Allomby.
1690	
1691/92	William Wilson, Thomas Allomby.
1692/93	Willis Wilson, William Armistead.
1693	Anthony Armistead, William Wilson.
1694	
1695	
1696	November- Captain Anthony Armistead. April-October- Mathew Watts, Captain Willis Wilson.
1696/97	Anthony Armistead, Willis Wilson.
1698	Anthony Armistead, Captain Willis Wilson.
1699	Anthony Armistead, Captain Willis Wilson.
1700	William Wilson, William Armistead.
1701	
1702	William Wilson, William Armistead.
1703	Anthony Armistead, William Armistead.
1704	Anthony Armistead, William Armistead.
1705	Nicholas Curle, William Armistead.
1706	
1707	
1708	
1709	
1710	Nicholas Curle, Francis Ballard.
1711	Nicholas Curle.
1712	Nicholas Curle, William Armistead.
1713	Nicholas Curle, William Armistead.
1714	William Armistead, Robert Armistead.
1715	William Armistead, Henry Jenkins
1716	
1717	
1718	Henry Jenkins, Thomas Wythe.
1719	
1720	James Rickets, Anthony Armistead.
1721	James Rickets, Anthony Armistead.
1722	James Rickets, Anthony Armistead.
1723	James Rickets, Thomas Wythe.
1724	Robert Armistead, Thomas Wythe.
1725	Robert Armistead, Thomas Wythe.
1726	Robert Armistead, Thomas Wythe.
1727	Robert Armistead, (Simon) Hollier.
1728	Robert Armistead, Simon Hollier.
1729	Robert Armistead, Simon Hollier.
1730	Robert Armistead, Simon Hollier.
1731	Robert Armistead, Simon Hollier.
1732	
1733	
1734	Simon Hollier, Merrit Sweny.

1735
1736 W. Westwood, Merit Sweny.
1737
1738 W. Westwood, Merit Sweny.
1739
1740 William Westwood, Merit Sweny.
1741
1742 William Westwood, Merit Sweny.
1743
1744 William Westwood, Merit Sweny.
1745 William Westwood, Merit Sweny.
1746 William Westwood, Merit Sweny.
1747 William Westwood, Merit Sweny.
1748 William Westwood, John Tabb.
1749 William Westwood, John Tabb.
1750
1751
1752 William Westwood, John Tabb.
1753 William Westwood, John Tabb.
1754 William Westwood, John Tabb.
1755 William Westwood, John Tabb.
1756 William Westwood, John Tabb.
1757 William Westwood, John Tabb.
1758 March-William Westwood, John Tabb.
September- William Wager, John Tabb.
1759 William Wager, John Tabb.
1760 William Wager, John Tabb.
1761 George Wythe, William Wager.
1762 George Wythe, William Wager.
1763 George Wythe, William Wager.
1764 George Wythe, William Wager.
1765 May- George Wythe, William Wager.
October- George Wythe, Wilson Miles Cary.
1766 George Wythe, Wilson Miles Cary.
1767 George Wythe, Wilson Miles Cary.
1768 George Wythe, Wilson Miles Cary.
1769 Wilson Miles Cary, James Wallace.
1770 Wilson Miles Cary, James Wallace.
1771 Wilson Miles Cary, James Wallace.
1772 Henry King, Worlich Westwood
1773 Henry King, Worlich Westwood
1774 Henry King, Worlich Westwood
1775 Henry King, Worlich Westwood

Order Book 1689-99, page 12, shows that on November 28, 1692, Captain William Marshall and Pasco Curle were paid for serving as Burgesses, besides the ones listed for aforesaid year.

0 0

CONVENTIONS of 1775-1776.

Assembled March 20, 1775.
Henry King, Worlich Westwood.

July 17, 1775.
Henry King, Worlich Westwood.

December 1, 1775.
Henry King, Worlich Westwood.

May 6, 1776.
Wilson Miles Cary, Henry King.

0 0

ATTORNEYS
1746

George Wythe
John Sclater
John Wright

0 0

JUSTICES

(The date given is the first record found listed.)

Allainby, Capt. Thomas	1688
Allen, John	1747
Armistead, Major Antho.	1699
Armistead, Lt. Col. Antho.	1715
Armistead, Booth	1755
Armistead, Robert	1721
Armistead, Robert	1759
Armistead, Westwood	1748
Armistead, Capt. William	1692
Armistead, Major Wm.	1715
Armistead, Lt. William	1762
Balfour, James	1762
Ballard, Capt. Francis	1715
Banister, Joseph	1720
Bayley, John	1715
Bayley, Walter	1699
Beverley, Robert	1700
Bland, Richard	1660
Bosell (Boswell), Capt. Wm.	1715
Brodie, John	1727
Brough, Coleman	1692
Cary, Wilson	1731
Cary, Wilson Miles	1762
Cay, Gabriel	1767
Curle, David	1759
Curle, David Wilson	1765
Curle, Joshua	1718
Curle, Nicholas	1767
Curle, Nicholas	1700
Curle, Nicholas Wilson	1767
Curle, Pascho	1695
Curle, Thomas	1692
Curle, Wilson	1734
Dunn, Pascho	1688
Gutherick, Quintilian	1688
Harwood, Thomas	1696
Hollier, Capt. Simon	1717
Holloway, Major John	1716
Howard, Lt. Thomas	1724
Hunter, John	1754
Hunter, William	1727
Irwin, Major Henry	1718
Jenings, Lt. Charles	1724
Jenkins, Capt. Henry	1688
Johnson, Mark	1715
Jones, Edward	1727
King Charles	1747
King, Henry	1767
King, Capt. John	1715
Lowry, John	1720
Lowry, William	1692
McCaw, Joseph	1767
McClung, Walter	1762
McKenzie, Alexander	1731
Michel, Cary	1762
Michel, Thomas	1732
Mingham, Thomas	1747
Minson, John	1699
Moore, Augustine	1692
More, John	1715
Myhill, Edward	1688
Proby, Peter	1692
Ricketts, James	1718
Robinson, Starkey	1759
Roscow, James	1720
Royall, Henry	1702
Selden, Cary	1747
Selden, John	1721
Selden, Joseph	1721
Servant, Bertram	1702
Servant, James	1718
Sweny, Edmund	1692
Sweny, Merrit	1731
Sweny, Samuel	1720
Tabb, John	1731
Tabb, John, Jr.	1759
Tabb, Thomas	1715
Tucker, Anthony	1749
Walker, George, Sr.	1759
Walker, George, Jr.	1764
Walker, Jacob	1721
Wallace, James	1720
Watts, Mathew	1696
Westwood, William	1727
Wilson, Major Wm.	1693
Wray, George	1734
Wythe, George	1755
Wythe, Thomas, Jr.	1688
Wythe, Thomas	1715

0 0

SHERIFFS

Allen, Henry. Deputy Sheriff	1769
Armistead, Anthony	1684 & 1710
Armistead, Robert, Jr. Undersheriff	1732
Armistead, Westwood	1759

Armistead, Capt. William 1695
Armistead, William 1768
Bailey, John 1719
Ballard, Francis 1706
Banister, Joseph 1730
Bayley, Walter 1700
Boswell, William 1717
Brodie, John 1732
Brough, Coleman 1699
Curle, Joshua 1723
Curle, Nicholas 1702
Curle, Pascho 1693
Curle, Wilson 1738
Hollier, Simon 1715
Jegitts, Joseph (Under Sheriff) 1760
Jenings, Charles 1759
King, Joshua 1721
Moore, John 1712
Selden, Joseph 1725
Tabb, John 1766
Tabb, Thomas 1708
Walker, George 1759
Walker, George, Jr. 1761
Walker, Jacob 1744
Wallace, James 1747
Wilson, Major William 1692
Westwood, Worlich 1791
Wray, George 1764

0 0

COUNTY CLERKS

Poole, Hardy (Henry) 1648
Jenings, Charles 1690
Irwin, Henry 1721
Mingham, Thomas 1723
Everard, Thomas 1742
Moore, Merritt 1795
Selden, Cary 1775
Tabb, Johnson 1784
Wager, William 1745
Walker, George 1679
Westwood, Worlich 1798

0 0

COUNTY SURVEYORS

Dixon, Richard 1768
Lowry, William 1698
Lucas, Robert 1759
Mallory, William 1695
Walker, Robert 1789
Westwood, James 1765

0 0

TOBACCO INSPECTORS

Johnson, George 1770
Puryear, Peter 1762
Wootten, Thomas 1768

0 0

COLLECTORS of the CUSTOMS

Cay, Gabriel 176-
Heyman, Peter 1698
Michell, Cary 1761
Michell, James 1748
Michell, Thomas 1725

0 0

COUNTY MILITIA OFFICERS

Armistead, Anthony ------ Major 1699
Cary, Miles Deputy Captaine 1698
Cocke, William Lieutenant of the Militia 1715
Wager, William Major of the Militia 1759
Wilson, William Lieutenant Colonel and Commander in Chief of the Militia 1699

Cary, Miles	Naval Officer	1769

ADDITIONAL CIVIL OFFICERS

1623. Officials for the Corporation of Elizabeth City: Captain William Tucker, John Downman, Edward Waters and Francis Chamberlaine.

1626. Commission for Elizabeth City: Captain Tucker, Captain Martin, Mr. Jonas Stogden, Lieutenant Purfrey, Mr. Edward Waters, Mr. John Baynum, Mr. Salford.

1628/29. Commission for Elizabeth City. Captain Thomas Purfrey, Captain Edward Waters, Lieutenant Thomas Willoughby, Lieutenant George Thompson, Mr. Adam Thoroughgood, Mr. Lyonell Coulston, Mr. William Kempe and Mr. John Downman. For holding and keeping of monthly courts, Captain Thomas Purfury and Lieutenant Edward Waters shall always be one with three of them to hear and determine all suits.

1632. Commission for Elizabeth City: William Tucker, William English, Thomas Purifie, George Downes, Thomas Willoughby, John Arundell and Adam Thoroughgood.

1649. Commission for Elizabeth City: Captain William Claiborne, Captain Leonard Yeo, Captain Nat. Oldis, Mr. Thomas Sely and Mr. John Shaunders.

Other Justices or Commissioners:

Chandler, John	1649
Elliott, Anthony	1649
King, Miles	1770
Mallory, Francis	1770
Mallory, William	1770
Moryson, Charles	1680
Oldis, Thomas	1639
Robins, John	1649
Tabb, Humphrey	1652
Wakelin, Mathew	1684
Westwood, James	1770
Westwood, Worlich	1770
Worlich, William	1649

__________ 0 0 __________

Additional Sheriffs:

Armistead, Robert	1797
Bailey, James Wallace	1775
Batt, William	1657
Booker, George	1793
Ceely, Thomas	1663/64
Hone, Theophilus	1656
Lowry, John	1740
Moore, Augustine	1697
Poole, Henry	1641

----- 0 0 -----

County Clerk for 1792: Solomon Tabb.

----- 0 0 -----

1628. Captain Thomas Purifoy, Commander-in- chief.
1695. Captain Henry Jenkins, Commander-in-chief.
1701. Captain William Armistead, Commander-in-chief.

----- 0 0 -----

First Feoffees appointed by the court in 1692: Thomas Allainby, William Marshall and Pascho Curle.

----- 0 0 -----

Francis Moryson was the Captain of Point Comfort Fort, Speaker of the House of Burgesses and acting Governor. 1655/56.

----- 0 0 -----

THE REVOLUTION

THE COMMITTEE OF SAFETY

1775

Chairman: William Roscow Wilson Curle

Allen, John
Armistead, Mosley
Armistead, Westwood
Bayley, James Wallace
Booker, George
Bright, Robert
Cary, John
Cary, Wilson Miles
Cooper, Edward
Cooper, Joseph
Curle, Wilson
Hollier, Simon
Jones, John
King, Henry
King, John
King, Miles
Mallory, William
Moore, Augustine
Parsons, John
Tabb, John
Wray, George
Wray, Jacob

Committee of Safety-November 21, 1774

Armistead, William
Cary, John
Cowper, Roe
King, Henry
King, Miles
Selden, Cary
Selden, Joseph
Tabb, John
Wallace, James
Westwood, Worlich
Wray, George
Wray, Jacob

Clerk, Robert Bright

Committee of Safety-1775

Allen, John
Armistead, Westwood
Bayley, James Wallace
Booker, George
Cary, Wilson Miles
Cooper, Edward
King, Henry
King, Miles
Jones, John
Moore, Augustine
Parsons, John
Tabb, John
Wray, George
Wray, Jacob

Chairman: William Roscow Wilson Curle

———— 0 0 ————

PUBLIC CLAIMS
List of Persons Who Furnished Supplies
(In State Archives)

Allen, Edward
Allen, Jane
Allen, Jean
Allen, Thomas
Armistead, Frances
Armistead, James B.
A Commissary
Armistead, John
Armistead, Moseley, Estate
Armistead, Moss

Armistead, Thomas Baker
Armistead, Major Thomas
Armistead, Westwood
A Commissary
Armistead, William
Ballard, William
Barron, James
Bayley, Hannah
Bayley, James Wallace
Bayley, William
A Commissary
Baylis, Thomas
Booker, George
Boutwell, Ann
Bright, Robert
Bryan, Richard
Burt, Richard
Carlavans, Joseph
Cary, John
Christian, Robert
A Commissary
Cooper, Joseph
Cowper, Edward
Cowper, Roe
Curle, Wm. Roscow Wilsons Estate
Cuttiler, Edward
Davenport, William
Captain of a Troop of Horse
Dewbre, Rebecca
Duberry, Rebecca
Dewbre, Samuel
Drewry, John
Drewry, William
Dunn, William
Face, Edward
Fields, Bartlet
Fields, John
Gillett, John
Gooch, William
Hawkins, James
Hollier, Simon
Hunter, Capt. John
Jenings, Thomas
Jones, John
Jones, Samuel
Kirby, Thomas
King, Henry, Jr.'s Estate
King, John
King, Miles
Kirk, Alexander
Latimer, George
Latimer, Thomas
Hill, Jamesby Cole Digges
Latimer, William
Lewellen, Alexander
Lewis, Thomas
Lowry, John
McLachlin, John Estate
Mallory, Edward
Mallory, Frances Estate
Mann, Thomas
A Commissary
Manson, Robert
Mingham, Elizabeth
Minson, Euphan
Mitchell, Edward
Moody, William, Jr.
Moore, Augustine
Moore, William
Morris, William
Moss, Shelden
Naylor, Jane
Needham, Joseph
Nichols, Joseph
Parsons, John
Parsons, Thomas
Ranals, John
Randal, William - a Pilot
Ross, Francis
Ross, Johnson
Rudd, Edward
Selden, Rev. William
Sinclair, John
Skinner, Ellyson
Skinner, John
Smelt, Joseph
Smelt, Robert
Smith, Bazzel Estate
Smith, John
Spruce, David
Stores, James
Tabb, John
Thompson, Lt. Robert
Wallace, Robert Estate, presented by Wm. Armistead the guardian of James Wallace, his orphan.
Watts, Samuel
Westwood, William Estate
Wootten, Thomas, Sr.
Wray, Jacob
Wythe, George
Yancey, Nathan
Yarbrough, Joseph
A Deputy Commissary.

__________0 0 __________

Services Listed in Virginia Soldiers of 1776
By Louis A. Burgess

Allen, Thomas -- Boatswain
Archer, Lt. John
Archer, Capt. Robert
Armistead, William --Paymaster
Barron, Commodore James
Barron, Midshipman James
Barron, Capt. Richard
Barron, Lt. Samuel
Barron, Lt. William
Brown, Dr. David

Bully, Edward Boatswain
Butler, Thomas Pilot
Chamberlayne, Lt. Philip
Cunningham, Capt. William
Cunningham, Wm. Roe Pilot
Haley, Lt. Samuel
Herbert, Lt. Pascow
Herbert, Capt. Thomas
House, William Gunner
Jennings, Capt. William
King, Miles Surgeon's Mate
Lewis, Mathew Carpenter's Mate
Marshall, Capt. James
Mossum, Capt. David
Parrish, John Pilot
Parrish, Mark Pilot
Parrish, William Pilot
Pasteur, Blovet Sailor
Payne, John Master in the State Navy
Read, Lt. John
Servant, Lt. Richard
Tarrant, Caesar Negro
Turnbull, Capt. Stephen
Wray, George Midshipman
(Above the records give service and much genealogical information.)

__________0 0 __________

Historical Register of Virginians in the Revolution
By John H. Gwathmey

Anderson, Capt. -----
Armistead, Robert
Armistead, William- Paymaster
Barron, Capt. -------
Barron, Commodore James
Barron, James- Midshipman and Aide-de Camp to his father, Commodore Barron.
Barron, Capt. Philip Navy
Barron, Capt. Richard Navy
Barron, Capt. Samuel Navy
Barron, Lt. William Navy
Bartlett, Surgeon Philip
Bright, Capt. Robert
Brodie, Surgeon John
Brodie, Surgeon Lodowick
Brough, Adjutant Robert
Brough, Capt. William
Burle, James Navy
Cary, Capt. John
Cary, Lt. Wilson Miles
Cayle, Wilson M.
Cooper, Major Roe
Counsel, Michael
Cowper, Major Roe
Cunningham, William
Dunn, William
Elliott, Col. Thomas (king Wm.)
Goecer, William
Gregory, Capt. -----
Hardyman, Lt. John
Harper, John
Harper, William Navy
Harwood, Major Samuel
Hollier, Capt. Simon
Isbell, Quarter Master Benj.
Jiggett, Ensign Edward Roe
Johnston, Doctor William
King, Lt. John
King, Capt. Miles
Latimer, Lt. Edward
Latimer, George Pilot
Latimer, Thomas Pilot
Mallory, Lt. Col. Francis
Marshall, Capt. James
Meredith, Col. Samuel
Moore, Capt. William
McClung, Surgeon Walter
Parrish, John Pilot
Parrish, Mark Pilot
Pasture, Blovet Navy
Paul, John Pilot
Selden, Ensign Joseph, Jr.
Skinner, Howard Pilot
Turnbull, Capt. Stephen
Walker, Capt. -----
Webb, Armiger Pilot
Wray, Midshipman George

__________0 0 __________

The History of Virginia's Navy of the Revolution
By Robert Armistead Stewart

Allman, William. Gunner. Boat Liberty, N. B. J. 1777.

Ballard, Edward. Pilot and Lieutenant. Proved by testimony of James Barron. July 27, 1832. "He rendered important services during the whole war, as did also Edward Cooper, William Roe Cunningham, William Watkins and James Latimer, Pilots. Mr. Ballard was promoted to a Lieutenancy for his patriotism, shortly before the close of the war. The rank of a Pilot in those days corresponded to that of a Junior Lieutenant".

Banks, James. Sailing Master, L. B. P.
Ballard, William. Pilot. 1783.
Barron, James. Commodore, Virginia State Navy.
Barron, James, Jr. Midshipman, later Captain.
Barron, Richard. Captain, given leave October 11, 1780 to go to the West Indies for the recovery of health.
Barron, Samuel. Lieutenant Commander, later Commodore.
Barron, William. First Lieutenant and then Captain.
Barthlett, Philip. Surgeon. Came from New York.
Booth, William. Sailing Master and Pilot.
Brown, David. Surgeon.
Bulley (Bully), John. Boatswain.
Bully, Edward. Boatswain.
Bully, Thomas. Enlisted in 1778, on Schooner Patriot.
Burk, James. Gunner.
Burk, John. Brother of James Burk.
Cain, Joshua. Pilot.
Chamberlaine, Philip. First Mate, later Captain.
Cooper, Edward. Pilot.
Cowper, John. Captain of Nansemond and Hampton.
Cunningham, William Roe. Pilot.
Davis, John R. Lieutenant of the Marines.
Dobson, Robert. Sailing Master.
Fiveash, Peter. Sailing Master.
Gibson, James. Seaman, later Gunner.
Gibson, John. Seaman and later Gunner.
Godwin, James. Midshipman and Lieutenant.
Graves, William. Lieutenant.
Haley (Healey), Samuel. Lieutenant.
Ham, William. Lieutenant.
Hardyman, John. Captain of the Marines.
Herbert, John. Carpenter and Midshipman.
Herbert, Pasco. Lieutenant.
Herbert, Thomas. "Silver Fist"- so called from a silver device that took the place of the left hand he had lost.
House, William. Gunner.
Humphlett, John. Midshipman.
Humphlett, Thomas. Lieutenant.
Jennings, John. Sailing Master.
Jennings, Thomas. Captain. Entered the service at 16.
Jennings, William. Seaman and Pilot.
Johnston, William. Surgeon's Mato.
Latimer, James. Pilot.
Lewis, Mathew. Carpenter's Mate.
McClurg, Walter. Surgeon.
Marshall, Joseph. Sailing Master.
Massenburg, Alexander. Midshipman.
Mitchell, Ross. Carpenter.
Parish, John. Pilot.
Parish, Mark. Pilot.
Pasteur, Blovet. Seaman.
Patterson, John. Midshipman and Clerk.
Poole, John. Enlisted in 1778 under Barron.
Ralls, George. Captain.
Rogers, John. Lieutenant and Captain.
Selden, Wilson Cary. Surgeon.
Servant, Richard. Lieutenant.
Servant, Samuel. Entered service June 24, 1777.
Skinner, William. Lieutenant and Captain.
Watkins, George. Pilot.
Watkins, William. Pilot.
Webb, James. Pilot.
Williams, John. Pilot.
Wood, Allen. Pilot.
Wood, James. Pilot.

Wood, William. Pilot.
(All of these references in Burgess contain much genealogical material.)

____________ 0 0 ____________

MARRIAGE LICENSES

William Cofield of Nansemond and Elizabeth Sheppard. January 5, 1694/95.
Moses Baker and Elizabeth Browne. January 12, 1694/95.
Thomas Carey of Warwick and Elizabeth Hinds. January 8, 1694/95.
William Long and Jane Proby. April --, 1694/95.
Pascho Dunn and Hannah Powers. April 8, 1695.
Mr. James Wallace, Clerk, and Mrs. Ann Wythe. July 11, 1695.
Mr. Thomas Harwood and Mrs. Ann Wythe, Sr. September 7, 1695.
John West of New Kent and Judah Armistead. October 15, 1695.
John Knox and Winifred Conner. October 21, 1695.
Thomas Walker of Yorke County and Elizabeth Johnston. October 21, 1695.
John George of Nansemond and Frances Servant. June 16, 1696.
Thomas Harvie and the Widow Hendrick. June 16, 1696.
Charles Goring and Elynor Allainby. October 27, 1696.
Charles Ceeley and Elizabeth Saunders. November 3, 1696.
William Minson and Easter Perrin. August 4, 1697.
William Smelt and Elizabeth Traverse, widow. October 21, 1697.
John Skinner and Jane Smith. 21 day of Xber 1697.
William Davis and Rebecca Skinner. April 5, 1698.
William Wilson and Jane Davis. September 16, 1698.
------------ and Sarah -------. July 5, 1698.
Francis Rogers and Apphya Miller. October 15, 1698.
Martin Bean and Ann Allen. 8 day of 8ber 1698.
William Sheldon and Hannah Armistead. December 10, 1698.
Richard Harshly and Mary Naylor, widow. 10 day of Xber 1698.
John Francis and Mary Savey. 19 day of Xber 1698.
John Colwell and Elizabeth Tucker. January 5, 1698/99.
John Fryby and Mary Tucker. January 5, 1699.
John Poole and Elizabeth Sheppard, widow. October 10, 1699.
Thomas Gray and Bathya Crooke. October 10, 1699.
Philip Johnson and Jane Trawell, widow. October 15, 1699.
Francis Ballard and Mary Servant. December 25, 1699.
Francis Beelman (Bulman ?) and Sarah Woods. April 18, 1700.
Nicholas Curle and Elizabeth Gutherick. June 14, 1700.
Samuel Neale and Elizabeth Exeter. June 29, 1700.
Robert Taylor and Elizabeth Hudson. February 20, 1701.
Henry Turner and Sydwell Minson. March 9, 1701.
Edward Myhill and Ann Johnson. 5 day of Xber 1701.
George Luke, Esq. and Elizabeth Baskins or Boikin. June 31, 1701.
Joshua Curle and Sarah Curle. March 2, 1702.
William Bossell and Elynder Brough. March 2, 1702.
James Priest and Margaret Ross. April 13, 1702.
Colonel Miles Cary and Mary Roscow. April 13, 1702.
Bruan Penney and Bethya Gray. May 3, 1702.
Charles Jennings, Jr., and Elizabeth Westwood. July 20, 1702.
Roger Daniel and --------------. March 13, 1720.
Francis Massenburg and -----------. April 13, 1721.

Marriages returned during 1719 and 1720.

Leonard Whiting and Easter Minson.

Thomas Wythe and Margaret Walker.

Thomas Milner and Mary Selden.

William Greenwood and Mrs. Harrington.

George Yeo and Elliner Boswell.

John King and Rebecca Armistead.

Robert Grives and Ellinor Wandless.

John Young and Elizabeth Ryland.

Francis Mallory and Ann Myhill.

____________0 0 ____________

John Holt and Elizabeth his wife, came into Court and acknowledged bond for the estate of William Hunter. 1745. *Tyler's Quarterly*, Vol. IX, page 204.

HAMPTON

America's Oldest Continuous Town

By
V. King Pifer

Three hundred and thirty-three years ago, the exact date being April 30, 1607, the first white man set foot on the Lower Peninsula and three years later in 1610, the first colonists decided to establish themselves at Hampton. Their presence here has been continuous and the "Gamecock Town" proudly lays claim to the honor of being the oldest continuous English speaking settlement in the United States. Through these 333 years runs a thread of participation in Colonial, Revolutionary and National history that sheds added luster on the community's fame and importance.

But to return to that historic day 333 years ago: Captain Christopher Newport had successfully brought his three tiny ships to anchorage off Cape Comfort, so named by the weary voyagers because of the deep water and the "good comfort" the harbor afforded. Here Captain Newport caused a shallop to be manned and towed to the mainland, on which was located an Indian village of 18 wigwams, bearing the name Kecoughtan. This village occupied the present site of the Veteran's Administration Facility and is well within what is known as the Hampton area.

The personnel of this first landing party has not been recorded, but one of the number must have been Captain George Percy, who told of that first meeting between white men and savages and of what may be regarded as the "first smoker" on the American continent.

"When we came first aland they made a doleful noise, laying their faces to the ground, scratching the earth with their nails. We did think they had been at their idolatry. When they had ended their ceremonies they went into their houses and brought out mats and laid upon the ground. The chieftest of them sat all in a rank; the meanest sort brought us such dainties as they had, and of their bread which they made of Maiz or Gennea wheat. They would not suffer us to eat unless we sat down, which we did on a mat right against them. After we were well satisfied they gave us of their tobacco which they broke in a pipe made artificially of earth as our are, but much bigger with the bowl fashioned together with a piece of fine copper. After they had feasted us, they showed us in welcome, their manner of dancing, which was in this fashion: One of the savages standing in the midst singing, beating one hand against the other, all the rest dancing about him, shouting, howling and stamping against the ground with many antics, tricks and faces, making noise like to many wolves or devils. One thing of them I observed; when they were in their dance they kept stroke with their feet just one with the other, but with their hands, heads, faces and bodies, every one of them, had a several gesture; so they continued for a space of half an hour. When they had ended their dance, the captain gave them beads and other trifling jewels.

KECOUGHTANS WERE FRIENDLY

It is fortunate that the name Kecoughtan has been preserved for the tribe of Indians bearing that name certainly proved to be friends of the white man until they had been conquered by the more powerful Powhatan, and disappeared from the community. The names of none of its chieftains have been preserved.

The first colonists did not tarry long at Kecoughtan, but proceeded up the broad James to Jamestown Island where the first settlement was made. In December 1607, Capt. John Smith paid a visit to the Indians at Kecoughtan for trade and returned to Jamestown with a good supply of fish, oysters, corn and deer meat which he had secured from them for a few glass beads. Smith stopped here again in July, 1608, when he returned from the exploration of Chesapeake Bay and on several other occasions found it convenient to sojourn with the hospitable Kecoughtans, stating on one occasion that he had been feasted "with great mirth". The next year a party including Capt. Francis West, Capt. George Percy and Capt. John Smith spent Christmas week among the savages. There own account was: "We were never more merry, nor fed on more plenty of good oysters, fish, flesh and wild fowl and good bread, nor never had better fires in England than in the dry, smoky houses of Kecoughtan.

FIRST FORT AT OLD POINT

While the first colonists were struggling to establish themselves at Jamestown, Kecoughtan was recognized as a strategic point, and after Capt. Smith had returned to England in October 1609, Capt. George Percy, then president of the council, sent Capt. John Ratcliffe down to the mouth of the river to erect a fort. He selected the present site of Fortress Monroe and named the first rude stockade "Algernourne Fort" in honor of President Percy's ancestor, William Algernourne de Percy. Other small forts, Henry and Charles were built and settlers began to move into the Hampton district. This year, 1610, marked the beginning of Hampton.

In 1616, John Rolfe reported that there were at Kecoughtan 21 men under Capt. George Webb and of the number William Mease was minister and 11 were farmers who maintained themselves. In 1619, when the first legislative assembly had met at Jamestown and formulated systems of government for the various settlements, Elizabeth City Corporation sprange into being, the name to remain closely associated with that of Hampton until the bonds between the two historic areas were finally dissolved with the beginning of the present year. Elizabeth City County, Kecoughtan and Hampton meant much the same thing in the early history of the Lower Peninsula.

EARLY CHURCH ESTABLISHED

The establishment of the Church of England was coincident with the building of the Hampton colony. Services were held each Sunday and the first house of worship was erected in 1737, eastward from Hampton River. It was in this first church that Sir John Harvey read his commission as governor. The building had a rather brief existence and its site was unknown until about a half century ago when the foundation stones were uncovered. The Daughters of the American Revolution later erected a marker and for many years services have been held on the historic site, annually, with ministers of the Episcopal Church officiating. A few gravestones have been found.

About 1667 a second church was built in the western part of Hampton, on what was known as the Pembroke Farm. This second church, like the first, long since has disappeared, but the foundation stones again remained dimly to outline its dimensions. Here are a few tombstones, with the inscriptions still legible, one of them marking the resting place of John Neville, vice admiral of the British Navy, who died August 17, 1697. Other graves are those of Peter Haymen, collector of customs, who died on April 29, 1700; Thomas Curle of Sussex County, who died on May 30, 1700 and the Rev. Andrew Thompson, who died September 1, 1719. He was a native of Scotland.

By 1727 the Pembroke church was in ruins and Old St. John's

sprang into being. It is one of the most famous in Virginia as well as one of the oldest.

During the 90 years from 1610 to 1700 the Hampton settlement showed a slow but steady growth.

FIRST FREE SCHOOL

Near the west bank of Hampton River and within the limits of the city stands the Syms-Eaton School building, undisputed descendant of the first free school in America.

In 1680 the General Assembly passed an act creating centers of population in the interests of trade and in 1691 the town for Elizabeth City County was decreed to be built "on the west side of Hampton River, on the land of Mr. William Wilson, lately belonging to Mr. Thomas Jarvis, deceased, the plantation where he late lived and the place appointed by a former law, and several dwelling houses and warehouses already built." By 1699 Hampton was a place of sufficient importance to require the services of a special constable and records show that considerable property changed hands, that building lots were sold and that the streets of the infant town were beginning to take outline. The main roadway was known as Queen street, a name that has been preserved to the present day and the roadway still continuing to be the most important one in the city and the main highway leading from Old Point Comfort and Phoebus to the upper districts of the Peninsula and state.

THRIVING BUSINESS CENTER

By 1710 Hampton was a town of more than 100 houses, boasted of many ordinaries, or public places for the accommodation of visitors and had the largest business of any place in Virginia. Men-of-War made frequent trips to the harbor, trading vessels saild in and out almost daily and the residents of Hampton learned much of what was going on in the principal centers of New York and Pennsylvania with whom a lively and profitable trade was being carried on.

From the first colonization period, Hampton was destined to have a part in every war in which the colonies and later the nation were to engage. It would require pages to tell of the achievements of the inhabitants of the "Gamecock Town" and only brief mention can be made here. But the town believed in preparedness. The small colony had been preserved from Indian Massacre through the vigilance of its people and ancient records show Hampton always had a military organization of some sort. In 1752 the town's defense force consisted of one company of militia and two troops of horse, containing 66 and 60 men respectively.

BRITISH ARMY LANDS

One of the most interesting historical events in the story of Hampton has been given little attention in many authentic recordings and in others it has been entirely forgotten. It was the landing of Gen. Edward Braddock's British army in 1755, the army that later was to be defeated by the French and Indians at Fort DuQuesne, now Pittsburg. The landings from the British warships were made near the foot of what is now Victoria Avenue and in close proximity to the Hampton Yacht Club. The British erected a camp, built a hospital and went through a general reconditioning while awaiting General Braddock, who did not reach the peninsula until several months later. Here he conferred with officials of the colony and its military leaders. Undoubtedly Col. George Washington, who later was to save the remnants of Braddock's defeated army, was among the number.

Later the first British army sailed up Chesapeake Bay to the head of Elk, in Maryland, from which the expedition across to the junction of the Alleghany and Monongahela rivers, in Pennsylvania, made its start, an expedition that was to end in dire disaster, the death of Braddock and the scattering of the army.

BRITISH FLEET DRIVEN OFF

Just 20 years later the inhabitants of Hampton greeted another British fleet, but in a different manner. The colonies were in rebellion against the mother country. On October 21, 1775, Capt. Mathew Squires appeared in Hampton River with six armored boats and attempted to make a landing. The guarding Hamptonians under the command of Capt. George Nicholas from the bushy banks of the river poured such a deadly stream of lead into the boats that the attempt to land had to be given up. It was one of the few instances in history where militia-men defeated a naval force. Many buildings in Hampton were damaged by fire, following the heavy British bombardment, and one house was burned. After the repulse of Squires no more attacks were made on Hampton, although its militia-men had frequent encounters with marauding troops from the many British ships of war that continued to ply the waters of Hampton Roads and Chesapeake Bay. From the shores of the peninsula many of the inhabitants must have witnessed the coming and going of many men-of-war, including the arrival of the French fleet that was to take part in the siege of Yorktown, only a few miles distant, a brief siege that was to culminate in the surrender of Cornwallis and make certain the establishment of the American Republic.

Peace followed, the town on the banks of Hampton Roads prospered and again came grim war-the War of 1812. Admiral Cockburn, who had been ravaging the entire Hampton Roads area, landed a force of more than 2,500 men on June 25, 1814, and opposing them was a small party of militia. The latter put up a hard battle, but were obliged to retreat up the peninsula. The town was given over to pillage, insult and outrage. Old St. John's Church was wrecked and many homes destroyed by fire. It was Hampton's darkest period. But the "Gamecock Town" came back, as did the entire Lower Peninsula.

STILL DARKER DAYS

After war had been declared between the Southern States and those of the North and the conflicts of 1861 had ended disastrously for the forces of Gen. George B. McClellan, he planned for the capture of Richmond by way of the Virginia Peninsula in the spring of 1862. The residents of Hampton strongly espoused the cause of the Confederacy and with the outbreak of hostilities in 1861 were quick to throw all their available manpower into the Confederate ranks. And again the "Gamecock Town" was to know the tragedy of war. The Battle of Big Bethel, the first engagement of the war, had been fought only a few miles distant and by mid-summer much of the region had been taken over by the Federal troops, then strongly entrenched at Fortress Monroe.

Late in the summer the defending Confederates were strongly of the opinion that Hampton if taken over completely by Union forces, would prove a strong military post. Gen. John B. Magruder, then commanding the Confederate soldiers in the region, gave the command that the town be burned and the order was carried out. No house of any size, no public building, no church survived the conflagration and all the inhabitants were dispersed. The wisdom of the town's destruction long has been a subject for sharp controversy, many declaring that no useful purpose was served. When McClellan's immense army landed at Fortress Monroe early in 1862 it swept through the ruins of Hampton without a stop.

The war ended in 1865 and more old Hampton families flocked back. One of the first tasks was the rebuilding of old St. John's Church and the resumption of services. A school house was erected and the education of the children resumed. In March, 1866, Gen. Samuel C. Armstrong became superintendent of contrabands and head of the Freedman's Bureau and founder of the Hampton Institute, the leading school of the country for the education of Negro youth. In 1870 the old Chesapeake College was purchased and taken over by the government as a home for disabled veterans. The Hygeia Hotel at Old Point Comfort came into prominence as a resort, to be followed later by the Chamberlin. The extension of developments at Fortress Monroe also added to the expansion of the community which included the prosperous and growing town of Phoebus, across Mill Creek from the military reservation. The development of the oystering, crabbing and fishing industry was adding greatly to the material wealth of the area.

GREAT MILITARY CENTER

The even life of Hampton was twice disturbed by war in the years that followed. Military units participated in the Spanish-American War, the campaign on the Mexican border and the World War. During the latter conflict the National Soldiers' Home became a general hospital and thousands of veterans received treatment there. The institution has since been greatly enlarged, including the construction of a million dollar hospital building, equipped with the most modern appliances.

The World War brought in its wake the establishment of Langley Field, now one of the country's leading aviation centers. The field is less than three miles distant from the city with the connecting link being a modern concrete highway and a handsome bridge spanning Back River. In addition to the military establishment at Langley Field the laboratories of the National Advisory Committee for Aeronautics are located there.

The city of Hampton has undergone many changes during recent years, all of them along the lines of progress and enterprise. The city continues to be one of the leading seafood centers of the eastern seaboard. Thousands of dollars have been expended for the improvement of streets, the extension of sewers and the general beautification of the waterfront. The city government made an extensive appropriation for the deepening of the Hampton River channel. A new city hall has been erected, the Hampton High School building has been enlarged several times and a concrete stadium built. Along the main streets old wooden structures are rapidly giving place to buildings of modern construction.

This, in brief, is the record of Hampton for the past 333 years, a record that has been honorable, notable and patriotic and one that will be preserved and cherished throughout the coming years by its loyal and faithful people.

(Printed in the _Norfolk Virginian-Pilot_ and copied by consent of the author)

----- 0 0 -----

ELIZABETH CITY COUNTY RECORDS

For an interesting account of the history and destruction of the court records of this county see <u>The First Plantation</u>, by Marion L. Starkey, page 90.

Books which have been preserved:

Court Records and Deeds, 1688 (circa)-1699
Court Records and Deeds, 1715-1721
Court Records and Deeds, 1721-1725 (Recently acquired by the State Archives)
Court Records and Deeds, 1723-1729 (This volume is incorrectly marked 1704-1730)
Court Records, 1731-47
Court Records, 1747-1755
Court Records, 1755-1760
Court Records, 1760-1769
Court Records, 1784-1788
Court Records, 1798-1802
Minute Book 1803-1809
Court Records, 1808-1816
Court Order Book, 1816-1822
Court Records, 1827-1835
Court Records, 1844-1861
Court Records, 1865-1872
Court Records, 1872-1878
Court Records, 1878-1882
Court Records, 1882-1885
Court Records, 1885-1888
Minute Book of the Board of Supervisors, 1870-1894
Deeds and Wills, 1758-1764
Deeds and Wills, 1763-1771
Photostats of wills, 1701-1904 (The originals are also in the courthouse.)
Deeds, Volume 34, 1787-1800
Deeds and Wills, Vol. 33, 1805-1818
Deeds and Wills, Volume 32, 1820-26
Deeds and Wills, Volume 31, 1823-1831
Indentures, Volume 38, 1825-1831
Will Book Number I, 1865-1885
Re-recorded Deeds, 1834-1869-seven volumes
(The records are intact after the War Between the States. Many of the above books have been restored by Patriotic Societies and several of them have been renumbered.)

ADDENDA